UNIVERSITY OF PENNSYLVANIA
THE UNIVERSITY MUSEUM
PUBLICATIONS OF THE BABYLONIAN SECTION
Vol. I No. 2

SELECTED SUMERIAN AND BABYLONIAN TEXTS

BY

HENRY FREDERICK LUTZ
Harrison Research Fellow in Semitics

PHILADELPHIA
PUBLISHED BY THE UNIVERSITY MUSEUM
1919

CONTENTS

BIBLIOGRAPHY AND ABBREVIATIONS

AJSL *American Journal of Semitic Languages and Literatures.*

BA *Beitrage zur Assyriologie und sem. Sprachwissenschaft.*

BAGO Dennefeld, L.: *Babylonisch-Assyrische Geburts-Omina* (Assyriologische Bibliothek), Leipzig, 1914.

BB Ungnad, A.: *Babylonische Briefe aus der Zeit der Hammurapi Dynastie* (Vorderasiatische Bibliothek), Leipzig, 1914.

BE *Babylonian Expedition of the University of Pennsylvania,* Series A.

BMBI Barton, George A.: *Miscellaneous Babylonian Inscriptions,* New Haven, 1918.

Br Brünnow, R. E.: *A Classified List of Cuneiform Ideographs,* Leyden, 1887.

CPN Clay, A. T.: *Personal Names of the Cassite Period* (Yale Oriental Research Series, Vol. 1), New Haven, 1912.

CRT Craig, J. A.: *Assyrian and Babylonian Religious Texts* (Assyriologische Bibliothek, Vol. 13, Pt. 1 and 2), Leipzig, 1895–97.

CT *Cuneiform Texts from Babylonian Tablets in the British Museum.*

DHWB Delitzsch, F.: *Assyrisches Handwörterbuch,* Leipzig, 1896.

DPB Deimel, A.: *Pantheon Babylonicum* (Scripta Pontifici Instituti Biblici), Romae, 1914.

DSG Delitzsch, F.: *Sumerisches Glossar,* Leipzig, 1914.

EBL Lutz, H. F.: *Early Babylonian Letters from Larsa* (YBT, Vol. 2), New Haven, 1917.

ESB Thompson, R. C.: *The Devils and Evil Spirits of Babylonia* (2 vols.), London, 1903–1904.

HAV *Hilprecht Anniversary Volume,* Leipzig, 1909.

HK Holma, H.: *Die Namen der Körperteile im Assyrisch-Babylonischen* (Annales Academiae Scientiarum Fennicae, Ser. B, Vol. VII), Helsingfors, 1911.

HL Harper: *Assyrian and Babylonian Letters, belonging to the Kouyunjik Collections of the British Museum,* Part I-XIV, Chicago, 1892–1914.

JRBA Jastrow, M., Jr.: *Die Religion Babyloniens und Assyriens* (2 vols.), Leipzig, 1905–1912.

KAG Knudtzon, J. A.: *Assyrische Gebete an den Sonnengott für Staat und königliches Haus aus der Zeit Asarhaddons und Asurbanipals* (2 vols.), Leipzig, 1893.

KB Schrader, E.: *Keilinschriftliche Bibliothek* (Vols. I–VI), Berlin, 1889–1900.

KEAT Knudtzon, J. A.: *Die El-Amarna Tafeln* (Vorderasiatische Bibliothek), Leipzig, 1915.

KMS King, Leonard W.: *Babylonian Magic and Sorcery*, London, 1896.

LSS Behrens, E.: *Assyrisch-Babylonische Briefe kultischen Inhaltes aus der Sargonidenzeit* (Leipziger Semitistische Studien, II, 1), Leipzig, 1906.

KM Küchler, F.: *Beitrage zur Kenntnis der Assyrisch-Babylonischen Medizin* (Assyriologische Bibliothek, Vol. 18), Leipzig, 1904.

MAD Muss-Arnold, W.: *A Concise Dictionary of the Assyrian Language*, Berlin, 1905.

Maqlu Tallquist, Knut L.: *Die Assyrische Beschwörungsserie Maqlu, Acta Societatis Scientiarum Fennicae*, Tom. XX, No. 6, 1895.

MSAI Meissner, B.: *Seltene Assyrische Ideogramme*, Leipzig, 1909.

OBW Barton, G. A.: *The Origin and Development of Babylonian Writing*, Leipzig, 1913.

PBS University of Pennsylvania: *The Museum Publications of the Babylonian Section* (New Series).

PPN Pöbel, A.: *Die Sumerischen Personennamen zur Zeit der Dynastie von Larsam und der ersten Dynastie von Babylon*, Breslau, 1910.

IV R Rawlison, H.: *The Cuneiform Inscriptions of Western Asia*, Vol. IV.

RCL Radau, H.: *Letters to Cassite Kings from the Temple Archives of Nippur*, BE Vol. XVII, part I, Philadelphia, 1908.

SBR Frank, C.: *Studien zur Babylonischen Religion*, Strassburg, 1911.

SHG Schollmeyer, A.: *Sumerisch-Babylonische Hymnen und Gebete an Šamaš* (Studien zur Geschichte und Kultur des Altertums), Paderborn, 1912.

SS Scheil, V.: *Une saison de fouilles à Sippar*, Le Caire, 1902.

UBL Ungnad, Arthur: *Babylonian Letters of the Hammurapi Period* (PBS VII), Philadelphia, 1915.

ZA *Zeitschrift für Assyriologie.*

ZB Zimmern, H.: *Beiträge zur Kenntnis der babylonischen Religion: die Beschwörungstafeln Šurpu; Ritualtafeln für den Beschwörer, Wahrsager und Sänger*, Leipzig, 1896–99.

ZDMG *Zeitschrift der Deutschen Morgenländischen Gesellschaft.*

PREFACE

Under the title "Selected Sumerian and Babylonian Texts" appear in the present volume ninety-five letters, Sumerian and Semitic codes of laws, a medical text, hymns, prayers and incantations. To these texts have been added a few literary school texts.

This medley of so widely different texts needs an explanation. It was occasioned by the fact that the epistolary material offered here completed the publication of all the letters owned by the University Museum, with the exception of a small number of very fragmentary letters of the Cassite period, the condition of which would have made their publication worthless. I decided therefore to publish with these letters all such literary texts which had not yet been assigned to scholars. All the incantation texts in the possession of the Museum have been copied by me and are incorporated in this volume. But also the number of these texts proved to be too small and I have added on this account all such material that would insure the interest of the Assyriologist. The volume thus presents a considerable variety of texts, a variety, generally not favored with text editions, that was caused by the shortage of epistolary and incantatory texts.

I take this opportunity to express my thanks to Professor Morris Jastrow, Jr., for many helpful suggestions and criticisms. To Professor Jastrow I owe particularly the correct reading and the meaning of the heretofore enigmatic reading of *Ê-nu-ru*, *Ê-nu-sub* or *Ê-nu-šub*. The reasons for his reading

Ê-nu-šub = "House of exorcism" Professor Jastrow will submit in the forthcoming number of the *Journal of the American Oriental Society*. My thanks are also due to the Director of the University Museum, Dr. George B. Gordon, for many courtesies during the preparation of this work.

H. F. LUTZ.

PHILADELPHIA, PA., July 16, 1919.

TRANSLATIONS

I

No. 108

A Prayer to Marduk During an Eclipse of the Moon

Obverse

[anaku] ^{ilu}*Šamaš-šum-ûkin* *[mâr ili-šu]*	I, Shamash-shum-ukin, the son of his god,
[ša ilu-šu] ^{ilu}*Marduk* ^{ilât}*Ištari-šu* ^{ilât}*[Ṣarpanitum]*	whose god is Marduk, whose goddess is Sarpanitum,
[ina lumun[1]*]* ^{ilu}*atali* ^{ilu}*Sin ša ina arḫi Kislimu ûmi 10-[kam*[2] *išakna*$^{(na)}$*]*	in the evil of an eclipse of the moon which has taken place in the month Kislimu, on the tenth day,
[lumun] idâti^{meš} *ittê*^{meš} *limnûti*^{meš} *la ṭâbâti*^{meš}	in the evil of the powers, of the signs, evil and not good,
[ša ina] ekalli-ìa û mâti-ìa ibašâ-a	which are in my palace and my country,
[pal]-ḫa-ku ad[-ra-]ku [û šu]-ta-du-ra-ku[3]	I fear, I tremble and I am cast down in fear!
[ina lib]-bi-ia damiqta rabiti û mati-ia	In my heart great grace and my country
a-na-ša(?)-a-na(?) a-na	I bear for . . . .
[i-na k]i-bi-ti-ka ṣir-ti	At thy exalted command
[lu]-ub-luṭ lu-uš-lim-ma[4] *lu-uš-tam-mar ilu-ut-ka*	let me live, let me be perfect and let me behold thy divinity!
[e]-ma ú-ṣa-am-ma-ru lu-uk-šu-ud	Whenever I plan, let me succeed!
[šu]-uš-kin kit-ti ina pi-ia	Cause truth to dwell in my mouth!
[šub]-ši a-mat damiqtu$^{(tu)}$ *ina lib-bi-ia*	Let a word of grace be in my heart!
ti-ru û na-an-ẓa-ẓa liq-bu-ú damiqtu$^{(tu)}$	May the watchman and guardian command favor!
[ili]-ia li-iẓ-ẓiẓ ina imni-ia	May my god stand at my right hand!
^{ilât}*Ištari-ia liẓ-ẓiẓ ina šumêli-ia*	May my goddess stand at my left!

Reverse

[ili]-ia šal-lim-[mu ina idi-ia lu-u]-ka-a-a-an	May my god, who is gracious, stand firmly at my side!
[šur]-gam-ma qa-ba-a [še-ma]-a û ma-ga-ru	to shout, to command, to listen and to be gracious!
[a]-mat a-qab-bu-ú ki-ma a-qab-bu-û lu ma-ag-[rat]	Let the word I speak, in the fashion I do speak, be propitious!
$^{[ilu]}$*Marduk bêlu rabû-ú napištim*$^{(tim)}$ *lu-ú*[5]	O Marduk, great lord, life!
[ba]-laṭ napištim $^{(tim)}$*-ia qi-bi-im*	Truly do thou command the life of my soul!
[ma]-ḫar-ka nam-riš a-tal-lu-ku lu-uš-bi	Before thee splendidly have I come, let me be satisfied!
$^{[ilu]}$*Enlil(!) urru-ka* ^{ilu}*E-a liriš-ka*	May Enlil be thy light, may Ea cry unto thee with joy!
[ilâni]^{meš} *ša kiš-šat lik-ru-bu-ka*	May the gods of the universe be favorable unto thee!
[ilâni^{me}*]*^{š} *rabûti*^{meš} *lib-ba-ka li-ṭib-bu*	May the great gods please thy heart!
[inim-]nim-ma šu-il-la ^{ilu}*Marduk-kan*	Prayer of the raising of the hand—it is to Marduk.

II

No. 121

A Prayer to a Goddess Against Witchcraft

Obverse

. . . .	. . . .
. . . . *lu ar-ru-ú mikda*[6] *limnutim*$^{(tim)}$	. . . . I am surrounded with the power of evil,
[ša ina zumri]ia-ši-im la idi[7] *kis-pi ru-ḫi-e ru-si-[e]*	which is in my body, is not known to me. Sorcery, witchcraft, poisoning,
ár-ša-še-e limnûti^{meš} *la ṭabu ša amelûti*	the evil, not good, tricks of mankind,
di-bal-la ĝul-gig ka-dib-bi-da-ge	deceit, seduction, stuttering,
zi-tar-ru-de-e ša a-we-lu-tim	raping of mankind,

ša bêl ik-ki-ia ša ṣi-ri-ia ša bêl dini-ia	of the lord of my oppression, (of the lord) of my enmity, of the lord of my judgment,
ša bêl dababi-ia ša bêl limnûtim(tim)*-ia*	of the lord of my reflection, of the lord of my mischief,
ša ip-ša bar-ta ù limnûtam(tam) *ša ú-še-pi-ša*	of sorcery, rebellion and evil which they did
is-ḫu-ra-am ekimam[8] *e-ni-en-na*	surrounded me, seized me. Now
an-ḫu-šu nu-ḫu e-še-'i pa-ni-ki	I am weak through it. Comfort I see before thee!
ina kabiti-ki ṣir-tim ša la innakaru(ru)	By thy exalted command, which does not change,
an-ni-ki ki-ni ša la in-ni-en-nu-ú	(and) thy true grace, which does not alter,
linnasiḫ ina zumri-ia ki-ma piššat ṣumbi-ki	let be torn away from my body like the grease of thy wagon
ma-am-ma la ṭâbu	whatsoever is not good!
ni-lil murṣi-ia ma-am-ma a-? a-šib	Let . . . . my sickness, whatsoever I . . . . . I dwell.
di-na liqi di-na di-in	Take up the judgment, render judgment!
purussa-a-a pur-si	Decide my decision!

Reverse

lu ar-ru-ú mikda[6] *limnûtim*(tim)	I am surrounded with the evil power
ša amêl kaššapi ù *sal**kaššapti*	of the sorcerer and the sorceress!
ina ki-bi-ti-ki	Through thy command
û an-ni-ki	and thy grace
limna eni-ia qarna rêši limnûtam(tam) *ša ina zumri-ia*	the evil of my eye, the horn of the head, the evil which is in my body,
šêri-ia riksati-ia ba-šu-ú linnasiḫ(iḫ) *zumri-ia*	my flesh, my members, let be torn away from my body.

AG.AG.BI[*ina muši*[9]]*gušuru mû illu tasalaḫ*	Perform the following: In the night sprinkle a bough with pure water.
ana pân kakkabi šib-zi-an-na (?) *qāna azag tanadi*(di)	At the presence of the star Shib-zianna, thou shalt throw a pure cane.

qān urrugalli tu-za-qap šipâta ǵe-gal tanaši[10]	An urrigallu-reed thou shalt set up. Wool of great abundance thou shalt carry.
šipâta za-gin-na . . -ga-ṣu teppuš mû tu-la-aḫ	Of pure wool a . . . . thou shalt make. Water thou shalt sprinkle.
ina libbi qān urrigalli GI.GAB tukân$^{(an)}$	Amongst the urrigallu-reed thou shalt set up a drink-offering.
. . . . *tuballal*(?)	. . . . thou shalt mix (?)
šiptam 3-šu tamannu	The incantation thou shalt recite three times.
. . . . *ki-za-za*	. . . .

Rest too fragmentary for translation.

III

No. 115

An Incantation Text

This text, together with another text published in this volume (No. 112), contains but implorations to the evil spirit to depart. Judging from the size of the tablet, it seems that only a few lines of the top of the obverse are lost, so that we may conjecture that this tablet, like tablet No. 112, began immediately with the formula: *zi X ǵe-pad niš X utammika.*

Obverse

. . . .	. . . .
[*zi gig-ge ù-ku-ku-e-ne*]*-ge ǵe* [*niš m*]*u-šu û mu-uṣ-la-lu*	By the night and those who sleep mayest thou be exorcised.
[*zi mul-mul gig-ge*] *nigin-bi ǵe* [*niš kakkabani*]$_{\text{I}}^{meš}$ *mu-ši-tum nap-ḫa-ri-šu-nu*	By the totality of the nightly stars mayest thou be exorcised.

[ẓi nam-tar-ri] ĝe [niš] šim-ti-ši-na

By their decree mayest thou be exorcised.

[ẓi dingir Babbar ê'-ta ẓi] dingir Babbar-šû-a ĝe [niš ṣi-it šamši]$^{(ši)}$e-rib šamši$^{(ši)}$

By the rising and the setting sun mayest thou be exorcised.

[ẓi dingir Babbar-ra udu-ge] dingir Giš-bil(?)gê-da ĝe niš ^{ilu}Šamaš ša û-mi ^{ilu}Sin ša mu-šu

By Shamash of the day, by Sin of the night mayest thou be exorcised.

ẓi ud te-ge mu-a ĝe niš ûmu ub-bak û šat-ti

By the turning day and year mayest thou be exorcised.

ẓi kur-bar-ra ẓi kur-šàg-ga ĝe niš ša-ḫat ša-di-i niš ki-rib ša-di-i

By the exterior of the mountain, by the interior of the mountain mayest thou be exorcised.

ẓi laĝ gê-gêg-ga ĝe niš nu-ru ik-li-ti

By the light of darkness mayest thou be exorcised.

ẓi ĝar-ra-an kaš-an ĝe-en-du ka-kaš[11] *kalam-ma-ge ĝe niš ur-ḫu ḫar-ra-an ṭu-du pa-da-nu ša ma-a-tu*

By the highway, the road, the path, the way of the land mayest thou be exorcised.

ẓi ub-da-da úr giš-gê ki-gub-bu-ne ĝe niš ṭup-ki ša-ḫa-ti du-tu ṣil-lu šub-tu man-ẓa-ẓa

By the side of the foundation, the shade of the dwelling-place mayest thou be exorcised.

ẓi ud-ge a-ab-ba nu-gi-gi-da-ge ĝe niš šal-šam(?) tam-tim la ta-a-ri . . . . .
. . . .

By the third sea of no return(??) . . .
. . . . mayest thou be exorcised.

ẓi an-ki-bi-da i-ri-[pad ĝa-ba-ra-du-un][12] *niš šamê û irṣitim$^{(tim)}$ lu[-ú ú-tam-me-ka lu-ta-at-ta-lak]*[12]

By heaven and earth I exorcise thee that thou mayest depart.

[en-na] su lù-gišgal-lu du[mu dingir-ra-na] a-di ẓumru$^{(ru)}$ amêl ili-šu

Until from the body of the man of his god

ba-ra-an-ta-ṛi-en-na ba-ra-an-[ta] ta-as-su-ú ta-[as-su-ḫu][13]

thou removest and thou departest

ú ba-ra-an-da-ab-kú-e [a ba-ra-an-da-ab-nak-e] a-ka-lu e[14] *ta-kul me-e [e tal-ti]*

food thou shalt not eat, water thou shalt not drink

a-na ẓumri-šu ĝa-ba-ra-ê'

From his body go out!

. . . . *ana man-ẓa-ẓi-ka* . . . .

. . . . to thy resting-place (return?).

. . . .
. . . .

. . . .
. . . .

Obverse, Col. II, Lower Piece

zi dingir Nin-sig-kur ....niš ^{ilâti}ditto be-lit ê ....
By Ninsigkur, the mistress of the temple of..........mayest thou be exorcised.

zi dingir Giš-bil sag nun-eš [kur-ra-ge ĝe][14] *niš ^{ilu}ditto a-ša-rid ša-[ka-nak-ka irṣitim(?)]*[15]
By Gishbil, chief high-priest of the earth mayest thou be exorcised.

zi dingir Da-mu a-su-gal [dingir-ri-e-ne-ge ĝe] niš ^{ilu}ditto a-su rabû ilâni$^{[meš]}$
By Damu, the chief physician of the gods mayest thou be exorcised.

zi dingir Ka-nun-ra .... niš ^{ilu}ditto me-dul(?) ....
By Kanunra, the........mayest thou be exorcised.

zi imma bil...................... niš.........................
By the burning thirst....mayest thou be exorcised.

zi šub.........................
By the prayer of......mayest thou be exorcised.

zi............................
By the........mayest thou be exorcised.

Reverse

zi dingir Nin-šar gir-lal ê-[kur ĝe] niš ^{ilu}ditto na-aš paṭ-ri ša Ê-[kur]
By Ninshar, the sword-bearer of Ekur mayest thou be exorcised.

zi dingir Azag-sug sanga maĝ [dingir An-na-ge ĝe] niš ^{ilu}ditto ša-an-gam-ma-ḫu ša ^{ilu}A-[nim]
By Azag-sug, the high-priest of Anu mayest thou be exorcised.

zi dingir Egir mu-gal din[gir An-na-ge ĝe] niš ^{ilu}ditto mu-gal ša ^{ilu}A-nim
By Egir the great representative of Anu mayest thou be exorcised.

zi dingir Nin-ma-da ba di[ngir An-na-ge ĝe] niš ^{ilâti}ditto ka-zal ša ^{ilu}A-nim
By Ninmada, she who implores Anu mayest thou be exorcised.

zi dingir Nidaba nin nig-nam-ma-ge šu-el [?-la ĝe] niš ^{ilâti}ditto be-el-ti mu-su(?)................
By Nidaba, the mistress of the pure treasure of fate (?) mayest thou be exorcised.

zi dingir Ĝa-ni bulug an sal-me-me gi-e[n ĝe] niš ^{ilu}ditto mu-kin pu-lu-[uk šami-e rapšâti]
By Hani, the establisher of the boundaries of the wide heavens mayest thou be exorcised.

zi dingir La-ma dingir lamma da.... niš ^{ilu}ditto ilu nam-.............
By Lama the protecting deity..... mayest thou be exorcised.

zi dingir En-lil-la an-na-ge [ĝe]
By Enlil of the heavens mayest thou be exorcised.

ʒi dingir Nin-lil-la an-na-ge [ǵe]	By Ninlil of the heavens mayest thou be exorcised.
ʒi dingir Ma-mi dingir . . . . niš ^{ilât}*ditto*[16] *be-lit . . . .*	By Mami the mistress of . . . . mayest thou be exorcised.

IV

No. 126

A Hymn to the Sun-god

For the restoration of this hymn compare IV R. 20 and IV R. 28.

Obverse

[en dingir Babbar an-ur-ra ǵi-i-ni-bu ^{ilu}*Šamaš ina i-šid šamê*$^{(e)}$ *tap-pu-ḫa-am-ma*	Incantation. O Shamash, at the foundation of the heavens thou flamest up.
giš si-gar aʒag an-na-ge nam-ta-e-gál ši-gar šamê$^{(e)}$ *ellûti tap-ti*	The lock of the brilliant heaven thou hast opened.
giš-gál an-na-ge gál-im-mi-ni-kid da-lat šamê$^{(e)}$ *tap-ta-a*	The bolt of the heaven thou hast removed.
dingir Babbar kalam-ma-ge sag-ga-na-šu mi-ni-ni-il ^{ilu}*Šamaš a-na ma-a]-ti ri[-ši-ka taš-ša-a]*	O Shamash, to the earth thou hast lifted up thy head.
[dingir Babbar me-lam an-na ^{ilu}*Šamaš me-lam-me] šamê*$^{(e)}$ *ma-ta-a[-ti tak-tum kur-kur-ra ne-tul]*	O Shamash, thou hast covered the earth with heavenly splendor.
[igi kalam-ma] ana ni-aš (!) ma-a-tu nu-ri ta[-ša-kan laǵ gar-ra[17]*-ne]*	When thou lookest upon the land establishest thou light.
[gir-kalam]-ma ki-bi-is ma-a-tu[18] *lu [-u tuš-te-ši . . . . -ne]*	The way of the land truly guide thou!
[maš]-anše niʒ-ʒi-gal bu-ul ṣêri ši-kin napišti [tι-ša-kan u-me-ni-gar][19]	The beasts of the field, the living creatures thou hast created.
dingir Babbar ama[20] *a-a-bi-da [gištug gar-gar-ra-ne]*[21]	To Shamash, like unto a father and mother they listen.
^{ilu}*Šamaš ki-ma a-bi û um-ma uʒ-na ši-[it-ku-nu]*[21]	

ú im-ši-in-kú-e-ne[22] *šam-mi ik-ka-la*	Food they are fed.
dingir Babbar a-sag ^{ilu}*Šamaš a-ša-rid ilâni at-*[*ta dingir-ri-e-ne-ge me-en*]	O Shamash, the chief of the gods art thou!
palil dingir A-nun-na-ki me-en[23] *a-lik maḫ-ri ša* [*A-nun-a-ki at-ta*]	He who goes before the Anunaki art thou!
an dingir Enlil-bi-da-ta [*lugal nam-lu-gišgal-lu me-en it*]*-ti* ^{ilu}*A-nu û* ^{ilu}*En-lil šâr amelûti* [*at-ta*]	With Anu and Enlil a king of mankind art thou!
[*id*]*-ag-ge un-ki*[24]*-šar-ra-ge* [*si-ne . . .*] [*te*]*-rit kiš-šat niši* [*šu-te-šir*]	Guide thou the law of all the people!
dingir nig-si-di mi-[*ša-riš*] *ina šamê*$^{(e)}$ *ka-a-a-nu at-t*[*a an gub-ba me-en*]	O god of justice in the heaven eternal art thou!
dingir nig-gi-na kit-tu bi-rit uz-na ša ma-ta-a-t[*u at-ta kur-kur-ra igi-gal me-en*]	Thou art the justice and the wisdom of the land!
zi-du mu-un-zu ki-na ti-di rag-gu ti[*-di nig-erim mu-un-zu*]	Thou knowest the pious, thou knowest the wicked.
dingir Babbar nig-si-di ^{ilu}*Šamaš mi-ša-ri ri-is-su i-na-aš*[*-ši-ik*] [*gu-bi ma-ra-an-ri*]	O Shamash, righteousness lifteth up to thee its head.
dingir Babbar nig-erim-e[25] *usan-dim* [*im-ma-ra-an-nun-ki-ta*] ^{ilu}*Šamaš rag-gu ki-ma qin-na-zi* [*it-tar-rak-ka*]	O Shamash, wickedness like a whip becomes torn through thee.
dingir Babbar iskim-ta[26] [*an dingir En-lil me-en*] ^{ilu}*Šamaš tu-kul-ti* ^{ilu}*A-nim* [*u* ^{ilu}*En-lil at-ta*]	O Shamash, the helper of Anu and Enlil art thou.
dingir Babbar di-kud [*maǵ an-ki-bi-da me-en*] [^{ilu}*Šamaš da-a-a-nu ṣi-ru ša šamê*$^{(e)}$ *irṣitim*$^{(tim)}$ *at-ta*]	O Shamash, the exalted judge of heaven and earth art thou.

Reverse

. . . .*-am-a-ni-šu* ^{ilu}*Šamaš*	. . . . .Shamash
. . . .	. . . .
[*lugal-e dumu dingir-ra*]*-na ta-gab-bu-na* [*ǵe-gub*] [*šarru mā*]*r ili-šu ina šu-mē-li-šu* [*li-zi-iz*]	The king, the son of his god, may stand at his left.

[dingir lù-gal-lu dumu]-a-ni-šu mú-un-na-an-gub a- . . . . ù ilu amêli aš-šu ma-ri-šu aš-riš iz-za-az-ka	And the god of man on account of his son devoutly steps before thee.
me silim me nam-ti-la [u-gar-ra-ab] pa-ra-as šul-me pa-ra-as ba-lá-[tu šu-kun-šum-ma]	A command of peace, a command of life establish for him!
ka silim šàg ǵul-la ina sa-li-mu ḫu-ut lib-bi	In loving kindness of a joyous heart . . . .
ka-gar sig-ga ina e-gir-ri-e dam-ḳi	In gracious thoughts . . . .
dingir Babbar lugal dingir-ra-na su-a ǵe-en-da-ab-[bi] ^{ilu}*Šamaš šâr mâr ili-šu liq-bi ša a-na qa-tu . . . .*	May Shamash, the king of the son of his god, speak, so that into the hand . . . .
en ki-gal kul-unu-ki kalag kalam-a-ni-šu rag-ga- . . . . be-el ša ki-gal-e ša kul-la-bi ka-a-ša	Lord of the kigallu of Kullab to thee, the hero in his land . . . .
dingir Babbar di-kud maǵ [en nun kur-kur-ra-ge me-en][27] ^{ilu}*Šamaš da-a-a-nu ṣi-ri bêl rabû*$^{(u)}$ *ša [ma-ta-a-ti at-ta]*	O Shamash, the lofty judge, the great lord of the lands art thou.
lugal nig-zi-ga [šà-lá-sud kalam-ma-ge me-en] be-lim šik-na-ti napištim$^{(tim)}$ *rim-nu-[ú ša ma-ta-a-ti at-ta]*	The lord of living creatures, the merciful of the lands art thou.
[dingir Babbar ud-da] ne-e[28] *lugal*[29] *dumu dingir-ra-[na u-me-ni-el u-me-ni-laǵ-laǵ* ^{ilu}*Šamaš ina ûmi]*$^{(mi)}$ *an-ni-e šar-[ri mâr ili-šu ul-lil-šu ub-bi-ib-šu]*	O Shamash, at this day purify and cleanse the king, the son of his god.
[nig-nam ǵul-dim]-ma su-a ni-ga[l-la bar-bi-ta ǵe-en-zi-zi] [mimma e-piš] limnûtim$^{(tim)}$ *ša ina zumri-[šu ba-šu-ú ina a-ḫa-a-ti li-in-na-si]*	Whatever evil sorcery, which is in his body, may it be removed.

Rest destroyed.

V

No. 118

Another Hymn to Shamash

A duplicate fragment of this text is found in Langdon's Grammatical Texts, PBS. XII, No. 1, plates 32 to 35. The text, however, where the duplicate comes to assist in its restoration, is still too fragmentary in the first column of the reverse to allow a running translation. It is probable that also text No. 27 in the work of Langdon represents but an excerpt of the present hymn. Below is offered a transliteration and translation of the second column of the reverse only. The obverse of the tablet is nearly completely destroyed.

Reverse, Col. II

dingir Babbar ana ʒagin-ta ê'-[a]	O Shamash, come forth from the shining heaven!
ù-gin ana aʒag-ga-ta sag-tu-tu	Go forth from the brilliant heaven, O first-born!
dingir Babbar en-gal-bi dingir Babbar lugal-á-[bi me-en?]	O Shamash, its great lord; O Shamash, its mighty king art thou.
dingir Babbar en-gál bàr-bàr-e-ne	O Shamash, lord of the throne-chambers,
dingir Babbar lugal-gal an-ki-ki	O Shamash, great king of heaven and earth,
dingir Babbar kid-a ʒ(?) dingir-e-ne-ge sag-ka maš-sag a-a a-nun-na-e-ne	O Shamash, encloser(?) of the gods, chief, leader, father of the Anunaki,
dingir Babbar še-ir-ʒi^{30} *ʒid-da an-ki-a* ^{mul}*ana*	O Shamash, true glory, in heaven and earth the Anu-star,
dingir Babbar ušum-gal nir-lugal šàg ê'-a	O Shamash, hero, lord of the interior, king, come forth!
dingir Babbar dingir šar-ra gal-ʒa an-na me nu-un-laġ-laġ	O Shamash, god of the totality, thy greatness in heaven does not remove presage.

ub-šu an[31]*-na-ge sag la kur-bi me-en*	In the sphere of the heavens thou art the chief of the fullness of its region.
. . . . .*lu igi(?) edin-na gú-nu-má-má me-en*	The foremost in the desert, who does not humble himself, art thou.
. . . .*palil me-en lù-tab-ba za-e me-en*	The first art thou, a companion art thou.
dingir Babbar lù . . . .*á-duǵ-a nir(?)-e me-en*	O Shamash, who . . . . . .in increase of might, thou art a lord.
dingir Babbar lu ê'-a(?) ki-gub-a-ni ib-ǵa-e	O Shamash, who having gone forth to his place of position, teemeth with might.
ǵul-gál-e . . . .*-a-ni-bi ǵe-šu-kud*	The evil . . . . may be cut off.
dingir Babbar lugal nun-ra me(?)-na . . . .*ni-zu*	O Shamash, king, who maketh known to the prince his command of . . . .
kur zagin šu-úr maǵ gú-bi	The brilliant mountain, the great bolt, its neck . . . .
dingir Babbar-ka [2] *šàg ana-ge gal-bi*	O Shamash, inmidst of the heaven greatly . . . .
šàg kur-ra-ge û dagal-bi ni-tuš	Inmidst of the world (and) its wide desert thou dwellest.
dingir Babbar di-kud dingir Babbar ka-aš-bar	O Shamash, judge, O Shamash, decider,
dingir Babbar di-kud dingir-e-ne-ge	O Shamash, judge of the gods,
dingir Babbar ka-aš-bar a-a a-nun-na-ge	O Shamash, decider, father of the Anunaki,
dingir Babbar ad dingir En-lil-la tu-tu-ud-gá-gá	O Shamash, born of father Enlil,
dingir Babbar en-kal-gál ana azag-ga	O Shamash, powerful lord of the splendid heaven,
dingir Babbar dingir nig-si-di di-kam	O Shamash, just god of judgment,
dingir Babbar sib a-a sag-gig-a	O Shamash, shepherd, father of the black-headed,
dingir Babbar sag di-kud kalam-ma-ge	O Shamash, chief judge of the land,
dingir Babbar di-kud-ge(?) za-a-am	O Shamash, a judge art thou!
dingir Babbar ka-aš-bar-ra za-a-am	O Shamash, a decider art thou!
dingir Babbar nig-gi-na za-a-am	O Shamash, truth art thou!
dingir Babbar nig-zi . . . .*za-a-am*	O Shamash, life . . . . .art thou!

dingir Babbar a-ab-ba igi-nim ẓa-a-am	O Shamash, above the ocean art thou!
dingir Babbar a-ab-ba sig-a ẓa-a-am	O Shamash, below the ocean art thou!
dingir Babbar kur-aš šu-di-na tur-ra ẓa-a-am	O Shamash, into the mountain . . . . .entering art thou!
dingir Babbar sig-ga-aš esig-ga-ra gá-nu ẓa-a-am	O Shamash, raging in might towards the strong one art thou!
dingir Babbar nu-tuk-ki gul-la ẓa-a-am	O Shamash, one who does not own destruction art thou!
dingir Babbar nu-mu-un ku-si-da ẓa-a-am	O Shamash, the seed of Kusida art thou!
dingir Babbar ẓa-men nu-ê' di-kud nu-kud ka-aš nu-bar-ra	O Shamash, if thou dost not come forth, judgment will not be rendered, decision will not be made.
dingir Babbar ẓa-men nu-ê' igi-a-šu lu-ru-tiq di-kud nu-kud	O Shamash, if thou dost not come forth, in the presence of the oppressor (?) judgment will not be rendered.
dingir Babbar ẓa-men nu-ê' giš-gu-ẓa nam-lugal-la-šu nu-gub	O Shamash, if thou dost not come forth, the throne in the kingship will not stand (firm).
dingir Babbar ẓa-men nu-ê' pa nam-lugal-la-šu nu-gá-gá	O Shamash, if thou dost not come forth, the scepter in the kingship will not exercise.
dingir Babbar ẓa-men nu-ê' giš-dug(?) nam-lugal-la-šu nu-laǵ	O Shamash, if thou dost not come forth, the good lord in the kingship will not lead.
dingir Babbar ẓa-men nu-ê' lugal erin-ne á la ba-ag-gi	O Shamash, if thou dost not come forth, the king's men will not exercise power.
dingir Babbar ẓa-men nu-ê' giš-lugal dingir-ra-ẓu sig-aš nu(!)-sig-ga	O Shamash, if thou dost not come forth, the royal lord through thy divinity will not be filled with fullness.
dingir Babbar ẓa-men nu-ê' lù-maǵ dam igi-bar nu-ẓu	O Shamash, if thou dost not come forth, the mighty one will not know the look of a woman.
dingir Babbar ẓa-men nu-ê' ur-bar-ra -ge nu-ub-ba-šù-šù	O Shamash, if thou dost not come forth, the jackal will not rush about.
ur-maǵ esig-ga nu-ub-si-ga kur-gal ka-	The lion will not be filled with strength, the great mountain . . . .

VI

No. 127

An Utukku Limnutu Text

Obverse, Col. I

en ê-nu-šub	Incantation of the house of exorcism.
utug-ĝul lù-e (?) *gig-ga*	The evil demon has smitten man with sickness.
á-úr-da du-du	It causes the limbs to toss in pain.
e-sir-ra šu-šu	It rushes into the street.
galla-ĝul-gál	The evil devil
edin-na šú-bar-ra	Is let loose in the plain.
sa-gaz šú-nu-gi	The robber is not turned back.
dingir-dim-me	The hag-demon
dingir-dim-a	The ghoul
galu-ra su-su	Have rushed upon the man.
[*šàg*][33]*-gig libiš-gig*	With heart-disease, madness,
[*tu-ra*] *sag-gig*	Sickness (and) headache
[*uru-lu-galu*]*-ra dul-la*	They cover the man.
[*lù gin u*]*-dim*	Scorching the wanderer
[*mu-un-da*]*-ru-uš*	Like the day.
[*ṣi-na*]	With bitterness
[*ba-ni-in-su-eš*]	They fill him.
lù-gal-bi [*zi-ni-ta*]	This man from his soul
ni-bal-bal-[*e zi-gim mu-un-zi*]	Is torn and tosses like the billows.
dingir Asar-lù-dug igi-im-ma-an-sum	Marduk saw him.
a-a-ni dingir En-ki-ra	Unto his father Ea
ê-a ba-an-ši-tur	Into the house he entered.
gù-mu-un-na-dé-e	He spoke:
a-a-mu utuk-ĝul galu-e gig?-ga	O my father, an evil demon has smitten man with sickness.
á-úr-da du-du	He causes the limbs to toss in pain.
e-sir-ra šu-šu	He rushes in the street.
a-du 2-kam-ma-aš	Twice
ù-ub-dug[34]	Let him say it.
[*a-na ib-aga*]*-en na-bi nu-zu*	What he has done he does not know,
[*a-na ni*]*-íb-ge-ge*	Nor how he shall be relieved.
[*dingir En-ki du*]*mu-ni*	Ea unto his son
[*dingir Asar-lù-*]*dug*	Marduk
[*mu-un-na-ni-íb-ge-ge*]	Answered:

Col. II

dumu-mu a-na nu-e-zu	O my son, what dost thou not know?
a-na a-ra-ab-daǵ-e-en	What can I add unto thee?
dingir Asar-lù-dug	O Marduk,
a-na nu-e-zu	What dost thou not know?
a-na a-ra-ab-daǵ-e-en	What else can I add unto thee?
nig-má-e ni-zu-a-mu	That which I know
ù-za-e in-ga-e-zu	Thou knowest also!
gin-na dumu-mu	Go, my son
dingir Asar-lù-dug	Marduk!
a an-za-am-ma	Water from the asammu-vessel
ù-me-ni-dé	Pour out.
giš-šinig ú-in-nu-uš	Tamarisk and mashtakal-plant
šàg-ba ù-me-ni-šub	Place on his heart.
galu-ba ù-me-ni-gur	This man atone!
[*nig*]*-na gi-bil-la*	Censer and torch
[*ù-me-ni-e*][35]	Cause thou to go forth.
[*nam-tar kuš galu-ka*]	The curse which is in the body of man
[*nig*]*-gál-la* [*a-gim*]	Like water
ǵe-im-ma-ra-an-zi-[*zi*][36]	May run away!
urudu nig-kalag-ga	The copper of strength
ur-sag an-na-ge	Of the hero Anu
za-pa-ag ǵu-luǵ-ǵa-ni[37]	Whose terrifying roar
nig-ǵul ba-ab-ur-ri (*šu ù-me-ti*[38])	Seizes away whatsoever is evil, take!
ki za-pa-ag sum-ma	Where its roar is given out
ù-me-sum	Bring it!
sag-tu-uk-zu[39] *ǵe-a*	Verily it shall be thy supporter!
urudu nig-kalag-ga	May the copper of strength
ur-sag an-na-ge	Of the hero Anu
za-pa-ag me-lam-m[*a-ni*]	With its awful roar
[*ǵu*]*-um-ma-daǵ-*[*e*][40]	Help thee!

Col. III

utug-ǵul a-la-ǵul	May the evil demon, the evil spirit
ǵa-ba-ra-ê'	Go forth!
gidim-ǵul galla-ǵul	May the evil ghost, the evil devil
ǵa-ba-ra-ê'	Go forth!
dingir-ǵul maškim-ǵul	May the evil god, the evil fiend

ǵa-ba-ra-ê'	Go forth!
ka-ǵul uǵ ǵul-dim-ma[41]	May the evil mouth, sorcery, evil deed
ǵa-ba-ra-ê'[41]	Go forth!
dingir-dim-me dingir-dim-a	May the hag-demon, the ghoul
galu-ra šu-šu	Having rushed upon man
ga-ba-ra-ê'	Go forth!
šàg-gig libiš-gig	Heart-ache, madness
tu-ra [*sag*]*-gig*	Sickness, headache
uru-lu-galu-ra dul-[*la*]	Which cover the man
ǵa-ba-ra-ê'	May go forth!
[*ẓi dingir*]*-gal-gal-e-ne-ge*	By the great gods
[*i-ri*]*-pad*	Mayest thou be exorcised
ǵa-[*ba-ra-du*]*-un*	That thou mayest depart!
inim-nim-ma [*utug-ǵul*]*-a-kam*	Prayer against the evil spirit.

---

en ê-nu-šub	Incantation of the house of exorcism.
utug-ǵul a-la-ǵul	O evil spirit, O evil demon,
lù gig-ki-a-šu[42]	Who have power by night
sil-a kil-ba	Over the street,
gidim-ǵul gal-la-ǵul	O evil ghost, O evil devil,
lù gig-ki-a-šu[42]	Who have power by night
e-sir-ra[43] *kil-ba*	Over the path,
ud-bat[44]*-ša*	O thou that mightily
an-ša-ša	Afflictest
nig-na-me nu-un-kad-kad	And leavest nothing untouched,
ǵul-gál lù[45] *igi-ǵuš-a*	The evil one whose face is angry,
me-lam-ma ẓag-sir	Girt about with splendor
ka-du-a[46]	(Which is) terrible

Col. IV

šug-ga nu-un-ẓu-a	Knoweth no kindness.
galu-ra ǵul-gál-ta	To man it gleams full of disaster
mul-dim sur-ru-da	Like a star.
lù šu-lá-a	It binds
šú-nu-un-bar-ri	And does not set free.
lù gig-ki-a	It in the night
ê-a-ni-šu ra-a	Goes to his house

galu-ra ba-te	And approaches the man
[*gú*][47] *ni-in-sum*	Cutting the throat
. . . *-bi-šu mu-un-ru*	Fastening in his . . . . .
ê-a-ni-šu ba-an-te-ga	It draws near unto his house.
giš-gi-en-na-ni ba-an-da-ĝa-lam	It destroys his members.
igi-ni til-til	It tears out his eye,
lù igi-nu-un-bar-ri	So that he cannot see.
. . . *igi-bi lù-bi?* . . . *-ne-* . . .	The . . . . . of its eye man . . . . . .
lù . . . . *-na*	Who . . . .
lù-gal-bi	Man . . . .
ĝul-dib-bi[*galu-ra*]*dib-dib*	Evil has seized the man.
azag gig[*su-na*]*mu-un-šu-šu*	White leprosy? covers his body.
dingir Asar-lù-dug igi-im-ma-an-sum	Marduk saw him.
nig-má-e ni-zu-a-mu	What I know
ù-za-e in-ga-e-zu	Knowest thou also.
gin-na dumu-mu dingir Asar-lù-dug	Go my son Marduk!
dug-bur-šar-ra ù-me-ni-si	A suharratu-vessel fill!
a-gub-ba dingir En-ki-ge	The pure water of Ea
ù-me-ni-tum	Bring!
nam-šub nun-ki-ga	The incantation of Eridu
ù-me-ni-sig	Perform!
lù-gal[*-lu dumu dingir*]*-ra-na*	Unto the man the son of his god
giš-nad-k[*a? tum*]*-ma*	At the bed bring (it).
ù-me-ni-sug-sug	Sprinkle him!
urudu nig-kalag-[*ga*] *ur-sag an-na-ge*	The copper of might of the hero Anu

COL. V

giš-ma-nu giš-ku kalag-ga-ta	May the tamarisk the powerful weapon
za-pa-àg me-lam-ma-ni	The roar of its splendor
ĝu-mu-ra-ab-daĝ-e-en	Help thee!
zid-sur-ra en-nu-un kalag-ga	Smear meal-water,
ù-me-ni-sur	The powerful protection!
kán-na-ne-ne-a zid-sur-ra	Smear the doors
ù-me-ni-sur	With meal-water!
giš-gál ê-e-ka	The house-door
giš-sagil ê-e-ka	The bolt of the house!
šu šab-šab-bu	The hand that tears (it) off
ù-me-ni-šab-šab-bu	Cut off!

[ut]ug-ĝul a-lá-ĝul	O evil spirit, O evil demon,
[lù] ge-ki-a-šu sila-a kil-ba	Who has power by night over the street
[zi] dingir-gal-gal-e-ne-ge	By the great gods
[ĝe-ri]-pad	Be thou exorcised!
[nig-ĝul]-gál-e ê-a-na an-ri-i	The evil that has gone to his house
nig-ĝul-gál-e ê-a-na an-tuš-a	The evil that has dwelled in his house
giš-gál ê-e-ka	The door of the house
nam-mu-un-da-an-tu-tu-ne	May they not enter!
da lù ê'-da-ta	Having gone forth from the man
nam-mu-un-da-tu-tu-ne	May they no more enter!
giš-gu-za-na nam-ba-tuš-ù-ne	May they not sit in his seat!
giš-nad-da-na nam-ba-ù-ne	May they not lie on his couch!
ur-šu nam-[ba-gibiš]-ne	May they not rise over his fence!
ê-ki-tuš-a-na nam-ba-tu-tu-ne	May they not enter into his chamber!
zi dingir-gal-gal-e-ne-ge	By the great gods
i-ri-pad	The evil that has gone to his house
ĝa-ba-ra-du-un	That thou mayest depart!
zi an-na ĝe-pad	By heaven mayest thou be exorcised!
zi ki-a ĝe-pad	By earth mayest thou be exorcised!
inim-nim-ma u[tug-ĝul-a]-kam	Prayer against the evil spirit.

Col. VI

[en ê-nu-šub]	Incantation of the house of exorcism.
................*-ĝul*	........................evil
................*-ĝul*	........................evil
................*-zu*	........................knows
........*-ê-ta ê'*	.......from the house take forth
.........*ê-gal-ta*	.........at the temple
ù-mi-in-gar	Is placed.
du-gab ê-gal-ta ê'-a	The offering (?) take forth from the temple!
šu-a im-mi-in-gar	Place it into the hand!
ur-gig-gi	A black dog's
ka mu-ni-íb-....	Tooth................
ur-babbar.....	(With) a white dog's.......
lil mu-un-na-ab(?)-dul	Tall grown cover him.

ur gur-a ur-ẓu il(?)	The dog turn away, thy dog carry up.
dug-[48]*ga*	The word ....
ẓu an-na	The knowledge of heaven ....

Ten lines destroyed.

....*ẓu dingir-ri-e-ne-ge*	Unto the ....of the gods
galu mu-un-ši-gi-gi	Man has turned.
dingir Asar-lù-dug	O Marduk
dumu nun-ki-ga-ge	Son of Eridu
[tû]-tû-e ẓu-ab	The incantation of the Deep
[nun]-ki-ga-ta	Of Eridu
[nam]-mu-un-da-an-bur-ri	Let never be loosened!

VII

No. 119

An Invocation to Nergal

A duplicate of this text is published in King, Magic and Sorcery, No. 27.

Obverse

[šiptu be-lum gaš-ru ti-iẓ-ḳa-ru bu-kur ^{ilu}*NU.NAM.NIR]*	Incantation: O mighty lord, hero, first-born of Nunamnir.
[a-ša-rid ^{ilu}*A-nun-na]-ki be[-el tam-ḫa- i]*	Leader of the Anunaki, lord of battle,
[i-lit-ti ^{ilu}*KU.TU.ŠAR šar-ra-tum rabîtum*$^{(tum)}$*]*	Offspring of Kutusar the mighty queen,
^{ilu}*Nergal kaš-kaš ilâni*^{meš} *na-ram* ^{ilât}*NIN.MIN.NA]*	O Nergal, mighty one of the gods, the beloved of Ninminna,
[šu-pa-ta ina šamê$^{(e)}$*] illûti*^{meš} *ša-qu man-ẓa-ẓa-ka*	Thou treadest in the lofty heavens, lofty is thy place.
ra-ba-ta ina arallî	Thou art exalted in the underworld.
ma-ḫi-ra la(!) ti-ši[49]	A rival thou hast not.
itti ^{ilu}*A-nim ina puḫur ilâni*^{meš} *me-lik-ka šu-ṭur*	With Anu among the multitude of the gods write thy counsel.
itti ^{ilu}*Sin ina šamê*$^{(e)}$ *û irṣitim* $^{(tim)}$ *ta-ši-i 'gim-ri*	With Sin in the heavens and the earth thou seekest everything.

id-din-ka-ma^{ilu}*En-lil abu-ka*	And then has Enlil thy father given unto thee
ṣal-mat qaqqadu pu-ḫur napištim$^{(tim)}$	That the blackheaded, all living creatures,
[*bu*]-*ul* ^{ilu}*Nergal nam-maš-ša-a qa-tuk-ka ip-qid*	The cattle of Nergal, animals, thy hand should take into care.
[*ana* ^{ilu}*Šamaš-šu*]*m-ûkin mâr ili-šu*	Unto Shamash-shum-ukin, the son of his god,
[*ša ili-šu* ^{ilu}*Marduk*] *ištari-šu* ^{ilât}*Ṣar-pa-ni-tum*	Whose god is Marduk, whose goddess is Sarpanitum
[*lumun idāti*^{meš}] *itâti*^{meš} *limnûti*^{meš} *la ṭabâti*^{meš}	In the evil of the powers, of the signs, evil and not good,
[*ša ina ekalli*]-*ia ib-ša-a-ma*	Which are in my palace,
[*pa-ḫa-ku ad*]-*ra-ku û šu-ta-du-ra-ku*	I am afraid, I tremble and I am cast down in fear.
[*a-na ekalli*]-*ia a-na mati-ia*	To my palace, to my land
[*iq*]-*ba-a-a-nim a*[50] *a-mat an-ni*	They spoke a word of sin.
[*našâḫu u ḫu-lu-uq*][51]-*qu-ú ib-ba-šu-ú ina biti-ìa*	Destruction and insurrection are in my house.
[*qa-bu-ú la še*]-*mu-ú it-tal-pu-in-ni*	Speaking, not listening they distress me.
[*aš-šum gam-ma-la-ta* ^{ilu}*Nergal be*]-*lum* [*as-sa-ḫar ilu-ut-ka*][52]	Because thou art well-wishing, O lord Nergal, I turn to thy divinity.

REVERSE

[*ag-gu lib-ba*]-*ka li*[-*nu-ḫa*]	Let thy angry heart have rest!
[*pu-ṭur an*]-*ni ḫi-ṭi-ti û si-la-ti*[53]	Loosen my sin, my offence and my presumption.
[*na*(?)-*ṣir lib*]-*bi ilu-ti-ka rabîti*[54]	Thy great divinity protect my heart!
[*luš-ta*]-*mar sartani pa-da-ám-ma*[54]	Let me see the untruthfulness and set me free.
[*ilu û*] *ištaru ẓi-nu-tum šab-su-tum*[55]	O god and angry and incensed goddess
[*dum-qa*] *ma-ḫar-ìa lu-ut-pu liš-li-mu itti-ìa*	Favor let come before me and deal graciously with me.
[*nir*]-*bi-ka lu-ša-pi*[56] *dá-lí-lì-ka lud-lul*	Let me proclaim thy greatness, let me bow in humility before thee.
inim-nim-ma šu-il-la ^{ilu}*Nergal-kam*	Incantation of the raising of the hand. It is to Nergal.
šiptu šu ǵul(?)*nu mul-mul-kam*[57]	Incantation......of the *mulmullu*-star.

VIII

No. 124

A Consecration Text for the Building of House and City

For the restorations of this interesting, but poorly preserved, text compare Scheil, Sippar 36.[58]

Obverse

šiptu ^{ilu}*E-a* ^{ilu}*Šamaš û* ^{ilu}*[Marduk ilâni rabûti]*	Incantation: Ea, Shamash and Marduk the great gods
muteppušu û da-an-[ni]^{meš} (?)*ina âli [at-tu-nu-ma]*[59]	The builders and the fortifiers (?) in the city (are you?)
mu-šap-pa-lu MÚR.NIR [muballiṭu kāl mimma šumšu ša tabna]	You dug deep the large circuit. You revived every creature that you have created.
ala an-na-a [ša te-pu-šu][60]	This city which you have built
ina amat-ku-nu ki-ma šadê$^{(e)}$ *li[-kun ki-bit-ku-nu . . . .]*[61]	Through your word may stand firm like the mountains. Your command . . . .
ana ^{ilu}*Šamaš-šum-ûkin mâr [abi-šu arad pa-liḫ-ku-nu]*	Unto Shamash-shum-ukin, the son of his father, the servant who fears you,
ana amātu$^{(tu)}$ *parsı balāṭa [kal i-li-šu lid-din]*	Command through a word that his god may give strong life!
šiptu ^{ilu}*E-a* ^{ilu}*Šamaš û* ^{ilu}*[Marduk bêlê šamê û irṣitim]*	Incantation: O Ea, Shamash and Marduk, lords of heaven and earth
e-piš âli û bîti [at-tu-nu-ma]	The builders of the city and the house are you!
da-[an?]-nu di-in . . . . [-ma zêru muš-te-še-ru te-ni-še-e-ti]	Strong is the judgment of . . . . the leaders of mankind.

Reverse[62]

bul-liṭ AN	Call into existence (?) . . . .
at-ta ^{ilu}*? amel mu-[te-puš uṣur?]*	Thou O . . . . . . protect the builder(?)
âla^{ki} *an-na-a ša* ^{ilu}*Šamaš-šum-[ûkin]*	Unto this city of Shamash-shum-ukin

ala an-na-a^{ki}[63] *u âlani*^{ki} [^{meš} *ša mâti(?)*]	This city and the cities of the country
ṣilla û damiqta-ka at-⌈ta li-šim-ma]	Mayest thou decree gracious protection and thy favor
itta-ka damiqtam$^{(tam)}$ *ina âli* [*tašakanu(?)*]	Thy sign of favor place into the city.
martam$^{(tam)}$ *la šur-ru-ú*	Not shall grow up bitterness
ina âli ka-a-tu	In the city . . . .
i-nun-bi-ṭu	They shall shine . . . .
ina âli ^{ilu}*Šamaš-šum-ûkin*	In the city of Shamash-shum-ukin
. . . .	. . . .

IX

No. 112

An Exorcism[64]

Obverse

[*zi dingir* . . . .] *ge-pad*	By . . . . mayest thou be exorcised.
[*zi dingir* . . . .] *ge-pad*	By . . . . mayest thou be exorcised.
[*zi dingir* . . . .] *ge-pad*	By . . . . mayest thou be exorcised.
[*zi dingir* . . . .] *ge-pad*	By . . . . mayest thou be exorcised.
[*zi dingir* . . . .] *kur-kur-ra ge-pad*	By . . . . of the lands mayest thou be exorcised.
[*zi dingir* . . . .] *kur-kur-ra ge-pad*	By . . . . of the lands mayest thou be exorcised.

Three lines destroyed.

zi dingir Dam-en-ki . . . . *ge*	By Damenki the . . . . mayest thou be exorcised.
zi dingir Ba-ú ama . . . . . *ge*	By Bau the mother of . . . . mayest thou be exorcised.

zi dingir Am-ma ama dingir an-ki-bi-ta-ge ǵe — By Amma the mother of heaven and earth mayest thou be exorcised.

zi dingir Šul-pa-ê' . . . . ǵe — By Shulpaë the . . . . mayest thou be exorcised.

Three lines destroyed.

zi dingir Šu?-ur-mu za- . . . . ǵe — By Shurmu the . . . . mayest thou be exorcised.

zi dingir En-ki uš-sa an-ki-a- . . . . ǵe — By Enki inmidst of the heaven and the earth mayest thou be exorcised.

zi dingir Dam-gal-nun-na dam dingir En-ki-ge ǵe — By Damgalnunna the consort of Enki mayest thou be exorcised.

zi dingir Asar-lù-dug gúb-gúb an-ki-a-šu ǵe — By Asar, the good Being, the *gubgubbu* in heaven and earth mayest thou be exorcised.

zi dingir Amar-udu inim-dug-ga ni-uš nig-ǵul(?) ni-ri ki-ta ǵe-pad — By Marduk, the spokesman . . . . . evil(?) who goes below mayest thou be exorcised.

zi dingir Ni-nun dingir . . . . . . gi-a in- . . . . ǵe — By Ninun the god in the . . . . mayest thou be exorcised.

Three lines destroyed.

zi dingir Taš-me-tum dam a-mu-ru-ki(?) ǵe-pad — By Tashmetum the consort Amuru(?) mayest thou be exorcised.

zi dingir Bu-bu-bu nu-tur kur-ra-ge ǵe — By Bububu the dwarf of the mountain mayest thou be exorcised.

zi dingir Á[65] *ama en-gur-ra-ge ǵe* — By Á the mother of the Deep mayest thou be exorcised.

zi dingir Ṣi dam en zu mu-da-ge ǵe — By Ṣi the consort of the lord of the knowledge of dreams mayest thou be exorcised.

zi dingir A-ra giš ab-zu-a ǵe — By Ara, the hero in the Deep mayest thou be exorcised.

zi dingir La-ǵa-ma ad-gal gu-gu-a(?) ǵe — By Lagama the ancestor in the gugu mayest thou be exorcised.

zi dingir Nannar kud nam-kud-da-ni-ge . . . . . bi-ib-la . . . . . ǵe — By Nannar the divider of divisions . . . . mayest thou be exorcised.

zi dingir Dam-gal-la(!) an-da-a-ge ġe
By Damgalla in the heavens mayest thou be exorcised.

zi dingir Dam-kešda dag-il-il-na ġe
By Damkeshda .... mayest thou be exorcised.

zi dingir .... gal-gal-la ġe
By .... the great mayest thou be exorcised.

Obverse, Col. II

zi dingir A-ra-su šúb-šúb-[ba] an-na-ge [ġe-pad]
By Arasu the implorer in the heavens mayest thou be exorcised.

zi dingir Ù-ra ġe-ê'-a zi [dingir ......] šag-ga ù-na-ge ġe
By Ura mayest thou go forth, by .... the gracious of time, mayest thou be exorcised.

zi ni-bu gu-za-lá ù-na-ge ġe
By Nibu the thronebearer of time mayest thou be exorcised.

zi an-ki še-ir-zi nam-kur-ra me-lam-ma ġe
By the perfection of the splendor and the brilliancy of heaven and earth mayest thou be exorcised.

zi dingir A-a-bu dumu-sal? dam-a-ni ġe
By Abu the daughter of his (her?) consort mayest thou be exorcised.

zi dingir Dam-bu(?) nig-si-na-aš-šu (?) ki nig-an-el-a ġe
By Dambu .... mayest thou be exorcised.

zi dingir Ka mu-gal azag-ga(?) ... dul-la-a ġe
By Ka the holy representative of ...... in the cavern mayest thou be exorcised.

zi dingir Ka-gi luġ bi-ib-la .... [ġe]
By Kagi, the priestly anointer .... mayest thou be exorcised.

zi dingir .... giš-ur-a bi-ib-la [ġe]
By .... mayest thou be exorcised.

zi dingir Nin-tir-mu ti-na-gi ġe
By Nintirmu she who turns the life mayest thou be exorcised.

zi dingir Na-na-a nir-gál-a-ni-dim ġe
By Nana who is like her hero mayest thou be exorcised.

zi dingir Ig-gal-e[66] *sag ki-kur a-a-ni-dim ġe*
By Iggal, the chief of the mountain country like his father mayest thou be exorcised.

zi dingir Da-da-a um-ma ad gal-gal-la(!) ġe
By Dada the mother of the great fathers mayest thou be exorcised.

zi dingir En-me-ġar-ra na a-šu maġ a kur-da-na ġe-pad	By Enmeharra the creature in the great water, in the water of the mountain mayest thou be exorcised.
zi dingir Dam- ....[*ġe*]	By.......................... mayest thou be exorcised.
zi dingir Ka- ....[*ġe*]	By.......................... mayest thou be exorcised.

Two lines destroyed.

zi dingir Lugal-er-ra ana-ka im-til ê'	By Lugalerra of heaven, the wind of life, go forth.
zi dingir Lu-eš-gal sib si-gal-la-ge	By Lueshgal, the shepherd of the living creatures mayest thou be exorcised.
zi dingir Dam-ki-gal-la dam šàg ki-gal-la-ge	By Damkigalla the mistress inmidst of the netherworld mayest thou be exorcised.
zi dingir Nin-giš-zi-da gu-za-lá kur-ra-ge	By Ningishzida the thronebearer of the land mayest thou be exorcised.
zi dingir En-'ur-na-gal en kur nu-gi-en-da ġe	By Enkurnagal the lord of the land of no return mayest thou be exorcised.
zi dingir Ġuš-bi-il(?) agrig kur-ra-ge ġe	By Gushbil the abarakku of the land mayest thou be exorcised.
zi dingir Dug-dug-ga-á gir-lal kur-ra-ge ġe	By Dugdugga-a the sword-bearer of the land mayest thou be exorcised.
zi dingir Ê'-ta-na dingir ê' kur-bal-ge ġe	By Etana the god who goeth forth to the hostile foreign land mayest thou be exorcised.
zi dingir Ka-ti ....[*ġe*]	By Kati........................ ......mayest thou be exorcised.
zi dingir Gál-? im-si nig-ši zagin [*ġe*]	By Gal......................... ....the brilliant mayest thou be exorcised.
zi dingir en-sig dam-sig en-nu dam-nu	By the god, the lord below, the mistress below, the lord of nothing, the mistress of nothing,

dingir en šilig dam-maǵ eš-.	The god, the lord, the potentate, the great mistress. . . . .
en-me-á-ra en-me-šar-ra[67]	By Enmeara, by Enmesharra,
en ama a-a azag-dul-la-ge-ne	By the lord, the mother, the father, the sanctity of the caverns and
nam-tar-ra-ge-ne ǵe-pad	Of the fates mayest thou be exorcised.
. . . . dingir-mu-gal	By . . . . the divine representative
ǵe-pad	Mayest thou be exorcised.

Reverse, Col. III

zi im-imin-bi zi an-ki ub-da-limmu-ba ǵe-pad	By the seven winds, by the four regions of heaven and earth mayest thou be exorcised.
zi gê-a si-si-ga ud-da-zal-a ǵe	By the night which overcometh the dawn mayest thou be exorcised.
zi zag-gar zag-gu-la kur-kur-šu[68] *šu-bi-eš im-sag*[69] *a-ab-ba a-da*[70]*-gal-gal-la ǵe*	By the pillar, the bolt, which submit the lands, the devastating wind of the ocean-floods mayest thou be exorcised.
giš-aš-a ba-ra-an-da-sir-ri	Not a single tree shalt thou root out!
gi-aš-a ba-ra	Not a single reed shalt thou pluck out!
giš . . . .-aš-a ba-ra	Not a single . . . . . .-tree shalt thou root out!
. . . . gar-ra-da ba-ra-an	. . . . shalt thou root out!
ṣu-a[71] *a-ma-da*[72]*-ge ba-ra-an*	No spreading shoots of the land shalt thou pluck out!
ṣu-a[71] *a-ab-ba-ge ba-ra-an*	No spreading shoots of the sea shalt thou pluck out!
dŭ-e bal-e ba-ra-an-da	That which has been made hostility shall not tear down!
dŭ-e sag-bal-e ba-ra-an-da	That which has been made the chief of hostility shall not tear down!
ki uku kur-ra-ge tur- tur-zu laǵ	From the place of the people of the land, to thy children go!

dingir Babbar sag-kal dingir-ri-ne-ge šu-na ù-si-ga[73]	Unto Shamash, chief of the gods, command him.
dingir Babbar sag-kal dingir-ri-ne-ge ĝul-bi su-na ĝa-ba-an-sir-ri	May Shamash, the chief of the gods, remove the evil in his body.
inim-nim-ma utug-ĝul-a-kam	It is a prayer against the evil spirit.

X

No. 128

An E-nu-šub Text

Obverse, Col. I

[*inim-nim-ma*] *utug-ĝul-a-kam*[74]	Prayer against the evil spirit.
[*en ê*]*-nu-šub*[75]	Incantation of the house of exorcism.
[*utug-ĝul-gál*] *edin-na laĝ-a*	The evil spirit which roves over the desert,
[*gidim-ĝul-gál*] *edin-na dul-la*	The evil demon which covers in the desert,
[*sag-gig*] *nig-gig*[76] *edin-na lá-a*	Headache, sickness which lies in the desert,
......*-ni maĝ-e dingir En-lil še-ir-zi-da*	..........the great, Enlil the brilliant,
.............*dingir En-ki dingir En-lil ban-da-bi*	...............Enlil the son of Ea.
.............*dingir A-nun-na-ge-ne urugal-la ri-a*	The..............of the Anunaki is begotten in the underworld.
.............*ki-dur-maĝ-a-zu*	................in thy great dwelling
......*la-*...*-zu bi-da-*....*-bu*[77]...	....
..............[*im*]*-te-gá-da-ba*	.......................themselves
.........*-gal-ne-a mu-un-tar-ri-eš*[78]	The..............in the......... they have decreed.
..............*-e ib-te-gi-eš úr-ra mu-un-ni-in-uš*[79]	..................they come near, on the foundation they take their stand.

[dingir] Asar-lù-dug igi-im-ma-an-sum	Marduk saw him.
[a-a-ni] dingir En-ki-ra ê-a ba-an-ši-tur gu-mu-un-na-dé-e	Unto his father Ea into the house he entered. He spoke:
[a-a-mu] utug-ĝul edin-na laĝ-a	My father, an evil spirit roves over the desert.
[gidim-ĝul] edin-na dul-la	An evil demon covers in the desert.
[sag-gig nig]-gig edin-na lá-a	Headache, sickness lies in the desert.
[. . . . . -ni maĝ-e] dingir En-lil še-ir-ʒi-da	. . . . the great, Enlil the brilliant
[. . . . . dingir En-ki dingir En-lil, ban-da-bi	. . . . Enlil, the son of Ea
[. . . . . dingir A-nun-na-ge-ne urug]al-la ri-a	The . . . . of the Anunaki is begotten in the underworld.
[. . . . . ki]-dur maĝ-ʒu-a	. . . . in thy great dwelling
[. . . . la- . . . ʒu bi-da]-bu	. . . .
[. . . . . im-te-gá-]da-ba	. . . . themselves
[. . . . . -gal-ne]-a mu-un-tar-ri-eš	. . . . they have decreed.
[. . . . . ib-te-gi]-eš úr-ra mu-un-n[i-in-uš]	. . . . they approach, at the foundation they take their stand.
. . . . ĝul-bi-ka	. . . . of his evil . . . .

OBVERSE, COL. II

a-a-[mu(?) . . . .]	My father . . . .
nam-tar	Fate . . . .
bar-šu ĝe-[im-da-gub]	May stand aside.
ạ-ĝul-gal ê'-a	Go forth, O evil power!
utug-ĝul a-lal-ĝul bar-šu ĝe-[im-da-gub]	The evil spirit, the evil devil may stand aside!
utug-sig-ga dingir-kal sig-ga ĝe-im-[laĝ-laĝ-gi-eš]	A kindly spirit, a kindly protecting deity may be present.
inim-nim-ma utug-ĝul-a-[kam]	Prayer against the evil spirit.
en ê-nu-šub[80]	Incantation of the house of exorcism.
utug-ĝul-gál gidim maš-tiq-gar [edin-na]	The evil spirit and devil who appear in the desert
nam-tar nig-ĝul-gál tag-ga-ʒ[u]	Fate, evil approached thee.
eme nig-ĝul-dim-ma lù mu-ri-in-[kešda-ge]	The tongue of evil is bound on the man.

dug-dim ǵe-gaz-gaz[81]	May they be broken in pieces like a cup.
dug-bur(!)-dim ǵe-maš-maš[82]	May they be smashed like a vessel.
giš-gam-ma giš-kan-na-ka	Through the bolt of the door
sag-nam-ta-bal-e-en[83]	May they not break through!
giš-i-tub-ba[84] *nam-ta-bal[-e-en]*	Through the .... may they not break!
utug-ǵul edin-zu-šu a-lal-[ǵul edin-zu-šu]	O evil spirit to thy desert! O evil devil to thy desert!
utug-ǵul(!)[85] *ê-a-til-la šu[-nu-gar-ra-zu-šu]*	O evil spirit that dwells in the house not will spare thee
dingir lù-gal-[lu-ge]	God and man
utug-ǵul a-lal-ǵul gidim-[ǵul mulla-ǵul dingir-ǵul maškim-ǵul la-dug-bur-zi dug-qa-bur-dim]	Whether it be an evil spirit, or evil devil, or evil demon, or evil god, or evil fiend, like the sherd that is thrown away by the potter
an-aš-an-a[86] *ǵe-im-mi-[gaz-gaz]*	May they be cut to pieces in the main-streets.
inim-nim-ma utug-ǵu[l-a-kam]	It is a prayer against the evil spirit.
en ê-nu-[šub]	Incantation of the house of exorcism.

Reverse, Col. III

ki lù-na me	The place of man ....
lù an-ta ri-ri	Who goes above ....
lù ki-ta nu-bal-da	Who below not breaks through .....
nin-ra sag-me-da(?) gar nin-(?)	To the lady ....
sag-gig gig-giš-na	Headache, sickness of the members,
....	....
šàg-gig-ga-šu	In sickness of heart ....
lù šàg-gig-ga	Whose heart-ache ....
utug-ǵul sag-da	The evil spirit at the head ....
ù-ǵul nig-	The evil man ....
dingir-ǵul nig-	The evil god ....
inim-nim-ma zu-ab-ba a-ra-ab-im-mu-ne-en	The incantation of the Deep shalt thou mention to him.
lù-galu dumu dingir-ra-na	The man, the son of his god,
šu-íl-íl-la-zu ba-ra-an-da-te-ne-en	With thy raised hand thou shalt not approach.

lù tab-tab-ba-zu ba-ra-an-da-ná-ne-en
With thy companions mayest thou not lie down,

ka-ǵu-luǵ-ǵa-zu ba-ra-an-da-dug-ne-en
With thy fearful mouth mayest thou not speak,

sag-ki sur-ra-zu ba-ra-an-da-?-n[e-en]
With thy angry face mayest thou not . . . . ,

igi-ǵuš-a-zu ba-ra-an-da-ru-e-ne-en
With thy angry look mayest thou not turn about.

ní-me-me-ne-zu ba-ra-an-da-dib[87]*-dib-ne-en*
With thy commands of fear mayest thou not seize,

ka-zu-ta nig na-an-ta-ê' . . . .
From thy mouth nothing may go forth . . . .

eme-zu-ta nig-ǵul na-an-gá-g[á-ne-en]
Through thy tongue evil mayest thou not do!

šàg-zu gar-nu-ǵu[š-ǵuš-ne-en]
Thy heart may not inspire fear!

zi an-na ǵe-[pad zi ki-a ǵe-pad]
By heaven be thou exorcised! by earth be thou exorcised!

en-na [su lù-gal-lu dumu dingir-ra-na ba-ra-an-ta-ri en-na ba-ra-an-zi-ga-en-na-aš]
Until from the body of the man, the son of his god thou art removed, until thou goest off

ú na-[an-da-ab-kú-e a na-an-da-ab-nak-e][88]
Food thou shalt not eat, water thou shalt not drink!

Reverse, Col. IV

[utug-ǵul-gál kalam-ma nigin-e][89]
O evil spirit which hunts over the land,

[utug-ǵul-gál nig]-zi-gál dib-dib-bi
O evil spirit which seizes living creatures,

[utug-ǵul]-gál nam-tar-šú šur-ra [90] [91]
O evil spirit which rages (?) over destiny,

[utug]-ǵul-gál kalam-mà ǵul-a[92] *lu(!)*[93]*-a*
O evil spirit which violently troubles the land,

utug-ǵul-gál a-ra-su šú-nu-sir
O evil spirit which receives not prayer,

utug ǵul-gál tur-tur-lal ǵa-dim a ban-su[94]*-a*
O evil spirit which draws out the children like fish from the water,

utug-ǵul-gál gal-gal-e zu-gal mu-un-ru-ru-a
O evil spirit which throws down the great intentionally,

utug-ǵul-gál um-ma ab-ba-bi-da(?)-ge(?)mu-un-dun-dun
O evil spirit which strikes father and mother,

utug-ġul-gál sila dagal-la mu-un-dib-dib-bi	O evil spirit which seizes the wide street,
utug-ġul-gál edin dagal-la mu-un-si-si-ga	O evil spirit which fills the wide desert,
utug-ġul-gál i-lu-ma kabar-kabar-ri	O evil spirit which dives into the spring,
utug-ġul-gál dim-ma kalam-ma šub-šub-bu	O evil spirit which overthrows the work in the land,
utug-ġul-gál kalam-ma si kab-kab	O evil spirit which overthrows the horn of the land,
utug-ġul-gál á-e si-si ba-ri-a	O evil spirit which walks at the side of the weak,
utug-ġul-gál lù-ra ú(?) nu-kú	O evil spirit which to man food does not give to eat,
utug-ġul-gál dam(?)....û-ra dun-dun	O evil spirit which............ to the.........strikes,
utug-ġul-gál sag-li-tar tar-ra-bi	O evil spirit which tears to pieces him who is attentive,
utug-ġul-gál kur-ra šú laġ-laġ-gi	O evil spirit which washes the hand in the mountain,
má-e lù-tû-tû sanga-maġ dingir En-ki-ga me-en	I am the exorciser, the high-priest of Ea.
en-e mu-un-ši-in-gi-en	The lord has sent me.
má-e giš tu-ra-ka[95] *mu-un-ši-in-gi-en*	He has sent me to the sick man.
egir-má-a-ra nam-ba-ab-giš-gi-en	They shall not follow behind me.
egir-má-ka nam-mu-un-ra-ra	They shall not walk behind me.
lù-ġul-gál šú-nam-ba-zi-zi-in	May the evil man be removed!
utug-ġul-gál šú-nam-ba-zi-zi-in	May the evil spirit be removed!
zi an-na ġe-pad zi ki-a ġe-pad	By heaven mayest thou be exorcised! by earth mayest thou be exorcised!
[*inim-nim-ma utug-ġúl-a-kam*]	It is a prayer against the evil spirit.

Reverse, Col. V[96]

[*sila-a gin-gin ab-ba šu-šu giš-šagil*] *tu-tu-da*[97]	Walking the streets, attacking dwellings, penetrating bolts,
[*galu-ġul*] *igi-ġul*	Evil man, whose face is evil,
[*ka-ġul e*]*me-ġul*	Whose mouth is evil, whose tongue is evil,
[*uġ-ġul, uġ-zu*] *uġ-ri-a*	Evil spell, sorcery, witchcraft,

[gar-ša-a] gar-ĝul-dim-ma	Enchantment, evil deed
[ša-ê]-a-ta ê'-ib-ta[98]	Go forth from the house!
[zi an-na] ĝe-e-pad	By heaven mayest thou be exorcised!
[zi ki-a] ĝe-e-pad	By earth mayest thou be exorcised!
[lù-gal-lu dumu] dingir-ra-na	Unto the man, the son of his god,
[ba-ra-an]-na-te-gá-ne-en	Mayest thou not approach!
[ba-ra-an-gi-]gi-e-ne-en	Mayest thou go off!
[giš-gu-za-na nam-ba]-tuš-ù-ne-en	Mayest thou not sit in his seat!
[giš-nad-da-na nam-ba]-ná-ù-ne-en	Mayest thou not lie on his bed!
[ur-šu nam-ba-gib]iš-ne-en	Mayest thou not rise over his fence!
[ê-ki-tuš-a-na nam-ba-tu-t]u-ne-en	Mayest thou not enter into his chamber!
[zi an-na-ki-bi-da-ge i-ri-pa]d	Mayest thou be exorcised by heaven and earth!
[ĝa-ba-ra-du-un]	Mayest thou depart!

XI

No. 114

A Hymn and Incantation to Enlil

An excerpt duplicate text of this hymn is published in Barton, Miscellaneous Babylonian Inscriptions, No. 10.

Obverse

inim-nim-ma-bi inim-šúb-[ba-kam]	His exorcism is a word of blessing.
tû-tû-bi inim zur-[ra-kam]	His incantation is a word of imploration.
inim-bi ka-gar šag bar-šu giš-šub š[ub-ba]	His word is a good thought. It sets aside fate.
garza nig-kal-kal-la-[kam]	It is a command of preciousness.
ezen ìa-ga sud ĝe-gál-la daĝ-[ĝa]	He replenishes the feast with oil. He adds abundance.
giš-ĝar ka-ni(?) . . . . . . dagal?-la(?) silim-bi nig-gal-gal-la-kam	The barrier . . . . is wide(?). His well-being is a great treasure.

ud-šu-uš ezen peš-ša en-maǵ-ám	Daily he revives the feast. He is a lofty lord.
gan dingir En-lil-la kur ǵe-gál-la-kam	The field of Enlil is a mountain of abundance.
šu-gid igi-nim lal šu-sag nig-gig-bi	The extended hand above exorcises. His sickness of hand and head
ê-a[99] *en-bi ê*[99]*-da mú-a*	Go forth! His lord come forth! shine forth!
gur-bi-šu silim-ma ǵe-dŭ-ám	At his gracious intercession well-being is established.
abzu-sa-nun-bi-šu luǵ-ǵa tum-ma-meš	From his great Deep a cleansing they bring.
nu-eš-bi gag diš azag-gi dŭ-a-meš	His priests pull down one shining pluck.
engar-maǵ-bi sib-zid kalam-ma	His lofty Engar, the faithful shepherd of the land
ud dug-ga zid-de kur tu-da-a	In a good and true day brought forth the mountain.
uššu ê-dagal-la ǵe-dŭ-a-ám	The foundation of the wide temple is resplendent.
mur im-da-gub šuku dingir Nînni gal-gal-la-kam	An enclosure is erected. Many are the Ishtar-cakes.
eš-bi nu-mu-un-gub e-kur zagin dur	When his dwelling stood not, he inhabited Ekur the shining.
dingir En-lil á-dam azag ki-a mur-ra-a-za	O Enlil brilliant hero thou walkest on earth
dingir En-lil-ki uru ní-za ši-im-mu-un-ru-ru-a	Since Nippur thy city has been built through thy fear!
ki-ùr kur-ki-el-dim-a izi dug-ga	The gate of the underworld is like a pure mountain purified by fire.

Reverse

ub-da-limmu-ba[*šàg*]*-ga an-ki-ka ki-dur-e-*[*za*]	In the four quarters, in the midst of heaven and earth is thy dwelling-place.
saǵar-bi zi kalam-ma zi kur-kur-ra-[*ám*]	Its earth-heap is the life of the land and the life of the foreign countries.
murǵu-bi azag-ǵuš-a barag-ni ud zagin-na [*tur-zu*]	In its shining and brilliant brick enclosure, its sanctuary on a shining day thou didst enter.

am-dim ki-en-gi-ra si dingir-dingir ba-ni-ib-si-[il-la] — Like a wild-ox it lifts up to Sumer the horn of the gods.

kur-kur-ri[100] *sag ní-ʒu-uš*[101] *sig-gi* — To foreign lands it smiteth on the head with terror.

eʒen gal-gal-bi uku-e nam-ġe-a ug-ga mu-un-di-ni-ib-ʒal-e — Its great feasts fill the people with fullness of light.

dingirEn-lil urta[102]*-aʒag duġ-li dú-dú-a-ʒu* — O Enlil, holy seer, splendor thou increasest!

abʒu engur[103] *aʒag-ga*[104] *gal-bi tum-ma-ʒu* — Mightily thou sweepest along through the splendid watery Deep of the ocean.

kur sig X[105] *aʒag-ki im te-en-te-en-ʒu* — In the low mountain of the brilliant shrine(?) thou abatest the wind.

ê-kur ê ʒagin ki-dúr-maġ im il šub-ʒu — From Ekur, the shining temple, the lofty dwelling-place thou turnest away the stirred up winds.

nì-lam-bi[106] *an-ni*[107] *uš-sa*[107] — The fear of its splendor reaches the heavens.

giš-gê-bi kur-kur-ra-ša[108] *mu-un-lal* — Its shadow encompasseth the mountains.

muš-bi an-ša-ga-aš ša-mu-un-dim-gub[109] — Its form stands inmidst of the heavens.

en-en-e[110] *bàr-bàr-ge-ne* — The priests of the sanctuaries

šuku dingir Nînni[111] *aʒag-ga si-mu-ni-in-di-eš* — Prepare holy Ishtar-cakes.

inim-ʒur-ra ù-kul[112] *mu-na-gá-gá* — Prayer and imploration they make.

dingir En-lil-la[113] *igi-ʒi*[114]*-bar-ra-ʒu* — O Enlil, behold thou graciously!

gù-ʒid-dé-a kalam-ma il-la-ʒu — Through a faithful word raise thou up the land!

kur-[giš-ni][115]*-šu kur-ġuš*[116]*-ni-šu* — On the inaccessible mountain, on his brilliant mountain,

kur-ra ki-sud ug-ga gú-mu-na-ab-gá-gá[117] — The distant mountain, submission is rendered.

a-ri-sa-dim dú-a nig-ki-šar-ra-kam — Like a just shepherd appoint the affairs of the universe.

maš-da-ri-a[118] *gú kalam dugud-da-bi* — With produce make the surface of the land heavy!

šag-dug in-il ê nig-ga-ra-kam — Offerings (then) they will bring to the treasure-house.

ê-maġ-e[119] *šuku dingir Nînni si-ne-in-di* — In the lofty temple they will prepare Ishtar-cakes.

dingir En-lil sib-zid ní-ba dib-a	Enlil, the faithful shepherd will seize them for himself.
. . . . *nig-zi-gál-la-ka*	. . . . .of the living creatures.

XII

No. 122

An Incantation Against the Female Demon Lilitum

Obverse

[lil-la edin-na ni-kaš-kaš-eš-ám] li-li-tum ša [ina ṣi-rim it-ta-na-aš-rab-bi-ṭu][120]	Lilitum who struts in the desert
uǵ-zu uǵ-ri-[a?ba-ni-in-gar] ki-iš-pu ru-ḫu-ú it[-ta-aš-kan][121]	Has committed evil spell, sorcery.
ki-el kalag [ê-ur-a-ni-ta ba-ra-ê'] id-lam ù wa-ar-da[-tam ina biti-šu-nu ú-še-ṣi-i][122]	She drove forth the man and the maiden from their house.
ni-gin šar zu-ab kirrud-da da-šab . . . . .il-li-ik-ma ti-da(?)-am i-na absu i-na ḫu-u[r-ri . . .]	Thereupon she went . . . . . .into the Deep into the hole . . . .
ṣalam mu-un-dim da-šab-šú . . . . i-bu-uš-ma mu-ša-te-	A picture she made and . . . .
alam+bat-a-ni lù ba-an-[gaz] i-na li-ra-ti-šu a[melam i-nar-ru][123]	With her saliva she smites the man.
uǵ i-ni-in-dé ki-a[124] *ru-'-tam id-di-ma i-na ir-ṣi-tim-ma*	Spittle she threw down upon the ground.
uǵ-dug-dug[125] *nig-kú-kú-[a mu-un-šub-ba] ki-iš-bi i-pu-uš-ma i-na ma-ka-lim [id-di-ma]*	Evil spell she performed and threw it into the food.
uǵ bi-e dé-a eme nig-ǵul-bi	Spittle she threw into wine and badly the tongue it . . . .
ru-'-tim ina[126] *ši-ka-rum id-di-ma lim-ni-iš [lišânam . . . .]*	
[lù-gal-lu] pap-ǵal-la di nu-um-a-zu . . . . . .amêl mu-ut-ta-al-li-kam i-na la i-du-ú	The wanderer does not know . . . .

[lù]-galu-bi á-šú-gir-ni sa ab . . . . . . i-na ba-na-ni-šu	The man in his members rheumatism . . . .
zak-še im-gam-gam . . . . . . ga(?) ešir . . . . a-ḫa-a-šú ku-us -sa	His sides stoop down(?) . . . .
dingir Asar-lù-dug igi-ma-an-[sum]	Marduk saw him.
a-a-ni dingir En-ki-ra ê ba-ši-in-tur [gù-mu-un-na-an-dé]	Into the house of his father Ea he entered and spoke:
a-a-mu ĝul-gál igi-ĝul	My father, evil, the evil eye, ...
a-du 2-kam-ma-aš ù-ub-da a-na ni-ib-g[e-g]e	'Twice let him say it.' Whereby may he be relieved?
dingir En-ki-ge dumu-ni dingir Asar-lù-dug mu-na-ni-íb-g[e-g]e	Ea answered his son Marduk.
dumu-mu a-na a-an-na-e-zu a-na a-an-a-ra-ab-daĝ-e	My son, what dost thou not know? what else can I add unto thee?
gar-gá-e ni-zu-a-mu ù-za-e in-ga-e-zu	What I know thou knowest also.
ù-za-e in-ga-e-zu gá-e-ni-zu	Thou knowest what I know.
gin-na dumu-mu dingir Asar- ù-dug	Go my son Marduk!
a kar el-la-ta dug-šar ù-ba-e-ni-si me-e kar-ri el-lim i-na [saḫarruti][127] *mu-ul-li-ma*	Fill pure water from the dyke(?) in a saharrutu-vessel!
ᵍⁱˢšinig ú-in-nu-uš ᵍⁱˢ[gišimmar-du][128] *gi-sul-šar*	The cedar, the mashtakal plant, the suhushshu-plant, the reed of shalalu,
rig-li [erin]-babbar-ra	Cypress, white cedar,
[nà gab-ši-a n]à nini-[ši] nà muš-[gir][129] *[du-ša-a ḫu-la-la muš-gar-] ra*	The dushu-stone, the hulalu-stone, the mushgarru-stone
[šà a-gub-ba-šu ù-me-ni-šub ana lìb a-gub-bi-e i-di-ma]	Place into a laver!

Reverse

[ka-sar-ni ĝe-en-da-gab-gab][130] *ki-iṣ-ri-šu li-pa-aṭ-ṭi-ir*	May her knot be loosened!
uĝ-zu uĝ-ri-a-ni zur(?) tur-tur-ra-dim ru-ta ki-ma wa-ad-lum(?)ṣi-iḫ-ḫi-ru-tim	The spittle be like the *wadlum* of the little ones!
lù-šeš uĝ-ri-a-ni giš-tap-šu-uš-gal ĝu-gab-šu ša-lam-ti ka-aš-ša-ap-ti šu-a-ti li-is-ḫu-ub	May the corpse of that witch be thrown away!

dingir muš-dim šàg-bi-šu ģe-en-sur-ri-eš[31] *libbi-šu a-ia i-ni-eš*[31]	May she weaken in her heart like the serpent-god!
dumu gir-tab-ba-dim uģ-ri-a-ni..... *ģe-šub-bu(?)-uš ki-ma ka-ša-ap-tu šu-a-ti ki-iš-pu-ša li-ša-am-ki-tu-šu*	May the sorcery of that witch fall down like the young of a scorpion.
sa ud giš-bu-dim ka bad....... *ģe-ni-uš ši-ir-a-ni-ša ki-ma ga-ši-ši-im ka-ša-ap-tu šu-a-ti li-mur-ru-ú*	May that witch's................ like a pole.
uģ-im im-te-na-šu šú-ģa-ba-ab-zi ki-iš-pu-ša a-na ra-ma-ni-ša li-in-na-ad-ru	May her sorcery rage fiercely against her own self.
agan á u-a-na.............[132] *ģe-kud-kud-e zi-ri-iz-za i-na am-ma-[tim] li-ba-zi-ir*	May her breast be cut off by inches.
šú-si-ni zaģan-dim[133][..........]*-e ša ki-ma ba-*..............	May her finger like a............. ....

Two interlinear lines too fragmentary for translation.

[dingir N]in-ib ur-sag-[kalag-ga dingir En-lil-la-ge][134] *ģe-a*	May Ninib the mighty warrior of Enlil
.......*mu(?)-gal dingir-ri[-e-ne-ge] ģe-a*	May X the representative of the gods
dingir Nin-giš-zi-da gu-[za-lal kur-ra-ge] ģe-a ' su-ka-di....	May Ningishzida the throne-bearer of the land.............
dingir Nin-gi-ba-.............*ģe-a su-ka-di*...........	May Ningiba.................... ....

Five lines completely destroyed.[135]

lù-gal dumu dingir-ra-na [ģe-en-azag-ga ģe-en-el-la ģe-en-laģ-laģ][136]	May the man, the son of his god, become pure, become clean, become bright!
dug-bur-šagan-dim [ù-me-ni-ģu-luģ-luģ ki-ma bu-ri šik-ka-ti lim-te-is-si]	May he be cleansed like a vessel of lard!
dug-bur-ìa-nun-na-dim [ù-me-ni-su-ub-su-ub] ki-ma bu-ri [ḫi-me-ti liš-ta-kil]	May he be clean like a vessel of butter!

dingir Babbar sag-kal dingir-ri-e-ne-ge [*šu-na ù-me-ni-sum*] *a-na* [^{ilu}*Šamši a-ša-rid ilâni*^{meš} *pi-qid-su-ma*]	Entrust him to the care of Shamash, the chief of the gods!
dingir Babbar sag-kal [*dingir-ri-e-ne-ge silim-ma-na*]	Through Shamash, the chief of the gods, his welfare
šu-šag-ga dingir-ra-ni-šu [*ĝe-en-ši-in-ge-ge*][1] [7]	At the kind hands of his god may be attained!
dingir lù-ba-ge dingir En-ki dingir . . . . . . *i-li amêl šu-a-ti ù* [^{ilu}*E-a ilu*].	The god of that man and Ea, the god . . . .
. . . .	
lù-ba an-šu	. . . .

Rest destroyed.

XIII

No. 135

A School Exercise

The present text contains disconnected sentences in Sumerian with interlinear Akkadian translation. It represents obviously a scholar's exercise in a more advanced class. After having passed through a course of writing names of persons, animals, plants and so forth, he was advanced to a class in which he passed from word-lessons to lessons of sentences. It is true that the personal names contain already such constructions of sentences, yet they occur in such stereotyped forms that they must have been included in an elementary course rather than in a higher class. Personal names at that time, as now, were regarded as a word-unit. The clumsiness of writing in scholars' exercises containing personal names is ample proof that they constitute the work of beginners.

Obverse

. . . *zu-*	. . . .
. . . . *da-ra-da*	. . . .
ur-ri[138] ***ur-da*** . . . . *kal-bu it-ti kal-bi*	Dog with dog . . . .
ur-ri ur-ra-ta á . . . . — *a-na———na-mu-ud(?)* . . .	Dog to dog . . . .
an[139]***-ta-mu inim 1-ám li-mu-ba(?)*** *[ab-bi] tab-bi-e a-wa-tam is-ti-a-at a-ga-[ab-bi]*	To my companion one word I shall speak.
ê dingir Nannar im-te zu-ab mu-ni-lal *i-na———i-na ra-ma-ni— ——eš-te-ni-ki-[i]*	In the temple of Sin he himself raised high 'the Deep.'
ni-gab-ba[140] ***luǵ lù ê-a tur-tur lù-gal-[lu pap-ǵal mu-ni—tum?]*** ——*—mu-[ut]-ta-al(!)-ik bi-tim*	The door-keeper to him who enters into the house as wanderer a cleansing brings(?).
mu dingir Ba-ú nin ê-ka-e šub-ba ê dingir Nannar-kam *aš-šum be-el-ti-ia e-zu-ub i-na bitim*	On account of Bau, my mistress, I remained in the temple of Sin.
unugi ki-gub-ba nu-tuku-a *pa-ar-ṣa ù ma-za-za-am la i-šu-ú-ma*	A tomb and a dwelling they have not.
un(?)-mu-ta im-ri-a-mu-ta[141] *i-na ni-ši-ia ù ki-ši-ti-ia*	From my people and my war prisoners.
. . . . ***lù-e ê dingir Nannar-kam ba-ra-al-gál-la-e-kam*** . . . . . *amêli i-na— ——la i-ba-aš-šu-ú-ma*	The X of the man are not in the temple of Sin.
[mu ê] dingir Nannar-kam nig-na-me-šu nu-mu-ni-íb-te-ta[142] *aš-[šum] ša———a-na mi-im-ma šum-šu la te-ḫa-ku-ú-ma*	Concerning that whichever (belongs) to the temple of Sin, I do not draw nigh.
. . . . ***-ám muš-aga-a me en*** . . . . *-ma* . . . . . *-zu-uš-bu-tam ip-ši-e(?)*	[. . . . .] who has done [. . . . .] art thou.

Reverse

ù kalam-e mu-un-ki- . . . . *ù ma-tum*	And the land . . . .
nig-šam-ma nig-1-a-kam lù-na . . . . . *i-na ši-im 1 NIG ma-am-ma-an*	For the price of one object anyone . . . .

mu-mu nu-mu-un-pad šú-mi ú-ul i-za-kar	He does not mention my name.
ur-dur-ri[143] *ê'-ta-ab-ṣi-en kal-ba-am šu-ṣi-a*	Drive ye out the dog!
ur-dur-ri[143] *sir-ra-ab-ṣi-en ba-ab-en-na*[144] *ku-ši-da i-ga-ab-bu-ú*	Overpower ye the dog, they say!
ġar-ta-âm lù-palil-ge-ne ne-in-dug-eš-a i-na ki-a-am pa-nu-tu-ni iq-bu-ú	In this fashion spoke the chiefs.
gar nu-kú-a šu-mu-da-an-kar a-na la a-ku-lu šam-mi ḫa-mi-is ṣu-ba-ti	It was not in order to eat food that he took off the garment.
en-nu-un kalaga nu-me-a gê-da-kam ù-nu-mu-un-ni-ku-ku a-na la ma-ṣa-ar-ti-ia ka-la mu-ši-im ú-ul aṣ-li(!)-il	Not for the sake of my guarding did I not sleep all night.
ne-en-nam di-kud dingir Nannar-kam an-nu-ú-um di-nu ša ^{ilu}*Sin*	This (is) the judgment of Sin.
lù nig-šag-ga kú-a-ni ê-a-ni mu-un-ru ša du-mu-uq bi-ti-šu i-ku-lu id-du-ma	They have squandered of the good of the house that they have eaten.
me-en-ne ê-a-ni nig-na-me-šu nu-mu-ni-íb-te-ta ni-a-ti ša a-na bi-ti-šu a-na mi-im-ma šum-šu la tu-di-iḫ-ḫi	As for us, unto nothing which (belongs) to his house shall ye draw nigh!
nig-sag-il-la-aš mu-un-. . . . . *a-na la di-na-ni-šu*	In order not to . . . . . his bodily figure.
dingir En-zu-ra dúg-ne-in-gam-ma	To Sin he bowed the knees . . . .
a-na———ik-mi-is-ma	
ud-da ê-ṣu-šu nig-kam-. . . . . *ú-ma-am i-na biti-ka*	A day in thy house . . . .
nig-ê. . . . . *mi-im-ma šum-šu*	Whatsoever. . . . .

XIV

No. 129

A Fragment of an Incantation

. . . . *ša* . . . .
. . . . *ša ina zumri-ia* . . . .
. . . . *meš ittâte meš* . . . .
[*ka-dib-bi-da-ša*] *dababi-ša* [*li-kil-lu-šak-ša*]
[*it-ti mê ša zumri-ia û*] *KI-ME meš ša qata-ia liš-ša-ḫi-i*[*ṭ-ma*]
[*ana muḫ-ḫi*]*-šu û la-ni-šu lil-lik ilu Šamaš ta-*[*da-an-nu?*]
. . . . . *limnûti ana muḫ-ḫi-ša tur-ru-* . . . .
. . . . . . *ka-zu lim-šil-ma ana-ku lu-ut-bi*
[*ši-i*] *li-in-ni-gir-ma ana-ku lu-ši-ir*
[*ši*]*-i li-ir-te-si-ma ana-ku lu-bi-ib*
[*ši*]*-i li-mut-ma ana-ku lu-ub-luṭ*
. . . *ina di-ni-ka i-ša-ru-ut lul-lik*
. . . . *aš-šu la e-pu-ša-aš-ši-im-ma i-pu-ša*
. . . . *aš-šu la as-ḫu-raš-ši-ma is-ḫu-ra*
. . . . . . *šu al-ta-si ina muḫ-ḫi-šu mê a-ra-*[*muk*]
. . . . . . *qātā-ia u AM* (?)*-an-ni ki-ma mê* . . . .
. . . . *amâtu an-ni-tu iš-* . . . .
. . . . *gême* (?)*-mu û kalag-mu zu* . . . .
. . . . *-id-ma ina qāt* . . . .

XV

No. 120

An Incantation to be Recited with a Whispering Voice.[145]

Obverse

šiptu an-nu-ú šu-ú an-ni-tum ši-[*i*]	Incantation: He that one, she that one
i-la-as-su-ma[146] *arki-ia*	Goes to him and behind me
uš-ta-ma-aṣ-ṣa-a ana ṣa-ba-ti-ia	They reach out for my seizure.
ina pi-ša na-šat a-mat ma-ru-ša-ti	Into her mouth she takes a word of mischief.
šab-šat ina qatā-a-ša ru-ḫi-e zi-ru-ti	She turns in her hands witchcraft (and) hatred.

ma-la-a ki-e(?)-ma-ša utar ki-ri-ib (......)-ia	All her family she turns towards my ....
i-ḫar-ši-ma kal a-na ana amelûti$^{\check{s}un}$	She holds back and every condition to men ....
û ši-i kalbati[147] *ana lim-ni û lim-nûtim*[118]	And she (is) a bitch. For the purpose of evil and baseness,
an-ni-tum ......-ša i-la-[as-su-ma arki-ia]	That one's ....goes to him and behind me.
uš-ta-ma-aṣ-ṣa-a [ana ṣa-ba-ti-ia]	They reach out for my seizure.
aṣ-bat-ki ina ṣal-me [ša mu-ši?]	I seized thee in the blackness [of the night?]
ak-la-ki ina ár-ša-še-e	I held thee back in the enchantment ....

Rest of obverse too fragmentary for translation.

Reverse

ša e-piš-ti-iá ri-	Whatever my sorceress ....
ša muš-te-piš-ti-iá ú-tir û	Whatever my witch turned and ....
a-lik-ki ki-ma bêl ḫi-di-it-ti	I went to thee like a malefactor.
ú-ḫu-šu-ki ana abulli pi-ḫi-ı	They hastened to thee at the closed city gate.
ana mur-ḫu ša ^{ilu}*Šamšı pa-ni-ki ina ....*	At the approach of the sun thy face was in ....
ú-la-la la-na uzna lu-ú-ša-aṣ-bit abulla	They wash the body, the ear. Verily I took possession of the gate.
aš-šu-ia dimta limnûtim$^{(tim)}$ *tar-te-id(?)-di(?)*	On my account thou didst shed(?) evil tears.
marê$^{me\check{s}}$ *um-ma-ni mašmaše*$^{me\check{s}}$ *mušlaḫḫe*$^{me\check{s}}$[149]	The young sages, the mashmashu-priests, the "serpent-driver"-priests
li-pa-aš-ši-ru-ki-ma a-a-il-ki ú-pa-ṭu(!)-[ru]	May loosen thee! I have bound thee! They shall loosen!
šipta muṣṣaprata idî	Recite the incantation with a whispering voice!

Follows ritual and date.

"In the month Tebitu, on the twenty-fourth day. To Shamash-shum-ukin ...."

XVI

No. 107

An Incantation against Rheumatism[150]

Obverse

en ê nu-šub	Incantation of the house of exorcism.
sa[151] *gir-ne-a- su-a*	Rheumatism is on the feet (and) on the body.
dingir En-ki-šu ê-a mu-ši-tur	Unto Ea into the house he entered.
ur-keš-da-dim gir^{ga} *še-ba-bi*	Like a bound dog (he is). Gir-fish (constitutes) his sustenance.
ú-bi ša^{sar}*-dim ki-dar dun-bi*	His food is like Ša-plant. A crack is his hole.
kàš-šu ê'-a káš-šu gin-ni-a	Come forth in impetuosity! In impetuosity go!
ġuš-ni ba-ni-zu	His wrath is known.
ġuš-ni-ám šub-dim šid-šid	His wrath accounts for the work of destruction.
. . . .	. . . .

Reverse

ġar-ra-a-na mu-gál-a-na nu-mu-gál-la-bi	He who is inside, shall be no more!
bar-ra-a-na mu-gál-a-na nu-mu-gál-la-bi	He who is outside, shall be no more!
dingir En-ki-ne dingir Nin-ki-ne	O Enki and Ninki
nig-azag-ga an-na-dim šàg-ta-šu ġe-ba-ra-ab-sig-e	Splendor like that from the midst of the heaven may smite him!
mu-tar-a-aš ġe-im-me-e	May he be made a curse!
šàg lù-ê-ge aga lugal dingir En-ki-ge	Inmidst the human dwelling is the royal crown of Ea.
ê-ê nun-ki(!)[152]*-ka ġe-im-dù-dù-e*	Let the houses of Eridu be open!

XVII

No. 116

An Incantation

Obverse

. . . .	. . . .
[^{ilāt}*Dim-*]*a mar-ti* ^{ilu}*A-nim*	The ghoul, the daughter of Anu . . . .
. . . .*-ni*$^{(šu\text{-}ri\text{-}a\text{-}ni)}$	. . . .
. . . .*-ṣi-ṣi-ti-šu im-qut*	. . . . fell (into?) his . . . .
gin(?)-na dingir gub-bi sal ša šanga-ma itti ^{ilu}*Šamaš gub-bi*	Go! Place the god! The wife of the high-priest shall stand with Shamash.
ṣalma rukus ša ili šuati GAB-UB arki-šu riksa tašakan	Place into fetters an image of that god! A fetter place thou in front and behind him!
marê^{meš} *um-ma-ni GAB-UB arki-šu* ———*išakanu*	The young sage-priests shall place a fetter in front and behind him!
û ^{ilāt}*Nin-a-ḫa-kud-du*[153] *GAB-UB arki-šu*———*tašakan*	And Ninahakuddu shall place a fetter in front and behind him!
rabûti^{meš} *ipaṭaru*[*-šu*]	The great ones shall loosen him.
li-dur[154] *lim-nu ša pa-ni-ia uk-kiš a-a-bi ša tubqi*[*-ia*]	The evil Lidur of my face drive away the enemy from my side!
dingir Asar-lù-dug mašmaššu ilâni^{meš} *bêl ba-la-ṭú ir-ru-bu-*[*ša*]	Marduk, the purification priest of the gods, the lord of life enters unto her.
dingir Nin-ib ur-sag ilâni^{meš} *ir-ru-bu-ša*	Ninib, the hero of the gods enters unto her.
rabiṣu[155] *ẓi an-na ĝe-pad ẓi ki-a ĝe-*[*pad*]	O Rabisu, by heaven mayest thou be exorcised! by earth mayest thou be exorcised!
lù-lil-la ẓi an-na ĝe-pad ẓi ki-a ĝe-[*pad*]	O storm-demon, by heaven mayest thou be exorcised! by earth mayest thou be exorcised!
ki-el lil-la ẓi an-na ĝe-pad ẓi ki-a ĝe-[*pad*]	O maiden of the storm-demon, by heaven mayest thou be exorcised! by earth mayest thou be exorcised!

ki-el ud-da-kar-ra ẓi an-na ǵe-pad ẓi ki-a ǵe-[pad]

O maiden of the robber of the light, by heaven mayest thou be exorcised! by earth mayest thou be exorcised!

ka ǵul-ga bar-šu ǵe-[im-ta-gub]

May the evil mouth stand aside!

---

su lu-gàl-lu pap-ǵal-la-ge a-ba-an-[gi-eš]

Be removed from the body of the wanderer!

su-mu nam-ba-te-ga-e-ne bar-šu ge-i[m-ta-gub] ana ẓumri-ia a-a it-ḫu-ni ina a-ḫa-a-tu li-iẓ-ẓ[i-iẓ]

May they not approach my body! May they stand aside!

egir-mu nam-ba-gi[n-gin-ne] ana àr-ki-ia a-a illiku-ni

May they not walk behind me!

[ẓi dingi]r gal-gal-e-ne-ge ǵe-p[ad]

By the great gods mayest thou be exorcised!

[na-an-gu]b-bi-en ka-šar-bi ǵe-en-dù [a-a] ik-ka-lu ri-kiṣ-ṣu lip-pa-ṭir

May he not be held in bondage! May his fetters be loosened!

[lù gá-e] lù-tû-tû ga-šurru-maǵ dingir En-ki-[ge] [a-ši-pu] ša-an-gam-ma-ḫu ša ^{ilu}*E-a ana-ku*

I am the incantation priest of Ea.

[e-n]e-ne dingir nu-tuk-a-meš dumu dingir Lamga[156]*-a-[meš]*

They have no god, children of Lamga are they.

[utug]-ǵul gidim-ǵul galla[157]*-ǵul dingir-ǵul maškim-[ǵul]*

The evil spirit, the evil demon, the evil devil, the evil god, the evil demon Rabis,

[dingir dim-me]-a dingir dim-me bar(!) muǵ lù[158]*-ra šub-ba-a-[ne]* . . . . *ana a-aḫ-ḫa ša eli amêli i-ma-aq-qu-tu-šu-[nu-ti]*

Labartu, Labasu, rush to the side of the man.

[sila sig-ga gê-]ta-ge mu-un-laǵ-laǵ-gi-[eš] [ina su-qi ša-q]u-um-meš ina mu-ši it-ta-na-al-la-[ku]

Through the afflicted street by night they walk.

Reverse

[u-šu-uš ga-ba-da-an-k]ú ǵe-[me-en][159]

With whom should I have eaten on a day?

[u-šu-uš ga-ba-da-an]-nak ǵe-me-[en]

With whom should I have drunk on a day?

[u-šu-uš ga-ba-da-an]-šag ģe-me-[en]

With whom should I have made merry on a day?

[u-šu-uš g]a-ba-da-an-ku[160] *ģe-me-e[n]*

With whom should I have clothed myself on a day?

. . . .-a im-mi-in(?)-si-eš nam-dim ni-in-dul-dul-la dingir gig. . .

The . . . . they have attacked; that which is made they have overcome through an eclipse(?).

[lù-gàl]-lu-bi izkim-bi nu-un-[zu-zu] ša amêlu šu-a-tu it-ta-šu(!)[161] *ul ú-ta-ad-di*

They do not know the omen of that man.

dingir Asar-lù-dug dumu nun-ki-ga-ge šú-na ugu-na im-mi-in-[gar] nam-šub ba[-an-sum] ^{ilu}*Marduk mâr* ^{âlu}*Eridu qât-su eli-šu iš(?)-kun [šip-]ta id-di*

Marduk, the son of Eridu, placed his hand upon him. He performed the incantation.

---

nig-na gi-bil-la û-me-ni-ê'

Bring a censer and a torch,

nam-tar su lù-ka ni-gál-la a-dim ģe-im-ma-an-šur-šur-ra nam-ta-ru ša ina zu-mur a-me-lu ba-šu-ú ki-ma me-e li-iș-ru-ur

May the plague-demon Namtar, who is in the body of the man, trickle away like water!

urudu nig-kalag-ga ur-sag an-na-ge za-pa-ág me-lam-a-ni nig-ģul ba-ab-sir-ra šú-û-me-ti

Take the copper of might of the hero Anu, which by the roar of its splendor removes the evil.

---

a-lal-ģul dingir gig-a gin-gin šú bil-lá nu-te-ge-ne ģe-me-en

An evil demon art thou, a god who walks in the night, whose unclean hands do not know reverence.

a-lal-ģul lù-ra nà-a anšu-dim kabar-kabar-a ģe-me-en kimin ša e-li amêli rab-șu-[ma ki]-ma i-me-ri i-ša-an-šam at-ta

An evil demon art thou, who lies down (in wait) for the man, resting like an ass.

a-lal-gul zur-zur nu-un-zu-a [ku-kur-ge]-at-ge nu-tuku-a ģe-me-en kimin ša ni-qa-a la i-du-û-ma as-ḫa-ta la i-šu-ú kimin

An evil demon art thou who knows not sacrifice and who has no gifts.

---

e-sag[162] *ti-di-i ši-e-tam ù ku-ub-bit*

Disease thou knowest, snare and burden,

ina an-nim-ma ilu ḫa-di-iš

But in mercy the god gladly

ṭa-a-bi eli ilu Šamaš i-rab-šu[163] *dum-qu*	Vindicates good for him unto Shamash
šum-šu ú-lab u-ri. . .-du-ur u-mu	. . . . when
amata ina biti tu-kab-bit	Thou didst burden the maiden in the house.

XVIII

No. 104

Prayer of an Incantation Priest

This very interesting text contains the prayer of an incantation priest to the goddess Girazag in order to secure her divine assistance in re-establishing the good relations between a man and a maiden. An enemy, probably an evil spirit is intended thereby, has caused the separation of the maiden from the man. The maiden has gone away. The man was brought to the river to establish his innocence in the cause of this separation. His innocence was proven, or, to cite the passage in the text, "He is in the breath of life, he is established as a faithful man."

Obverse

lù-lù-ẓu ù-ne-. *sig-?-bi*	Thy men . . . .
murgu-bi lù-ģul-gál-ba šúb-šúb-[*ba*]	His enclosure. The one who was evil he implored.
šàg ìb-ba-bi-a igi-a e-ra[164] *babbar mi-ni-ib-g*[*ar*]	In the anger of his heart clear tears came into the eye.
ud eš-gub ê-kur bad-dim nì-bi-a-šu an-[*na uš-sa*][165]	When the dwelling Ekur was like a wall which in its awe reached to heaven
ki ka-(?)-tar-ri id lù-ru-gú-da-an[166] *ba-laģ-gi-eš*	To the place of reverence, the river, with him who was accused(?) they stepped.

zid-du erím gub-bar an-aga-ne si-di mu-un-ù-ga(?)

In truth they made the enemy to stand aside. Justice was performed.

erím-gál-la-ni-šu im-ri-ri-e-da-ni dul engur ne-gub

Unto his enemy with his kinfolks the well of the abyss shall be established.

ud-bi-a nin-e im-te-a-ni sal zid i-ri-bi-ám me-en

On this day as the mistress herself, the true woman, may I speak unto thee!

dingir Gir-azag dingir nun-gal-la-ge nì-di-šu al-e

O Girazag, goddess of Nungalla, protect in the awe of judgment!

nin me-en an-ni nam mu-un-tar má-e [gi-na] me-en

The mistress art thou of heaven. Fate thou decreest. Thou art true!

dingir En-lil-li nam-ma-aš ba-an-dù ê-gi-a-ni me-en

Enlil verily loosens! His bride art thou.

dingir-ri-e-ne me an-ki-a-šu mu-šu mu-gar-ri-eš

The gods have placed the command into heaven and earth:

ama ugu-mu azag dingir Nin-ki-gal-la ê-gal-ni-šu ĝe-ni-ba

"Let the holy mother Ninkigalla, she who bore me, in her temple express herself!"

Reverse

tab-zu kur-dingir-Babbar-ê' id maĝ mu-mi-ni-ri

Thy companion, the rising sun, has gone to the great stream.

ê-gal ki-dúr azag nam-lugal-la-ge má-e maš-bi me-en

Of the temple, the holy dwelling of the kingship the exorciser am I.

dingir Ninni-ra gal mu-un-da ne-sag-gál-la me-en

At the side of Ishtar the great I go. A leader am I.

dingir Nin-tu-ri ki nam-tur-zi-ka nam-da-an-gub-bi [me-en]

With Nintu in the place of life-giving verily I stand.

gi-dur kud-da nam-tar-ri-da inim šag-gi-ga mu-ba

Break the Dur-reed! Besides fate grant a word of grace.

nin izkim zid dingir En-lil-lá me-en nig-ga-ba nig-nig-nig

The mistress of the true presage of Enlil art thou. A treasure amongst his treasures(?).

erim nu-um[167]-ši-gi gá-a amat bad ma-da tab

Return to the city establish! The maid removed from the land join back!

uš-šàg-ne-gub gá-a amat lù la ba-ra-an-bal-li

Firm love of heart establish (in order that) the maid and the man do not break away (from each other).

sag-geg-ga igi-ge mu-un-gál-en nu-un-im-aga-e

The blackheaded sees that he has not done (anything wrong).

im nam-til-la-šu-gá mu-gál lù-zid ne-in-gub

He is in the breath of life; he is established as a faithful man.

erím gin á-gá la ba-ra-ê' nig-ġul-. . . . .

The enemy who came in strength may not go forth! Evil . . . .

XIX

No. 133

Prayers and Incantations of Shamash-shum-ukin[168]

Obverse

šiptu ^{ilu}Šamaš an-nu-ti e-piš ú-[. . . . .]

Incantation: O Shamash, this. . . . .

ṣalam kaššapi-ìa û kaššapti-ìa ṣalam e-piš-ìa û muš-te-piš-ti-ìa

An image of my conjurer and female conjurer, an image of my sorcerer and sorceress,

ṣa'am ra-ḫi-ìa û ra-ḫi-ti-ìa ṣalam bêl dababi-ìa û belît dababi-[ìa]

An image of my spoiler and female spoiler, an image of my male and female accuser,

ṣa'am bêl iq-qi-ìa û belît iq-qi-ìa ṣalam bêl di-ni-ìa û bel[ît di-ni-ìa]

An image of my male and female oppressor, an image of my male and female judges,

ṣalam bêl ṣir-ri-ìa û belît ṣir-ri-ìa ṣalam bêl qibi-ìa û be[lît qibi-ìa]

An image of the lord and the mistress of my crushing, an image of the lord and the mistress of my speaking,

ip-ša barta amât limnûtim^{lim} i-pu-ša ú- . . . .

Machination, rebellion, an evil word they have made, they . . . .

is-ḫu-ra u-še-is-ḫi-ra ana e-piš-ti ib-ši-ma . . . .

It surrounds me and lets me be surrounded through the sorcery it possessed . . . .

.....šer-ti dar-ri-ma iq-bu[-ú].....	........of sin...........and they commanded....................
.....an-nu-ti-šu-nu an-nu-ti ṣal-māni-[šu-nu.....]	The......of these their....,of these their images...............
[........izazzu] ṣalmāni-šu-nu ni-ba-ši elûti.............	..........they stand. Their images are.....the high..........
[ša ana ia]-ši kiš-pi ru-ḫi-e ru-si-e ár-[ša-še-e limnûti]	Who against me sorcery, venom, witchcraft, saliva, evil,
[ramu zaru] DI.BAL-A zi-tar-ru-da-a ṣibit pî nikis [napištim$^{(tim)}$]	Love, hatred, contention(?), anguish (?), dumbness, shortness of breath (?),
[kuš-ku-mal] igi-nigin-na íd-gur..... -gal tu-ra gig-ge........	Inactivity(?), indecision(?),......, great........., sickness of the night(?)...........
[.........-ne-mi pani ni-it] ṭe-me-ma-um qât ili [û qât] ištarati-ma qât mamit....................	.............distortion of plans, hand of god and hand of goddess, hand of curse,.................
[qât amelûti]-ma AN-UR(?)limnûtim$^{(tim)}$ rêš limnûtim ĠA-ZA mu-kil rêš limnûtim^{tim} [iš-ku-nu-ma]	Hand of man,........of evil, head of evil,............supporter of evil they established.
....-ma pi-ìa ú-ṣab-bi-tu kišadi-ìa ú-tar-ri-[ru lišâni-ìa ú-lab-bi-tu]	......My mouth they have seized. My neck they have wrung. My tongue they have seized.
....-qu-lu šinnê-[ìa][169] il-du-du ir-ti id[-i-pi lib-bi un-ni-šu]	They........... My teeth they have drawn. My breast they have crushed. My heart they have weakened.
........idâti^{meš}[170]-ìa ik-su-ú bir-ki-ìa [ik-su-ú ṣilli(?)-ia a-li-ka idi-ia(?)][171]	.... My hands they have bound. My knees they have bound. My shadow(?) which walks at my side(?)
[u-šim-su-ú(?) esenseri]$^{(ri)}$ iq-pu-pu pa-ni-ìa[172] uz-za-[-na-du[173].....-ia man-ga lu-'u-tam]	They have snatched away. My backbone they have bent. My face they swelled (?). My.... ....with disease and pollution
[ú-mal-lu-in-ni ša]rti-ìa im-lu-su [ulinni-ìa ib-tu-qu]	They filled me. My hair they have sheared. My girtle-cord they have cut.
[ru-ti-ìa il-q]u-ú epir šepê-ìa iš-bu-šu man-d[a-at la-mi-ìa ú-man-di-du]	My saliva they have taken. The ground of my feet they drew away (?). The measure of my form they measured.

[*ṣalmâni-ia lu*] *ša bini* [*lu ša* ^{iṣu}*erini*] *lu-û* [*ša lipî lu ša GAB-LÀL*]	My images, whether of tamarisk or of cedar or of tallow, or of baked cakes of honey
[*lu-û ša GAB šamaš*] *šammi lu-û* [*ša iddî lu-û ša ṭiṭṭi lu-û ša lî*]	Or of baked cakes of sesame, or of bitumen, or of clay, or dough,
.......$^{iṣu(?)}$ *bini(?)u mê(?)*^{meš} *ina* ^{iṣu}........................	..........tamarisk and water into a...vessel(?)..................
.........*-im-ki-*...............	....

Rest of obverse destroyed.

REVERSE

..............*e*]*-piš-ta-šu-*[*nu* ....]	.... their sorcery... ....
..............*-šu*]*-nu ana irṣit la* [*târi*] *li*[*il-li-ku*][174]	Their........may go to the land of no return(?).
[^{ilu}*Gibillu*] *agu russu li-ik-ta-na-*[*ni* ....]	O Gibil, may the magnificent diadem be set up.....................
[^{ilu}*Gibillu ša*] ^{ilu}*Nam-tar sukkal irṣitim*[175]......................	O Gibil, who......Namtar, the messenger of the lower world........
....*ša ana ia-a-ši kiš-pi ru-ḫi-e ru-si-*[*e ar-ša-še limnûti ipušu*]	...who against me sorcery, venom, witchcraft, saliva, evil have committed.
[*ilu*] *šarru bêlu û rubu*[176]*ni-si-ia*....	God, king, lord and prince have become enraged against me.....
[*k*]*i ili û ištar ú-zi-nu-nin-ni SA Ê-ŠAR-RA(?)* [*ú-lam-me-nu-in-ni*]	Since god and goddess turned in anger against me. With a rope of Esharra (?) they have maltreated me.
[*i-na*] *an-ni-tum*[177] *ina suqi pu-uḫ-pu-uḫ-ti*[178] *iš-ku-n*[*u-nim-ma*]	In it (and) in the street they established against me raping(?)
[^{ilu}*Šama*]*š ka-e-ti su-ú* ^{ilât}*A-a um-ma la tatâr-û*...........	Shamash........Aja, the mother, does not turn away and........
^{ilu}*Šamaš ša kaš-šap-ia û kaš-šap-ti-ia e-piš-ia û muš-*[*te-piš-ti-ia*]	May Shamash the sorcery of my sorcerer and sorceress, my male and female conjurers
ra-ḫi-ia û ra-ḫi-ti-ia kiš-pi-šu-nu itti ṣalam UD.KA id-ta-.....[*kima is-par-ri lib-bal-kit-su-na*]	My male and female spoilers with the image of..............break like a net.
[*epišân-šu*]*-nu li-ba-ru-šu-nu-ti* ^{ilu}*Šamaš UD.KA ma-su-ur-ma*	At their sorcery may they catch them. Shamash cut off(?)..... ......and....................

[*kı-ma*] *di-qa-ri ḫu-bu-šu(!)-nu*[179] *kima ti-nur*[180] *qu-tur-šu-nu li-ri-mu*[181]	Break them like an earthen jar. May he quench their smoke like an oven.
[*li*]-*ḫu-lu li-ẓu-bu û lit-ta-at-tu-*[*ku* . . . .]	May they melt, may they glow and may they run away . . . .
[*e-pi*]*š-ta-šu-nu ki-ma mê na-a-di liq*[-*tu-ú*]	May their sorceries cease like the water pouring forth.
[*šu-nu*] *li-mu-tu-ma ana-ku lu-ub-luṭ šu-nu li-ni-šu-ma ana-ku* [*lu-ud-nin*]	May they die, but may I live! May they tremble, but may I stand firm!
[*šu-nu l*]*i-ik-te-šu-ma ana-ku lu-paṭ-ṭar šu-nu li-iṣ-ṣab-tu-ma ana-ku lu-*	May they be bound, but may I be freed! May they be seized, but may I be . . . .
[*ana ki -bi-ti-ka ṣir-tu ša la innak-aru*[(ru)]	By thy exalted command, which does not change
[*û an*]-*ni-ka ki-nim ša la innu*-[*ú*]	And by thy true grace which does not alter
[*ana*]-*ku arad-ka lu-ub-lu-uṭ lu-uš-lim-m*[*a*]	May I, thy servant, live and prosper!
nar-bi-ka lu-ša-pi dá-lí-lí-ka ana nišê rapšâti[182] *lu-ud-l*[*ul*]	I will extol thy greatness. I will sing thy praise unto far dwelling people.
iluŠamaš šur-bi a-ši-pu-tu ša abkal ilânimeš i-pu-šu iluMarduk	O Shamash, exalt the exorcising priestship, which Marduk, the counsellor of the gods, has made.

XX

No. 113

Series of Incantations Against the Female Demon Labartu

Obverse

[*šiptu dingir Dim-me dumu an-na šumu-ša ištên*	Incantation: Labartu, daughter of Anu, is her first name.
ša-nu-ú a-ḫat ilâni ša su-qa-a-ti	The second: sister of the gods of the streets.
šal-šu paṭ-ru ša qaqqada i-nat-tu-ú	The third: the dagger, which smashes the head.

re-bu-ú ša iṣa i-nap-pa-ḫu
The fourth: who ignites the wood.

ḫa-an-šu il-tum ša pa-nu-ša šaq-ṣu
The fifth: the goddess, whose face is terrible.

seš-šu pa-qid qa-ti li-qat ^{ilu}*Ir-ni-na*
The sixth: committed to the care of, (and) taken into the hands of Irnina.

si-bu-ú nîš ilâni]^{meš}[183] *rabûti*^{meš} *lu-ú ta-ma-ta*
The seventh: by the great gods mayest thou be exorcised!

[it-ti iṣṣuri šamê]$^{(e)}$ *lu-ú tap-par-ši-ma*[184] *TÛ šiptu*[185]
Mayest thou fly away with the bird of the heavens. Exorcism. Incantation.

[šiptu dingir] Dim-me dumu an-na mu-pad-da dingir-ri-e-ne-ge
Incantation: Labartu, daughter of Anu, called by the name of the gods.

[dingir In]-nin nir-gál nin sag gig-ga
Innin, mistress, lady of the black-headed,

[zi a]n-na ge-pad zi ki-a ge-pad
By heaven mayest thou be exorcised! By earth mayest thou be exorcised!

[ú-ša]-ḫi-iz-ka[186] *kalba ṣalma qal-la-ka*[186] *aq-qi-ki mê*^{meš} *bûri*
I have given unto thee a black dog as thy servant; I have poured out for thee spring-water.

[pu-uṭ]-ri at-la-ku[187] *i-si-i û ri-e-qi*[188]
Go away! Go! Depart! and be far off!

[ina zumur ^{amêl}*ṣiḫri mâr ili-šu] an-ni-i ú-tam-mi-ki* ^{ilu}*A-nim û An-tum*
From the body of the child, this son of his god, I beseech thee by Anu and Antu,

[kimin ^{ilu}*En-li]l û* ^{ilât}*Nin-lil kimin* ^{ilu}*Marduk û* ^{ilât}*Ṣar-pa-ni-tum*[189]
Ditto, by Enlil and Ninlil, ditto, by Marduk and Sarpanitum

[kimi]n ilâni^{meš} *rabûti*^{meš} *ša šamê*$^{(e)}$ *û irṣitim*$^{(tim)}$
Ditto, by the great gods of heaven and earth,

[ša ana bît] an-ni-i taturrim-ma ša sil-la an-ni-i tatur-û-ma[190] *TE šiptu*
That thou turnest away from this house, that thou turnest away from this street. Exorcism, incantation.

[šiptu iz-zi-i]t ul i-mat na-mur-rat û ši-i-maš-šu(?)marât ^{ilu}*A-nim*
Incantation: angered, not speaking, terrible and . . . . .is the daughter of Anu.

[ina arantu][191] *ru-bu-us-su ina tibni ša immeri zikari*[192] *man-za-as-su*
In the cane-break is her resting-place, in the straw of the male sheep is her place.

[alpu a-li-ku][193] *i-kal-lu [pab]-ġal-la ....ú-paq-qar*
The ox who walks about she holds back, the traveler she annoys ....

[gu]-ub-bu-ru ú-gab-bar
The strong one she strengthens.

[n]u-up-pu-ṣu ú-nap-pa-ṣu
That which is broken to pieces, she breaks up.

..........-mi saq-qa-a mê^{meš} *bu-un-na*
Pour out ...., create waters!

......-lu-ut-šu-ma karpata arikta kima DI.BU ša marât ^{ilu}*A-nim*
Do ....her a wide vessel like the ......of the daughter of Anu.

[šu-kun rubût]-ka ^{ilu}*Šamaš TE šiptu*
Establish thy greatness, O Shamash! Exorcism, incantation.

Three lines too fragmentary for translation.

[i-bir nâra di-il-ḫa] iš-kun i-mid i-ga-ri lu-ḫum-[ma-a] ib-ta-ša-aš[194]
When she crosses a river she causes confusion; when she stands at a wall, she smears dirt.

[iz-ziz ši-i-ba] pašušatu$^{(tu)}$ *i-ga-bu-šu*[195]
When she steps near an old man, pashushatu she is called.

[iz-ziz edla an]-qu-la[196] *i-ga-bu-šu*
When she steps near a man, Anqulu she is called.

[iz-ziz ardāta] la-bar-tum i-ga-bu-šu
When she steps near a maiden, she is called Labartu.

[iz-ziz ^{amêl}*ṣiḫra] dingir Dim-me i-ga-bu-šu*
When she steps near a child, she is called Dimme.

[aš-šu tal-l]i-kim-mi tu-ṣab-bi-ta[197] *ši-kin pa-ni-šu*
Because thou hast come and seized the form of his face,

[meš-ri-t]i tu-ṣab-bi-ta[198] *tu-ab-bi-ta*[198] *mi-na-a-tu*[199]
Seized the muscles, seized the bodily form,

[tu-kas-sa-si] buânê ma-na-na[200] *tu-[kan]-na-ni*[201]
Didst cut the veins, didst bind the sinews,

[zi-i-mi tur-ra-]qi bu-un-na-an-ni-e t[u-uš-pi-e]l-li
The facial expression thou didst make pale, the bodily form thou didst change,

[a-]šu-uš-tum ta-nam-di-i
Thou imposest sorrow,

[girrâniš^{niš} *t]u-kab-ba-bi zu-um-ri*
Thou burnest the body like fire,

[ana nasâḫi-ki ana ta]-ra-di-ka ana la târi-ki ana [la ṭeḫî-ki
In order to remove thee, in order to drive thee away, so that thou mayest not return, so that thou mayest not come near,

[*ana našaḫi*]*-ki la sanâqi-ki la sanâqi-ki ú-*[*tam-me-ki*][202] ^{ilu}*A-nim*	In order to remove thee, not to draw near, not to draw near, I implore thee by Anu,
abi ilâni^{me} *rabûti*^{me}	The father of the great gods,
[*kimin* ^{ilu}*En-lil*] *šadâ*$^{(a)}$ *rabâ*$^{(a)}$ *kimin* ^{ilât}*be-lit rabîta ilâni*(?)^{meš} *kallâta*(?)[203]	Ditto, by Enlil, the great mountain; ditto, by the great mistress of the gods, the bride(?) of
[^{ilu} *Enlil?*][204] *abu šar-rat balâṭi pa-ti-qat nab-ni-ti*	Enlil(?), the father, the queen of life, the former of creation.
[*kimin* ^{ilu}*Sin bêl a-gi-e pâris*] *purussê mu-kal-lim ittâti-šu*[205]	Ditto, by Sin, the lord of the crown, the decider of decisions, he who lets his signs be seen.
[*kimin* ^{ilu}*Šamaš nûr elâ*]*ti*$^{(meš)}$ *ba-nu-ú kib-ra-te*[206]	Ditto, by Shamash, the light which is above, the creator of the world.
[*kimin dingir Asar-lù-dug bêl a-ši-p*]*u-tu kimin* ^{ilu}*Nin-ib ašarid ilâni* [*aḫê*]$^{(meš)}$*-šu*	Ditto, by Asar, the good Being, the lord of exorcism; ditto, by Ninib, the leader of the gods, his brethren.

OBVERSE, COL. II

ina ki[*-bi-ti ša šul-mi pu-uṭ-ri*][207]	At the command of salvation go out! . . . .
la[208] *ma-*[*ṣi-tú ša lib-bi-ša* . . . .]	Not having gone forth from its midst . . . .
ma-[. . . . .*-lu-ki a-ši-pu* ^{ilu}*Asar lù-dug*	. . . . .thee the exorciser Asar, the good Being.
ú-nak-kar [*i-mat-ki i-na-as-saḫ qâtâ-ki*]	He shall remove thy spittle, he shall tear off thy hands.
ú-ḫal-[*laq um-ma kuṣṣu ḫal-pa-a šu-ri-bu*]	He shall chase away heat, cold, frost, rain-shower.
ina zumur^{amêl} [*ṣiḫri mâr ili-šu an-ni-e* ^{ilu}*Asar lù-dug ú-tam-mu-ki*]	From the body of the child, this son of the god. Asar the good Being will exorcise
ši-pir-ki [*ú*]*-ri-e ú-la-pa aš-šu*[209]	Thy doing. An enclosure he shall put together in order
lu-ub-bu-tu-ka šaman šaḫê ikkib-ki [*ibašu aš-šu*][210]	To shut thee up. Lard shall be thy woe, in order to
edêli$^{(li)}$[211]*-šu-nu-tu šu-ṣi-šu-nu-tu ilâni*^{meš} *limnûti*[^{meš} *râbiṣe*^{meš} *limnûti*^{meš}]	Bar, to cause to come forth the evil gods, the evil lurkers,

šu-ut pa-ni-ki ša ina pa-ni-ki û arak-ki il[-la-ku]	Who are before thee, who go in front of thee and behind thee.
ki-ma na-al-ši ša kakkabâni^{meš} *ki-ma a-di-ki [ša a-pa-a-ti]*	Like the shower of the stars, like the passing of the clouds,
ki-ma[212] *sik-ki-e la ta-ḫal-lu-up*[213] *ṣi-ra-[niš]*	Like the dikes, which thou dost not cover up highly,
la ta-at-ta-nab-lak-ka-ti ḫa-ṣap r[a-a-ṭi][214]	Not shalt thou break a râṭu-vessel.
ú-lam-kip-ki[215] *šâri ir-bit-[ti]*	The four winds shall storm against thee.
ú-ma-al-li elippi-ki nam-ma-na-a-a	They shall fill up thy ship.........
....	....
e-piš[216] *a-da-pa abkal* ^{alu}*Eridu*	The work of Adapu, the sage of Eridu
ta-lak-ki[217] *ina* ^{alu}*Eridu i-na-ṭa-al-ki ka[-a-si]*	Thou shalt fall prey to. In Eridu he shall behold thee.
ú-nak-kar i-mat-ki i-na-as-saḫ qâtâ-ka ina zumur [^{amêl}*ṣiḫri mâr ili-šu an-ni-e]*	He shall remove thy spittle. He shall tear out thy hands. From the body of the child, this son of his god
pu-uṭ-ri at-lak TE [šiptu]	Remove, go away! Exorcism, incantation.
inim-nim-ma dingir Dım-me-kam	It is the exorcism of Labartu.
[šiptu iz]-zi-it šam-rat i-mat na-mur-r[at]	Incantation: Angry, raging, terrible, awful
[ul....iš-tu a-pi] i-lam-ma e-zi-zi iz-zi-[iz[218]*]*	Not........she rose up from the reed-thicket. In order to rage she stood.
..............*-bu*[219]*-te-šu ZU-AB-A il-la-ku*................	Her.............in the Deep come ....
bîtâte ḫar-ša-a-[ti.....]nir-ru-[bu(?)] [............................]	Houses of pregnant women......we entered(?).....................

Four or five lines destroyed.[220]

bi-il-la-nu [mârê]$^{(meš)}$ ***ki-na-tú [lu-di-ib-bu-ub]***	Bring the sons. Let me speak.... ....
ana pî mârâti$^{(meš)}$ ***ki-na-tu ul [lu-di-ib-bu-ub]***	Unto the mouth of the daughters not let me speak...........
il-lik-ma ana pân ^{ilu}***En-lil abi-šu i-qab-[bi]***	She came and in the presence of Enlil, her father, she spoke:

ša ir-ri-šu-ka bil-lu a-bu ilu*[En-lil]*	"What I have asked of thee, bring, O father Enlil.
šîr nam-lu-gàl-lu la ṭa-a-bi [dami nam-lu-gàl-lu niš-bu-ú-ti]	The flesh of man is not good; the blood of man is satiation."
aš-šu at-ta an-na-a tir-ri-ša-[221]*in-ni*	"Because such thou hast requested of me,
ša kur-ban-ni-e li-pu-šu bit[-ki]	Therefore may the 'collectors' make thy house.
li-bil-lak-ki ḳal-lat ṣi-ḫir-tum iṣu*ga[-ṣu še-bir-tum pilakkê ina libbi]*	Let them bring unto thee a young girl, a flayer's bench, an instrument of breaking (with) axes in it.
um-ma-ri ba-aḫ-ru-tu[222] *ša ina gu-ra-ru*[223] *ba[-aš-lu]*	(And) a pot with bahrutu-fruits, which are roasted in fire."
niš ilu*A-nim û An-tum niš* ilu*En-lil û* ilâti*Nin-lil [niš abulli û ne-ri-bi-e-ti]*	By Anu and Antu, by Enlil and Ninlil, by the doors and the entrances,
niš iṣu*kakki ḫar-bi ḫaṣbi zêri e-zi-bi*[224] *û mâ[ri-šu ú-tam-me-ki]*	By the weapons of destruction, the vessels of seed, the forsaken one and his son, I conjure thee
šum-ma ana bît an-ni-i taturrim-ma mâr an-ni-i tanasaḫ[225]	That thou turnest away from this house, that thou forsakest this son.
kussa[226] *uš-ša-bu tuš*[227]*-ša-bu šir-ri*[228] *ša ana ḫa-bu-ni[-ia a-na-aš-šu-ú]*	The chair which I occupy thou occupiest, the child which I take to my breast
[ana] ḫa-bu-ni[-ki] ta-na-aš-ši	Thou takest to thy breast.
*[*ilâti*Ištar pî] kalbi-ki ṣab-[ti]*	O Ishtar, seize the mouth of thy dog!
*[*ilâti*]Na-na-a ṣu-ub-bi-ti pî mi-ra-ni-[ki*[229]*]*	O Nana, seize the mouth of thy cub!
[ṣa]l-lu ina maiali a-a i-ir	He who rests on the couch shall not awake,
adi inappaḫa[230(ḫa)] ilu*šamši šûpû*[231] *ina ŠE.ḪAL-šu*[232] *TE [šiptu]*	Until the magnificent sun shines into his .... Exorcism, incantation.
[šiptu iz]-zi-it šam-rat i-mat na-mur-r[at]	Incantation: angry, fierce, terrible, frightful
[iz-zi-it bar-ba-rat i-mat ḫab-]ba-ta-[at][233]	Enraged, furious, terrible, rapacious is she.
[abu man-za-as-sa arantu ru-bu-us-sa]	Reed-thicket is her dwelling-place; cane-break is her resting-place.

Rest destroyed.

REVERSE

[*šiptu dingir Dim-me dumu an-na mu pad-da dingir-ri-e-ne-ge*	Incantation: Labartu, the heavenly daughter, called by the name of the gods.
dingir In-nin ner-gal nin-e-ne-ge	Inninni, mistress of the ladies,
šu-mu-un-du azag gig-a	Who has made the painful asakku-sickness
gàl-lu dugud-da nam-lù-gal-lu-ge	The heavy alu of man
dingir Dim-me ib-gul lù-ra nu-te-ga-e-ne]	Labartu, mighty one, do not draw nigh unto the man.
[*zi*] *an-na ĝe-pad zi* [*ki-a ĝe-pad*][234]	By heaven mayest thou be exorcised; by earth mayest thou be exorcised.
šiptu marat ^{ilu}*A-nim ša šamê*$^{(e)}$ *a-*[*na-ku*]	Incantation: The daughter of Anu of the heavens am I.
su-ta-ki[235] *šimtam gi-iṣ-ṣa-ku*[236] *na-mu-ra-*⌈*ku*]	A Sutaean am I, disrupting destiny am I, terrible am I.
bîta irrub umsāta$^{(ta)}$ *ubbal*[237] *bi-la-ni mârê*$^{(meš)}$ *ki-na-tu* [*lu-dib-bu-ub*]	The house I enter, want I bring. Bring unto me the sons that I may speak . . . .
ana pî marâte$^{(meš)}$ *ki-na-ta*(?) *ul lu-uš-šum-*[*ma*]	From the mouth of the daughters . . . . I may not hear(?).
iš-me-e-ma ^{ilu}*A-nim i-bak-ki*[238]	Anu heard it and wept,
ša ^{ilât}*A-ru-ru* ^{ilât}*be-lit ilâni*$^{(meš)}$ *il-si-šu ki-ma*[239]	Because Aruru, the mistress of the gods, spoke to him like (this):
am-me-ni ša ni-ib-nu-ú nu-ḫal-l[*ak*][240]	"Why shall we destroy what we have created?
û [*ša nu-ša*]*b-šu-ú ub-bal ša-a-š*[*a*][241]	And shall she take away, what we called into existence?
li-ki-ši-ma [*a-na tam-tim*] *ša mâti i-di-ma*[242] [*itti bîni a-bir*]	Take her and throw (her) into the ocean of the land. At a tamarisk bind her,
ù ku-ša-ri a-di[243] *ru-ku-us-su*	And a kusharu-tree, until she is bound
ki-ma ^{amêl}*miti la i-šu-ú* [*qab-ru*][244]	Like a dead person that has no burial-place,
ù ^{ilu}*Azag-sir la i-ni-qu GA.DAGAL*[245]	And does not pour out plenty milk unto Azagsir,
marât ^{ilu}*A-nim ki-ma kutri*[246] [247] *bita la i-naḫ*[*-ḫi-is TE šiptu*]	Thus shall not return unto the house like smoke the daughter of Anu. Exorcism, incantation.

šiptu šur-bat[248] *marât* ^{ilu}*A-nim mu-am-mi-lat la-'-ú-*[*ti*]	Incantation: Powerful is the daughter of Anu, who troubles the little ones(?).
rit-ta-šu[249] *al-lu-ḫap-pu ki-rim-ma-šu mu-*[250]	Her fist is a scourge. Her belly. . . . .
qaṣ-ṣa-at lab-bat en-ni-ni-it ik-ki-mat nak-ki-[*lat*[251] *ra-aḫ-ḫi-ṣa-at*]	Angry, raving, hostile, revengeful, cunning, crushing,
mut-tab-bi-lat mârât ^{ilu}*A-nim ú-lap-pat*[252] *lib-bi ša ḫar-ša-a-*[*ti*]	Abducting is the daughter of Anu. She turns upside down the inside of the pregnant woman.
ú-šal-lap[253] *šer-ri*[254] *ša ta-ra-a-*[*ti*]	She forcibly pulls out the child from the pregnant woman.
ú-še-niq[255] *ú-nam-ẓa-aẓ û it-tan-na-*[*al-lak*][256]	She nurses it; she sets it up, and lets it walk about.
rabu[*-ú uẓnê*]$^{(meš)}$*-šu nam-ši-šu bu-a-ni-šu uẓnê* ^{m}[^{eš}*-šu* . . . .]	Its ears become large, its members become movable. (Its) ears. . . . .
ka-[*diš-tu*] *mârât* ^{ilu}*A-*[*nim*]	A whore is the daughter of Anu,
ša ilâni [$^{(meš)}$ *ša aḫê*]$^{(meš)}$*-šu kaqqad-su kaqqad nê*[*ši*]	Amongst the gods, her brothers. Her head is the head of a lion.
šin-na-[*at imêri*] *šin-na-as-*[*sa*]	Her form is the form of an ass.
šaptâ^{meš}*-*[*ša*] *ẓiq-ẓiq-qu*[257] *ú-tab-ba-ka q*[*a-a*]?[258]	Her lips are in violent motion(?). They pour forth spittle.
iš-tu ku[*l-la*]*t šadî*$^{(i)}$ *ú-ri-dam-ma na-*[*'-a-rat ki-ma nêši*]	From the mountain district she descended. She . . . . like a lion.
uš-ta-na[*-a*]*l-ḫab kima kal-bat maš-da-a* [*a-na maš-di-i uš-ta-na-al-ḫab*]	She howls(?) like a bitch . . . . to . . . . she howls(?).
i-mur-ši-ma As[*ar-lù-dug*] *ana* ^{ilu}*Ea abi-šu a-mat i-g*[*a-bi*]	Asar, the good Being, saw her. Unto Ea his father he spoke the word:
a-bi a-mur mârâ[*t* ^{ilu}*A-n*]*im ša ú-šab-ba-šu*[259] *la-*[*'-ú-ti*]	"My father, I have seen the daughter of Anu, who troubles the little ones."
^{ilu}*E-a mâra-šu* ^{ilu}[*Marduk ip-pal*]	Ea answered his son Marduk:
a-lik ma-ru[260] ^{ilu}*Marduk* [*ina ši-pat ni-me*]*-ki tu*[*-um-me-ši*]	"Go, my son Marduk, exorcise her with the white exorcism."

Rest destroyed.

Reverse, Col. II[261]

[*šiptu dingir Dim-me dumu an-na mu pad-da*] *dingir-ri-e-ne-*[*ge*]	Incantation: Labartu, the daughter of Anu, called by the name of the gods,
[*dumu-sal dingir-ri*]*-e-ne-ge*	Daughter of the gods,
[*dumu-sal dingir-gal-gal-e-ne-ge*]	Daughter of the great gods . . . .
. . . .	. . . .
[*dumu na*]*m-lù-gal-lu-*[*ge* . . . .]*-gál-lu*	The son of man . . . .
. . . .	. . . .
. . . . *egir*]*-bi in-dib*	. . . . behind him she seizes,
[*i-gi lu pa*]*-ri*[262] *in-dib*	The eye, which is cut out(?) she seizes.
[*i-gi lu u*]*š-gi-im*[263] *in-dib*	The eye, which cried, she seizes.
[*tû-bi i*]*-gi-za-na in-dib*	Her incantation: igi-zana she seizes.
[*mê ba-ši ašri*] *in-dib*	The existing water of a place(?) she seizes,
[*mê ba-ši ašri ṭabi*] *in-dib*	The existing water of a good place(?) she seizes,
[*ú bur*] *in-dib*	Plants, caves(?) she seizes
[*giš-gal-t*]*a-a-an in-dib*	Each door she seizes
[*giš-sag-gul-t*]*a-a-an in-dib*	Each bolt she seizes
[*ê-šu dumu ê*]*-a-ge*[264] *nam-ba-ni-íb-tu-tu-ne*[265] *TÛ šiptu*	In the house of the son of the house they shall not enter. Incantation, exorcism.
[*inim-ni*]*m-ma dingir Dim-me-kam*	It is the incantation of Labartu.
[*TÛ*] *šiptu* ^{ilât}*Labarte*^{meš} *nu al-til*	The incantation, the exorcism of the labartus is not completed.

XXI

No. 123

An Early Enušub Text

Obverse

en ê-nu-šub	Incantation of the house of exorcism.
^{giš}*šinig* ^{giš}*gi*	The tamarisk, the reed,
^{giš}*ana ki el-li*	The heavenly tree in a holy place

mu-a	Grow!
ur-azag-zu šu-úr-a	Thy holy root lock up!
pa-zu-šu ǵa-šu-úr	With thy branch let it be locked up!

Reverse

a-gub-ba	The laver
dingir Nin-sulu-ǵa[266]	Of Nin-suluga
ni-tum-ma	Shall be brought.
nun-me-e šu el-la	The abkallu-priest with pure hand
ì-ni-tum	Shall bring it.

XXII

No. 91

A Sumerian Letter

[dingir]*En-lil-bar-zu ù-na-a-dug*	To Enlil-barzu speak!
Ka-[dingir]*Ninni na-ab-bi-a*	Ka-Ninni says:—
inim-na me-ma-an-dé-eš-da	In his word which was spoken(?)
lul-aš ba-ǵul-li	Strongly he rejoiced.
dingir Lamma ud-til-la-a kal-li lugal su	O protecting deity, strengthen in the days of life the stricken master!
Na-[dingir]*En-lil ù* [dingir]*En-lil-al-šag*	Na-Enlil and Enlil-alshag
ud-gê-a-šu palil zu-ne	In day and night take cognizance of the leader.
dingir Nin-gašan dingir-zu	Nin-gashan, thy goddess, and Nidaba
ù dingir Nidaba giš-ku-geštu dagal-la-ge	may give to thee a wide ear
giš-ku-pi ga-ra-ab-sum-mu-ne	To hear.
nig im-ma-aga šar-ri	About the matter which has been done write!
uru-šu bi nu-gi al-me-a nu-zu	He does not know that he was ordered not to return to that city.
2 gin kubabar 1 tug 2 [tug]*bar-si*	Two shekels of silver, one garment, (and) two bandages

lù gi-na[267] *šu-mu-ra-ab-*[*lag̀-lag̀*]	The faithful man causes to be brought to thee.
g̀a-la-da-da ama-zu	With the extensive portion of thy mother
šu-nam-ne-te-na-te-na	Be not content to ....
a-ma-ru-kam	Please!

FIRST DYNASTY LETTERS

XXIII

No. 2

An Appeal for an Interview

a-na Ibiq-Ištar qi-bi-ma	To Ibiq-Ishtar speak.
um-ma ^{ilu}*Enlil-lù-šág-ma*	Thus says Enlil-lushag:—
^{ilu}*Enlil li-ba-al-li-iṭ-ka*	May Enlil grant thee life!
ki-ma ti-du-ú e-bu-ru-um	As thou knowest, the harvest-time
ki-ru-ub	Is near.
la tu-ma-ga-a[268]	Be not negligent!
it-ti Na-din-iš-ša-al-mu-um	With Nadin-ishshalmum
al-kam-ma	Come and
ṭe-im bi-ti i ni-id-bu-ub	Let us discuss affairs of the house.

XXIV

No. 5

An Appeal to a Sister to Care for a Child

a-na Il-ta-ni	To Iltani
qi-bi-ma	Speak.
um-ma Ša-mu-uḫ-tum-ma	Thus says Shamuhtum:—
^{ilu}*Šamaš ù* ^{ilu}*Gu-la li-ba-al-li-ṭu-ki*	May Shamash and Gula keep thee healthy!

ú-ul ti-di-e ki-ma e-li-nu-uk-ki	Dost thou not know that I have no sister
a-ḫa-tam la i-šu-ú	Except thee?
ù a-na še-ir-ri-im	For the sake of the child,
ša aq-bu-ki-im	As I have told thee,
uṣ-na-a-a ma-di-iš	My attention is greatly
i-ba-aš-ši-a-ki-im	Directed toward thee.
[it-ti še-ir][269]*-ri*	With the child
la ta-.	Not thou . . . .
ki-ma ta-ta-am-ri šu-uṣ-im-ma	When thou readest bring forth.
a-na-ku lu-ul-li-ka-ak-ki-im	So indeed I shall come to thee.
gi-im-ri ma-la ta-ga-am-ma-ri	Everything as much as thou dost spend,
1 šiqlam kaspim 2 šiqlam kaspim	Be it one or two shekels of silver,
li-ib-ba[270] *šu-ú a-na-ku a-ap-pa-al-ki*	I will pay unto thee this in full.

XXV

No. 9

Seizure of Women Slaves for a Debt

m. Ilu-d[a-mi-iq.	Ilu-damiq . . . .
a-na mi-[im-ma] e-li-ia [i-ba-aš-šu]	For whatever is against me.
um-ma šu-ma	So he has said.
e-li Ḫa-ab-[lum] a-ḫi-ka	Against thy brother Hablum
1 ma-na 10 šiqlu kaspim i-na Na-ḫu-ur^{ki} *i-[šu-ú]*	They hold in Nahur one mina and ten shekels of silver.
an-ni-tam[271] *iq-bi-a-am-ma*	This he said to me and
2 ^{sal}*ni-pa-ti-ia it-te-bi*	Two of my women slaves held for debt he took.
m. Ilu-da-mi-iq	Ilu-damiq
ù ^{ilu}*Marduk-mu-ša-lim dekû*[272]	And Marduk-mushalim, the marshal,
ša e-li Ḫa-ab-lum a-ḫi-ia kaspam i-šu-ú	Who against Hablum, my brother, hold a claim for money,
ištên ardam	Caused one slave
ša Ḫa-ab-lum a-ḫi-ia	Of Hablum, my brother,
ú-še-ri-du-nim a-na kaspim id-di-nu-ma	To come down, and they sold (him) for money.

$\frac{1}{3}$ ma-na kaspim Ilu-da-mi-iq il-qi
ù $\frac{5}{6}$ ma-na kaspim ^{ilu}Marduk-mu-ša-lim il-qi
a-na ma-ḫar daiânê^{meš} al-li-ik
daiânê^{meš} a-wa-a[273]-ti-ni i-mu-ru-ma
ki-ma[274] a-na-ku aq-bu-[ú]
ù ^{ilu}Marduk-mu-ša-lim dekû
ki-ma $\frac{1}{3}$ ma-na kaspim Ilu-da-mi-iq
ù šu-ú $\frac{5}{6}$ ma-na kaspim il-qu-ú
ma-ḫar daiânê^{meš} iq-bi-ma
daiânê^{meš} ^{sal}ni-pa-a-tim wu-uš-šu-ra-[am-ma]
iq-bu-šum-ma
ú-ul ú-wa-aš-še-ir-ma
ki-a-am ú-lam-mi-da-an-ni
amêlê^{meš} ši-bi
mu-di a-wa-[a]-ti-šu
li-ki-ir-ri-bu-ni-ik-ku-[ma]
. . . .

$\frac{1}{3}$ mina of silver took Ilu-damiq
And $\frac{5}{6}$ mina of silver took Marduk-mushalim.
I went to the judges.
The judges investigated our case.
As I said,
Also Marduk-mushalim, the marshal, told in the presence of the judges
How Ilu-damiq took $\frac{1}{3}$ mina of silver
And he $\frac{5}{6}$ mina of silver.
The judges commanded him to free the women slaves held
For debt,
But he did not set (them) free.
Thus they informed me.
Witnesses
Who know his affair
They shall bring unto thee.
. . . .

XXVI

No. 4

A Request to Send Lead, Which Had Been Promised

a-na. . . . .
qi- [bi-] ma
um-ma ^{m}Sin-ma-gir-ma
^{ilu}Nin-ib li-ba-li-du-ka
aš-šum a-na-ki-im ki-a-am ta-aq-bi-a-am
um-ma at-ta-a-ma
ma-la ḫi-še-iḫ-ti-ka ú-ta-ba-la-ak-[kum]
at-ta-la-ak-kum-ma ú-ul li-[qi-aš-šu]

To. . . . .
Speak as follows.
Thus says Sin-magir:—
May Ninib grant thee health!
Concerning the lead thou hast spoken to me
As follows:—
Whatever thy need (may be) I shall send (it) unto thee.
I shall (then) come to thee. Do not get it

i-nu-ú-ma qu-um[275] *ḫa-tim tu-um-[mar]*	When thou seest the shortage of the white-smith.
ki-a-am ta-aš-pu-ra-am um-ma [a-na-ku-ma]	Thus thou hast written to me. I answer as follows:
a-na biltim ITU.ITU.GA a-al-la-[ka-ak-kum]	I come to thee for a talent of . . . . . .
i-na pa-ni-ia a-na-kam ub-ba-[lu-nim]	They shall send the lead into my presence,
ú-ul ta-at-ta-al-[kam-ma]	But thou shalt not come.
a-nu-um-ma 10 šiqlam kaspim ^{m} *Riš-i[li]*[276]	Now, ten shekels of silver through Rish-ili
uš-ta-bi-la-ak-kum	I cause to be sent to thee.
šum-ma i-na ki-it-tim a-ḫi at-ta	If in truth thou art my brother,
tuppim$^{(im)}$ *dam-ga-am ga-ti-ka ri-ši*	Gladden me with a good letter from thyself.
ṣi-bu-ti ma-di-iš id-na-šum-ma	As for my wish, let them give it full consideration.
ar-ḫi-iš du-ur-da-aš-šu	Send him quickly!
ri-gu-uṣ-ṣu la ta-da-ar-ra-da-aš-šu	Thou shalt not despatch him empty handed!
mi-im-ma šu-ku-ra-am	Everything is valuable for me!
ša ṣi-bu-ti-ka šu-up-ra-am-ma	Whatever thy wish (may be), write me
lu-[ú] it-ta-la-ak-kum	And indeed it shall come to thee.

XXVII

No. 13

King Samsu-iluna Asks That Reed-baskets be Sent to Him from Nippur

[a-na] be-el te-ri-e[-tim]	To the supreme commander[277]
[ù] daiânê ša Nippuru^{ki}	And the judges of Nippur
qi- bi- ma	Speak.
um-ma Sa-am-su-i-lu-na-ma	Thus says Samsu-iluna:—
a-nu-um-ma išten dekam ^{amêl}*NU.ŠÀG(?).KI*[278] *ga-du-um ummâni-šu*	I, now, despatch a sergeant-major of the quartermaster's corps with his troops.

at-ṭar-dam	
pisânnê$^{(ṣun)}$ *ša Zi-na-tum*	With the reed-baskets of Zinatum
ša i-na Nippuru^{ki} *ša-ak-na*	Which are deposited at Nippur,
bi-ik-da-ni-iš-šu-nu-ti-im-ma	Entrust them,
a-na ma-aḫ-ri-ia	And into my presence
li-ib-lu-nim	Let them bring (them).

XXVIII

No. 11

Letter from a Farmer to a Landlord Concerning a Deficiency of Fodder

a-na Amêl-^{ilu}*Nin-ib*	To Amel-Ninib
qi- bi- ma	Speak.
um-ma Ku-ru-um-ma	Thus says Kurum:—
^{ilu}*Enlil ù* ^{ilu}*Nin-ib*	May Enlil and Ninib
li-ba-al-li-du-ka	Preserve thy health!
aš-šum di-e-im tibni^{sun}	Concerning the information (regarding) the grain in head
ša ^{âlu}*Ki-lum ša pa-te-si*	Of the town Kilum of the patesi,
tibnu šu-ú ig-ga-mar-ma	That grain in head is consumed.
alpê^{sun}*-ka mi-nam i-ka-lu*	What will thy oxen eat?
a-di wa-aš-ba-a-ku ú-ul ú-še-ri-ib-šu-ma	As long as I dwell here I have not imported it,
1 qa tibni i-na ga-ti-i-ka	And thou holdest not (even) a single amphora of grain in the head in thy possession.
ú-ul ta-ṣa-ab-ba-at	
10 ^{gi}*GUR.DA*^{sun279} *šu-bi-lam-ma*	Have ten reed-racks brought to me,
a-di wa-aš-ba-a-ku lu-še-ri-ib-šu-ma	And then as long as I dwell here I will import it.
lu-up-ḫi-e-šu	I will keep it secure.
[nišê]^{sun} *na-aš-pa-ak 70 še gur*	Summon people for the storing of seventy gur of grain.
du- [uk- ki]	
aš-šum di-e-im kîrim	Concerning the information in regard to the garden . . . .
ša GU.EN.NA iš-tu arḫim 1-kam	Of the chief-sheriff: Since the first month

a-na Ê-DUB-BA[280] *ta-aq-bi-ma*	Thou hast told to the recording officer,
ta-ad-di-na-aš-šu	Thou hast given it.
a-na ṣa-ba-at ma-ri iš-te-en ma-ṣi	One (garden) suffices for the support (?) of a son.
mi-nu-um ša ^{m}*Ṭâb-pî-ša-ab-di warad ekallim*	How is it that Tab-pi-sha-abdi, the servant of the palace,
a-na ṣa-ba-at kîrim ša-a-tim	For obtaining(?) that garden,
kaspam$^{(am)}$ *na-šu-ú-ma wa-ar-ki*	Brings money? Henceforth
a-a ú-ti-im-ma it-ta-na-al-la-a-ku	Let him not concern himself about it. They have come repeatedly,
a-ša-ar ka-ti[281] *i-šu-ú*	And take thy place(?).
an-ni-tum tibnu e-ip-pi-eš	That grain in head does (its purpose).
. . . .*-a-ti i-na ga-ti-ia*	. . . . .are not in my
ú-la [*i-ba-aš-šu-ú*]	Possession.
li-[*iš-pu-ru-šu-nu-ši-im*]	Let them send for them.
a-na . . . .*-im da-pu-ul*	To the. . . . .
[*an-ni-ki-a*]*-am li-šu-ni-iq-qum-ma*	Immediately let it arrive.
e-li-šu ti-e	There is anxiety about it.

CASSITE LETTERS

XXIX

No. 80

Letter of a Caretaker to His Master

warad-ka ^{m}*I-ki-ša-*[*am*]	Thy servant Ikisham
a-na di-na-an be-li-[*ia lul*]*-lik*	May come unto the presence of my lord!
um-ma-a a-na be-li-ia-ma	The following speak unto my lord:—
^{isu}*adara*[282] *ša be-li iš-pu-ra*	(In regard to) the willow-trees about which my lord has written (I reply):
a-na mu-uḫ-ḫi 7 ^{isu}*adara*	In addition to the seven willow-trees
. . . .*-ši(?)-ni ù ašar kam-ri*[283]	A. . . . . . . .and a place of storage

be-li id-di-na	My lord gave unto me.
adara a-a-ú tu-šam-ma	Where didst thou buy the willows?
ia-'-nu adaru a-a	There are no willows (any more). I shall
a-na be-li-ia [uš]-še-bi-la	(However) not send (for others) to my lord.
še-e-ta[284] *ša be-li iš-pu-ra*[285]	When I have removed from the house
uš-tu[286] *bît ú-di-e ša ḫarrani*	Of the traveling utensils the hammock,
ki-i aš-ša-a a-na eli	About which
be-li-ia uš-še-bi-la	My lord has written, I shall send (it) to my lord.

XXX

No. 45

A Request That a Man Should Hasten to Reply to a Royal Letter

a-na ${}^{m\cdot}$*Amel-ia qi-bi-ma*	To Amelia speak.
[um]-ma ${}^{m\cdot}$*Ka-tar-SAḪ aḫ-ka-ma*	Thus says Katar-SAH, thy brother:
[a-na] ka-a-ša lu šul-mu	Greeting be unto thee!
[ilâni${}^{(meš)}$*] a-ši-bu ina* ^{âlu}*Qar-*^{ilu}*En-li*	The gods that dwell in the city Qar-Enlil
[nap]-ša-ti-ka li-iṣ-ṣu-rum	May protect thy life!
um-ma-a a-na ${}^{m\cdot}$*Amel-ia-ma*	The following (say) to Amelia:—
tup-pa ša šarrim	As to the letter which the king
ú-še-bi-al-ku[287]	Has caused to be brought unto thee
aš-šum eqlim ša ^{âlu}*Ka-du-ku-ú*	Concerning the field of the city of Kaduku,
ki-i pi-i tup-pi	According to the wording of the letter
ša šarru ú-še-bi-al-ku[287]	Which the king has caused to be brought unto thee,
ḫa-an-tiš šu-pu-ur-ma	Write quickly.
warad-ka ${}^{m\cdot}$*Ku-ub-bu-la*	Thy servant Kubbula
la i-kal-lu-ú-ma	They shall not detain.
lit-ta-al-ka	May he go!

XXXI

No. 76

A King Asks for a Footstool of a Subject's Chariot

a-na $^{m.\ ilu}$*Nin-ib-nadin-aḫê*	To Ninib-nadin-ahe
qi- bi- ma	Speak.
um-ma šarru-ma	Thus says the king:—
um-ma-a û-um tup-pi	When thou seest
ta-mu-ru	My letter.
$^{m.\ ilu}$*Šamaš-dajan*	Let Shamash-dajan
gištabba[288] *narkabti-ka*	Bring unto me
li-iš-ša-šum-ma	The footstool of thy chariot.
ḫa-mut-ta	Quickly
li-ik-šu-da	Let it come unto me.

XXXII

No. 25

A Report Concerning a Patient and an Inquiry Concerning Vessels to be Given to the King

warad-ka ^{m} *Ki-ša-aḫ-bu-ut*	Thy servant Kishahbut
a-na di-na-an be-li-ia	May come unto the presence
lu- ul- lik	Of my lord!
a-na bît be-li-ia	Unto the household of my lord
šu- ul- mu	Greeting!
um-ma-a a-na be-li-ia-ma	The following (speak): Unto my lord
a-na mâr be-li-ia	And unto the son of my lord
šu- ul- mu	Greeting
da-an-ni-iš	Much!
kurumat-su ik-ka-al	He eats his food
ù ši-ir-šu	And his omen (or flesh?)
ṭa-ab-šu	Is good.

ti-li-e[289] *šarri ša a-na be-li-ia*	The vessels of the king, which unto my lord
ú-še-bi-la be-li a-na ekalli	I have caused to be brought, my lord
it-ta-din-ma lu na-ad-nu	Should give to the palace. Verily are they given?
ù be-li ul it-ta-din-ma	But if my lord has not given (them),
li-kar-ru-ni[290]	Verily they will thirst(?).
til-lu-ú gu-ul-tum(?)[291]	. . . .-vessels
a-di-in-na[292]	At present . . . .
i-na âli^{ki} *ia-nu-[ú]*[293]	Are not in the city.

XXXIII

No. 23

A Notice Concerning the Dismissal of a Watchman

a-na ^{ilu}*Amurrû-ka-ra-bi-iš-me*	To Amurru-karabi-ishme
qi- bi- ma	Speak.
um-ma ^{ilu}*En-lil-al-šaḫ-ma*	Thus says Enlil-alshaḫ:—
^{m}*Aš-bi-ša-tu-ni*	Ashbishatuni,
ša ^{ilu}*En-lil-mu-ba-al-liṭ*	Whose watchman(?)
at-tu-ú-šu	Is Enlil-muballit
ù ša-šu ta-pi-šu	And that man was his associate,
muš-še-ir-ma	I have dismissed.
šu-ú liš-pu-uš	Let him be angry.
[at]-ta la ta-šap-pu-uš	Thou shalt not be angered.

XXXIV

No. 24

A Royal Summons for a Subject to be Brought to the King

a-na Amêl-^{ilu}*Marduk*	To Amel-Marduk
qi- bi- ma	Speak.
um-ma šarru[294]*-ma*	Thus says the king:—

um-ma-a a-na Amêl-^{ilu}*Marduk-ma*	(Say) the following to Amel-Marduk:
Apil-šadu-rubu-ú-a	Apil-shadu-rubua
it-ti-i-ka	With thee
a-na Babîli	To Babylon
li-qa-am-ma	Take
kul-da[295]	And arrive.

XXXV

No. 43

Report to a High Official Concerning the Collection of Taxes and Certain Irregularities in His Province

warad-ka $^{m.ilu}$*Nusku-teṣlîtam-išme*	Thy servant Nusku-teslitâm-ishme
a-na di-na-an be-li-ia lul-lik	May come unto the presence of my lord!
a-na ṣêri âli^{ki} *bît ili ù bît be-li šul-mu*	Unto the fields, the city, the temple of the god and the house of my lord greeting!
šu-ru-ub-ti bît ili ma-la i-ba-[296]*aš-šu li*[297]*-mad*	May the income of the temple of the god, whatever it is, be much!
um-ma-a a-na be-li-ia-ma	The following (speak) unto my lord:
sa mâr $^{m.ilu}$*Sin-ri-man-ni ša be-li*	As to the affairs of the son of Sin-rimanni about which my lord
iš-pu-ra 452 gur 140 qa šipâti$^{(ti)}$	Wrote to me, 452 ghors 140 amphoras of wool
ù ipra ṣâbê^{meš} *ma-ḫa-ar-šu*	And the food-payment for the workmen are in his possession.
te-lit 6 âlāni^{meš} *ša il-qa-a*	The contribution of six cities which he has received,
a-na be-li-ia ul-te-bi-la	He will cause to be brought to my lord.
ša 3 ṣâbê^{meš} *ka-lu-ti ša be-li iš-pu-[ra]*	As to the three men in imprisonment which my lord wrote about (I reply):
ma-ṣar-ta-šu-nu da-an-na-at	"Their guard is strong."
ka-a-a-na-am-ma a-na be-li-ia	Constantly unto my lord

lul-tap-pa-ra ša ḫa-du-ú Bît-Ki-[di-ni]	Will I write. As for the sin of Bit-Kidini,
ša be-li iš-pu-ra ù-lu[298]	Which my lord has written about, except
ul tu-še-el-ma a-na be-li-ia	Thou hadst not inquired, unto my lord
ul aš-pu-ra	I would not have written.
aš-šu 14 iṣṣurê^{meš} ša be-li iš-pu-[ra]	As for the fourteen birds which my lord has written about
um-ma-a ipra 14 iṣṣurê^{meš} ki-i [i-di-in]	As follows: "Give barley for fourteen birds," (I reply):
iṣṣurê^{meš} mi-i-tum[299] *i-lu-ṣu(?)* . . .	"The birds are dead . . . .
a-na qa-ti-ia la i-ša-ak-[ka-an]	Into my hand places not.
a-na mi-im-ma pa-na la a-[na-aš-ši][300]	I was not paying attention (to it) at all.
ul-tu kit-ta ù ta-ri . . . . *-a*	And while on justice and mercy . . . .
a-da-ab-bu-bu iq-li-e-[ma . . . .]	I was pondering, he seized . . . .
a-na pa-ni-ia pa-ar-[ka-ti ù][301]	Before me violence(?)
sa-ar-ta ip-pu-uš-ma [a-na ia-ši-im][302]	And rebellion he does and for me
i-kab-bi-it ul ša-am(?) . . . . *a-na-ku*	It is too heavy. Not . . . . I.
ù be-li i-di ša ḫi-tum [la ap-ri-ik][303]	And my lord knows that sin I did not commit.
a-ba-at-ti bâb mê	Now the water-gate of . . . .
ù tar-bat dul-li ip-pu-uš	And the greater part(?) of the work is made.
tup-pi te-li-ti ša-ši ṣêri	My letter referring to that offering of the fields
ù ^{mât}Babîli^{ki}	And the country of Babylon
a-na be-li-ia ul-te-bi-la	I have sent to my lord.
4 âlâni^{meš} ša kišad nâr Dur-Kib[304]	Four cities at the bank of the river Dur-Kib
i-šap-pu-šu-ma di-ma a-na be-li-ia	They tax, and the information unto my lord
a-šap-pa-ra	I shall send.

XXXVI

No. 19

A Request for Instruction about Works of Irrigation

[warad-ka X]	Thy servant X
a-na di-na-an be-li-[ia]	Unto the presence of my lord
lul- lik	May I come!
um-ma-a a-na be-li-ia-ma	The following (speak) unto my lord:
aš-šum ṣâbê^{šun} *ša be-li*	Concerning the men whom my lord
iš-pu-ra um-ma-a ṣâbê^{šun}	Wrote about, saying: "The men
li-qa-am-ma a-na ^{âlu}*Pa-laḫ-*^{ilu}*Adad*	Take and to the city of Palah-Adad
al-ka âli ḫi-il-ti[305]	Go." (I reply): Shall I dig
ša nâr Zu-mu-un-da-ar	Either the city-canal
ki e-ḫi-ru-ú âli ḫi-il-ti[305]	Of the river Zumundar
ša nâr Pu-rat-ti-i	Or shall I dig the city-canal of the
ki e-ḫi-ru-ú be-li	River Euphrates? My lord
ṭe-ma li-iš-pu-ra-am-ma	May send me information.
lu-um-mi-id-m[a]	Instruct (me) and
li-iḫ-ru-ú	They may dig.
ù aš-šum me-e ša $^{m.ilu}$*Nin-ib-aḫ-iddin*	And concerning the water of Ninib-ah-iddin,
ša be-li iš-pu-ra	About which my lord wrote
um-ma-a eqla-šu am-mi-ni	As follows: "Why does he not
me-e la i-ša-at-ti	Irrigate his field?
iš-te-en i-ša-at-ti-i-ma	A certain one shall irrigate."
lu-ú ul [i-ša-at]-ti	(I reply): He indeed does not irrigate.

Remaining one or two lines destroyed.

XXXVII

No. 71

A Physician's Report on the Condition of Several Women Patients

[warad-ka $^{m.}$*Mu-kal-lim]*	Thy servant Mukallim
a-na di-na-[an be-li-ia]	Unto the presence of my lord
lu- ul- li- [ik]	May I come!

a-na na-'-ri-[e]	Unto the lamentation priests
na-'i-ra-[a-ti]	The lamentation women,
^{sal}e-di-ir-[ti[306]]	The women of affliction
ù bît be-li-ia	And the household of my lord
šu- ul- mu	Greeting!
mārāt A-a-ri	Ari's daughter's
i-ša-ta-tum ša ir-ti-ša	Feverheat in her breast
ẓu-ú-ta[307] *it-ta-da-a*	Causes sweat to perspire.
ša mārāt Muš-ta-li	As to the daughter of Mushtali (I report)
ša ir-ti-ša-ma	That her breast also
ẓu-ú-ta it-ta-da-a	Perspires sweat.
ša mārāt [Ku]-ri-i	As to the daughter of Kuri (I report)
il-te-id-.......	That ....
ù [ša ^{sal}La-ta]	And of the lady Lata
ù [ša mārāt Aḫ-la-mi-ti][308]	As well as of the daughter of the Ahlamite
[ša ir-ti-ši-na]	(I inform thee) that their breast
[ẓu-ú'-ta it-[ta-da-a]	Perspires sweat.
[ša] mārāt $^{m\cdot}$Anu-i[p-pa-aš-ra]	Of the daughter of Anu-ippashra (I report)
2[309] *i-na ir-ti-ša*	Fever and chill in her breast
ẓu-ú-ta it-ta-da-a	Exude sweat.
ša mārāt Aḫu-ni	As to the daughter of Ahuni:
2 *i-na ir-ti-ša*	Fever and chills in her breast
ẓu-ú-ta it-ta-da-a	Exude sweat.
ša mārāt ^{sal}Ba-ba-ti[310]	As to the daughter of the lady Babati:
ù ^{sal}Bi-ta-ti	And the lady Bitati:
ẓu-ú-ta ul na-da-a	Sweat they do not exude.
a-na šu-ul-mi-ši-na	For their well-being
šu- ul- mu	Greeting!
8 *na-ad-ba(?)-ki*	Eight ....
uš(?)-ši-ki at-.....	....
[al]-ta-pa-[ra-ku][311]	I send unto thee.

XXXVIII

No. 35

The Conclusion of a Letter

Reverse

a-na mu-uḫ-ḫi-[ka]	Unto thee
a-bi-ia ù um-mi-ia	My father and my mother.
a-na ma-an-ni uz-[na]-a-a [i-ba-aš-ši]	Unto whom (else) should my attention be directed?
at-ta-ma ṣi-il-la	Thou establishest
i-na mu-uḫ qa-qa-di-ia ta-ša-ak-ka-an	A protecting shadow over me.
at-ta-ma tu-ba-al-la-ṭa-an-ni	Thou dost quicken me with life!
ù ka-am-ma ša^{312} *a-na be-el*	And as if(?) unto the lord . . . .
^{ilu}*Nin-ib ša i-na-aṣ-ṣa-ru-[ka(?)]*	Ninib who protects thee.
ša aš-pu-ra-ak-ku šu-bi-la-[am-ma]	What I have written to thee for, cause to be brought.

XXXIX

No. 70

A Notification That the Writer, Together with the Addressee's Brother, Will Set Out on a Journey

warad-ka ^{m}*Mu-li-[*^{ilu}*Šamaš(?)]*	Thy servant Muli-Shamash
a-na di-na-an be-l[i-ia lul-lik]	Into the presence of my lord may I come.
um-ma-a a-na be-li-[ia-ma]	The following (speak) unto my lord:
ša û-um be-li i-mu-[ru]	As to this, since my lord has seen it,
na-da-ku-ma it-ti	That I was neglectful and with
aḫ-ka ul al-lik	Thy brother I did not go.
i-na-an-na ki-i iš-pu-ra	Now, that he has written thus,

um-ma-a ri-da-a	My commissioner
ù ṣi-di-ti-ia	And my provender
be-li li(!)*-iš-pu-ra-am-ma*	Let my lord send.
ištu Nippuru^{ki} *ṣi-di-ti*	From Nippur the provender
qêmu ù GA-GAL^{meš}	Of flour and pure milk
li-pu-šu-ma i-tu-ú aḫ-ka	Let them provide. With thy brother
lu-lik ûm a-na ali	I will come. When unto the city
be-li-ia a-na-[bu?]	My lord I announce(?),
ki-i a-šap-pa-ru	As I write,
be-li i-di-e ki-i	My lord knows that
tir-ri i-tu aḫ-ka ia-nu	Mercy with thy brother (there is) not.

XL

No. 67

Concerning the Reception of Barley and Oil

a-na $^{m.}$*Amêl-ia ša a-ra-a-mu-uš qi-bi-ma*	To Amelia whom I love speak.
um-ma ^{ilu}*Marduk-šum-lišir aḫ-ka-ma*	Thus says Marduk-shum-lishir, thy brother:
a-na ka-ša lu-ú šul-mu	Peace be unto thee!
ilâni a-šib^{âlu}*Ak-ka-di nap-ša-ti-ka*	The gods that inhabit Akkad, thy life
li-iṣ-ṣu-ru um-ma-a a-na	May protect! The following (speak) to
Amêl-ia Nusku-e-a ša a-na li-it[313]	Amelia:—Nuskuea, whom unto
E-ne-ri taš-pu-ru	Eneri thou hast sent,
ul-tu ma-ḫa-ra ša še'ati	Since the reception of the barley
la iq-bu-ú ù ul-te-ip-ri-is(!)	He did not command and he withheld it,
e-nin-na Amêl-ia it-ti E-ne-ri	So may now Amelia (himself) with Eneri
lid-bu-um-ma ^{amêl}*tup-šar-ra-šu*	Consult, and his scribe
li-iš-pu-ra-am-ma	He may send to me and
še'atam li-im-ḫu-ru-ma u-sa-ta	Let them receive the barley. May god
ilu(?) *lit-ta-lik ša-ki-šum-ma-a*	Come to help! Do it!

amêl^{meš}*-e-a ma-la i-ba-aš-šu-ú*	My men as many as there are
li-si-ip-pi-i-iḫ	Verily he has scattered.
ù tuppam a-na muḫ-ḫi-ia	But a letter to me
liš (!)-ba-a[314] *ri-ša-am-ma*	May satisfy. Be glad!
[ma-am-m]a-an tuppam a-na na-še-e	I have no one to carry
ul a-ga-ša-ad ẓi-ri-im-ma[315]	A letter. Make an effort,
ki-pi-id-ma ḫa-an-tiš šup-ra	Give heed, hand quickly!
ù ša šamnu ša taš-pu-ra um-ma a-na Marduk-lim-ḫu-rum	And concerning the oil about which thou hast written to Marduk-lim-hurum, as follows:
ša tup-šar-ri ša tuppi-šu ṣa-bat-ma	"Take the document of the scribe and
šu-bi-lam-ma lib-bi liš-ša-ar-an-ni[316]	Cause it to be brought." My heart may lead me aright!
ù ša še'ati ša e-ri-ši-ka	And about the barley for which I have begged thee,
šup-ra-am-ma lu-ú i-na	Send (it) either to
^{ālu}*Ši-tu-la lu-ú i-na* ^{ālu}*Ma-še-e*	Shitula or to Mashe.
lid-di be-li id-be-tum[317]	The garments of my lord are lost.
it-ti-ia ta-na-ẓi-ik	Thou sufferest damage through me.
[ma]-ti-ma it-ti-ia i-ẓi-ẓu	At what time remained they with me?
ma-am-ma-na-a ul i-šu	No one has
uš-da-ka-dur	appropriated (them).

XLI

No. 68

An Inventory of Grain

[war]ad-ka $^{m.}$*Idin-*^{ilu}*Adad a-na [di-na-an be-li-ia]*	Thy servant Idin-Adad. May I come unto the presence
[lu-] ul- li- ik	Of my lord!
[4 (?)] gur 1 pi 30 qa še labiri	Four(?) gur, one pi and thirty qa (is the measure of) the old grain.
70 gur 3 pi 40 qa še ešši ša âli[^{ki}*]*	Seventy gur, three pi and forty qa (is the measure of) the new grain of the city.

9 gur 3 pi bêl makisi ša abulli	Nine gur, three pi (are with) the master of the tax-gatherers of the great gate.
napḫar[318] *80 gur 1 pi 40 qa še ša âli*^{ki}	(There is) a total of eighty gur, one pi and forty qa of grain of the city
48 gur miksu[319]	Forty-eight gur (is) the tax
še'im i-na Ru-ni(?)-šu-bur-ru^{ki}	Of the grain at Runishuburru
$^{m.ilu}$*Adad-šub-ši ma-ki-su*	Adad-shubshi (is) the receiver of the customs.
9 gur 3 pi 35 qa še labiri	Nine gur, three pi and thirty-five qa (is the measure of) the old grain.
46 gur 2 pi 30 qa še ešši ša âli[^{ki}]	Forty-six gur, two pi and thirty qa (is the measure of) the new grain of the city.
3 gur 1 pi bêl makisi ša abulli	Three gur and one pi (are with) the master of the tax gatherers at the great gate.
napḫar 49 gur 3 pi 3[0 qa še ša âli^{ki}]	The totality (is) forty-nine gur, three pi and thirty qa of grain of the city.
[b]êl ma[kisi]	The master of the tax gatherers
si-pi ṣi-ti [ša še'im ša]	Petition about the delivery of the grain
ma- ki- [su]	Of the receiver of the customs.
e-im âli^{ki} *ap-pa-al-[šu]*	Where (is) the city (to which) I shall send it?
a-na mu-uḫ-ḫi be-li-ia ú-še-bi-la	Shall I cause it to be sent to my lord?

NEO-BABYLONIAN LETTERS

XLII

No. 87

Report to a Superior Concerning the Arrest of Debtors

dup-pi $^{m.}$*Ṣil-la-a-a*	Letter of Silla
a-na Ninib-aḫ-iddina	To Ninib-ah-iddina,
bêl-ia ^{ilu}*En-lil ù* ^{ilu}*Nin-ib*	My lord. May Enlil and Ninib

šu-lum ù balaṭ ša bêl-ia	Command peace and health
liq-bu-ú a-na ^{amêl}*errišê*^{meš}[320]	Of my lord! Unto the farmers
ša ^{âlu}*Ab-ba-man-ta-nu*	Of the town Abba-mantanu,
ša lu a-na eš-ru-ú id-ku-ú	Whom they summoned on account of the tithe
a-na pan ^{amêl}*GU.EN.NA al-ta*[321] *a-na*	Unto the presence of the sheriff I.......
muḫ-ḫi-šu-nu bêlu la i-še-el-li	The lord shall not be angry against them
ú-il-tim ša 220 gur	A debt of two hundred and twenty gurs
ina muḫ-ḫi-šu-nu e-li-ka	Stands against them for thee.
ak-ta-la-šu-nu-tu	I have taken them in charge
um-ma a-ki-i	(saying) as follows: "According to
ši-piš-ti[322] *ša* ^{amêl}*GU.EN.NA*	The message of the sheriff, send
tuppa a-na arki	A document after Ea-iddina,
$^{\text{m.ilu}}$*E-a-iddina amêl ša eš-ru-ú*	The officer of the tithes."
šu-kun-'a a-ki-i ka-lu	Since they are held in restraint
ul il-lu-ku-'u	They shall not go.
ki-i ^{amêl}*ṣâbê*^{meš}*-'a*	Since as to my men
ú-il-tim ina muḫ-ḫi-šu-nu la te-el-li	A debt upon them rests not(?),
a-na ri-ik-si	So according to the contract(?)
[*ašar ú*][323]*-še-bi i-ta-ri*	They shall return where they live.
............*-šu-nu*	Their..................
.......*mârâtê*^{meš} *ša*......	........the daughters of.........

XLIII

No. 90

Instruction Concerning the Disposition of Dates

duppi $^{\text{m.ilu}}$*Marduk-zêr-ibni a-na*	Letter of Marduk-zer-ibni to
$^{\text{m.ilu}}$*Nabu-it-ti-ia aḫû-a* ^{ilu}*Nabu*	Nabu-ittia, my brother. May Nabu
ù ^{ilu}*Marduk a-na aḫi-ia lik-ru-bu*	And Marduk be gracious to my brother!
ina ma-aṣ-ṣar-ti ša suluppi	From the guarding of the dates
la ta-tel-li ma-la bašû	Do not go away. As many as there are,

suluppi ina lib-bi a-na man-ma
la ta-nam-din a-di
a-na $^{m\cdot}$*Ṭab-ia al-ta-par*
it-ti-ka
i-nam-ṣar

As to the dates therefrom to no one
Shalt thou give. Until
Unto Tabia I have written,
With thee
He shall keep (them).

XLIV

No. 89

An Order for Oil[324]

duppi $^{m\cdot}$*Ši-riq-tum-*^{ilu}*MAŠ*
a-na ^{m}*Gi-mil-lu*
aḫ-ia ^{ilu}*MAŠ û* ^{ilu}*MAŠ a-na*
aḫ-ia lik-ru-bu
1 gur 200 qa karpati lu-ú ša šamni ḫa-iṭ[325]
a-na $^{m\cdot}$*Nergal-iddin*
^{amêl}*malaḫu i-din-šu*
it-ti-šu
a-na Babili^{ki}
liš-ša-'a

Letter of Shiriqtum-Mash
To Gimillu,
My brother. May Mash and Mash.
Be gracious to my brother!
A one gur and two hundred qa jar of clear oil
To Nergal-iddin
The bootsman give.
Through him
To Babylon
Let it be brought.

NOTES

[1] For the restorations of lines 3 to 5 compare KMS. I: 12, 13.

[2] The wedge after the numeral 10 has been taken as the beginning of the sign *kam*, but it is also possible that it represents the lower left wedge of the numeral 4. In case we read 14, it is of interest to note what Bu. 88-5-12, 11 (CT. 5, 6) has to say of an eclipse that happens during the 12, or the 13, or the 14 day of the month *Kislîmu*. Lines 30 ff. read: *ina arḫi Kislîmu kimin* (i. e., *lû ûmu* XII-*kam lû ûmu* XIII-*kam lû ûmu* XIV-*kam adar* ^{ilu}*Sin naškun*^{un}) *ina erib bu-lim ana pân bu-lim mê tanaqqi*^{qi} ^{immer}*niqâ tanaqqi*^{qi} *dam niksi*^{si} *ašar-šu tamaḫḫaṣ bâbu is-sal-laḫ šegušsu KAL-GÊ ina bâbi šâri išten ta-ša-rap ina pân* ^{kakkab}*nimru* ^{kakkab}*aqrabu uš-kin balâṭu liṣip;* i. e., If in the month *Kislîmu*, either on the 12, 13 or 14 day occurs an eclipse of the moon: At the entering of the cattle, thou shalt libate water before the cattle, thou shalt sacrifice a lamb-sacrifice, with the blood of the butchering thou shalt sprinkle its place. The door shall be sprinkled. *Shegushshu*, black *KAL* thou shalt burn up at the gate of "one wind." He shall fall down before the panther-star, the scorpion-star. May he multiply life! See, Frank, SBR. pp. 118–128.

[3] Line 6 restored from KMS. IV: 42.

[4] With lines 10 ff. cf. KMS. IX: 10 to 21.

[5] Text reads *ki*. Read *lu-ú* with duplicate of KMS IX.

[6] *PEŠ=mikdu*, ZA. 9, 169, 31; MSAI. 4926.

[7] Cf. Maqlu, I: 87.

[8] Written *e-KAR-am*. *KAR=ekêmu*, CT. XII, 11, 19a; Br. 7740; MSAI. 5712.

[9] Restored according to KMS. XII: 2.

[10] It is doubtful whether *da* has the meaning of *našû* also in other cases for K. 247, Col. III: 15 limits the use of *da* to *našû ša amêli*.

[11] *ka-kaš=karaš=garaš*.

[12] Restore according to CT. XVI, pl. 30, lines 63 and 64; CT. XVI, pl. 39, Rev. Col. IV 1: 33 and other like passages.

[13] Cf. CT. XVI, pl. 11, line 19 ff.

[14] Text reads *um*, which is a scribal error.

[15] Restoration problematical.

[16] *Kimin*-sign omitted by scribe.

[17] Restoration of *gar-ra* is doubtful. Duplicate text IV R. 20, line 11 has only *ne* preserved.

[18] This text preserves the *ma-a-tu lu* but the verb is also missing as in IV R. 20, line 14. The reading of *tuš-te-šir* is a mere guess, based on *šir* preserved in the duplicate.

[19] With the additional readings of this text, the complete restoration of the line is almost certain.

[20] *Ama* omitted or placed after *a-a* in IV R. Our text again partially helps to restore the line.

[21] Or restore *uz-na ši-mi-e?* Subject Shamash? The horizontal wedge is however against the reading of *mi* or *me*.

[22] Probably nothing missing after *imšinkuene* and *ikkala*. There is hardly space for *a im-ši-in-nak-e-ne* with the Semitic translation. This line and the following one restore part of lines 19 to 23 in IV R. which are broken away.

[23] With line 14 the text corresponds with IV R. 28. Restore line 1 in R. according to this text. Also the following line.

[24] *ki* omitted by scribe.

[25] Text reads *e* with K. 11789 and omits *šu*.

[26] Duplicate reads *ti*.

[27] Text connects here again with IV R. 28 Rev. line 5.

[28] Duplicate reads *na*.

[29] Duplicate passage inserts *e* after *lugal*.

[30] *zi* omitted by scribe, or read simply *še-ir-zi-da?*

[31] Read *an*, rest erasure.

[32] *Babbar* omitted by scribe.

[33] With lines 11 to 19 cf. CT. XVI, pl. 24, Tablet A, lines 8 to 14; cf. also Col. III, line 12–14, of the present tablet.

[34] *adu 2-kam-ma-aš ù-ub-dug* refers to the incantation priest.

[35] Cf. with lines 49–51 CT. XVI, pl. 24, Tablet A, lines 21–23.

[36] Text reads *zi-(zi)* while duplicate has *šur-šur-ri*.

[37] Tablet A omits *ni*.

[38] *šu ù-me-ti* omitted by mistake by scribe.

[39] Notice the interesting phonetic writing of *daǵ, duǵ = tu-uk!*

[40] For *ǵu-mu-rab-daǵ-e*.

[41] Omitted in duplicate text.

[42] Duplicate reads *gig-bar-a-šu*.

[43] *ra* omitted in duplicate.

[44] Restore *ud* before *bad* in Tablet A. Instead of *bad* this text reads *ka*.

[45] Restore *ǵul-gal lù* in Tablet A.

[46] Cols. 2 and 3 of Tablet A may nearly completely be restored from here onward.

[47] Restoration doubtful.

[48] *in* erasure?

[49] KMS. 27:6 note: *ti-ši-'*.

[50] Mistake of scribe; omit.

[51] Here the text joins again with KMS. 27:13 ff.

[52] The lines broken away according to the duplicate text l. 16–19 are: (16) *aš-šum ta-a-ra-ta iš-ti-'-ú-ka(?)* (17) *aš-šum mu-up-pal-sa-ta a-ta-mar* . . . . (18) *aš-šum ri-mi-ni-ta at-ta-ziz pâni-ka(?)* (19) *ki-niš naplis-an-ni-ma še-mi qa-ba-a:* "Because thou art gracious, I seek thee. Because thou art one of compassion, I see . . . . Because thou art merciful, I stand in thy presence."

[53] KMS. 27:21 can now be restored completely from this text.

[54] Text restores also remainder of KMS. 27.

[55] On *šab-su-tum* see KMS. 12:55, *šab-su*.

[56] Duplicate reads *lu-uq-bi*.

[57] See III. R. 57, No. 2:14.

[58] In A. SCHOLLMEYER, *Sumerisch-babylonische Hymnen und Gebete an Šamaš*, p. 73–75. (*Studien zur Geschichte und Kultur des Altertums*, Paderborn, 1912.)

[59] Line 2 does not correspond according to the traces to line 2 in Sippar 36. The restoration of *attūnu-ma* is simply a conjecture.

[60] Conjectural restoration.

[61] *kibitkunu* is not the subject of line 4, but as this text shows the subject of a sentence the verb of which was contained in line 5 of Sippar 36.

[62] The reverse differs from Sippar 36 completely.

[63] *ki* misplaced by scribe.

[64] Surface of obverse badly defaced.

[65] In Tablet K, CT. XVI, pl. XLVI this goddess is mentioned in the following connection: *ina E-ri-du kiš-ka-nu-ú ṣal-mu ir-bi ina aš-ri el-lu ib-ba-ni zi-mu-šu uk-nu-ú ib-bi ša a-na ap-si-i tar-ṣu ša* [ilu]*E-a tal-lak-ta-šu ina E-ri-du ḫegalli ma-la-a-ti šu-bat-su a-šar ir-ṣi-tim-ma ki-iṣ-ṣu-šu ma-a-a-lu ša* [ilât]*Id*. The dark astragalus(?) it is here said has as its home the bed of *Id*. Since the goddess *Á* is here called the mother of the Deep it is most probable that *Id*, the river goddess, is to be identified with *Á* as one and the same mythological personage. Read *Id* also in this passage? In Tablet V, CT. XVI, pl. 13 the goddess *Id* is called the mother of *Ea*, which speaks also strongly for the identification of both goddesses.

[66] For the occurrence of this divine name amongst the published material see Lutz, EBL, No. I, line 5 and 37 and CT XXIV, pl. 20, l. 23. Luckenbill proposes the translation of "God of the sublime porte"; see AJSL. Vol. XXXV, p. 160.

[67] In Tablet V, CT. XVI, pl. 13 to *En-me-šar-ra* is prefixed the *dingir*-sign, and is followed by *dingir Nin-me-šar-ra*. It is, however, more probable here to read "the lord of a command of might, the lord of a command of abundance," according to the context.

[68] Read *šu*, instead of *ki*? For *šu* denoting accusative, see LANGDON, SG. No. 91, p. 73.

[69] On "*im-sag*" = *ḫarubtu*, see VIR. *Ištar* 25, 10.

[70] *a-da* = *age* > *ade* > *ada*, see LANGDON, SG. No. 50.

[71] On *ṣu-a*, see BE. XXXI, 72 note 13.

[72] *a-ma-da* < *ma-da;* cf. Tablet IV, CT. XVI, pl. 9 *ma-da-ma-da-bi* = *ma-a-ta ana ma-a-ti*.

[73] Text has *ù-si-ga*, while generally the verbal form is *ù-me-ni-sum*.

[74] For the restorations in Col. I, cf. CT. XVI, pl. 37, Tablet E. Our text probably contained also the twelve preceding lines.

[75] Omitted in Tablet E.

[76] The *dingir*-sign preceding *edin* is mistake of copy?

[77] Tablet E reads *bi*.

[78] Duplicate adds *a-an*.

[79] Present tablet helps to restore at least part of line.

[80] Here the text joins with the second part of the reverse of Tablet C in CT. XVI, pl. 32.

[81] Tablet C reads *ĝe-en-ta-gaz*.

[82] This line differs completely from the corresponding line of the duplicate, which reads: *a-dim ĝe-en-ta-de*, i.e., "Like water may they be poured out." The sign which resembles *bar* is a poorly written *bur*. For *maš-maš* = *parâru*, see Br. 1849.

[83] Duplicate has *na-an-ta-bal-e*.

[84] Restores text of Tablet C.

[85] *ĝul* omitted by scribe.

[86] Tablet C: *an-aš-a-an*.

[87] *šú-dib?*

[88] To Col. 3 I was unable to find any duplicate published.

[89] With Col. 4 compare CT. XVII, pl. 36, Tablet X. The present text restores a considerable number of lines, but Tablet X restores the first nine lines of the column.

[90] The only known meaning of *šur* is *ezzu*, *ezêzu*. The Semitic translation of Tablet X has *al-pu*.

[91] *utug-ĝul-gál kalam-ma ĝul-a nigin-na* omitted in this text.

[92] *ĝul* omitted by mistake of scribe.

[93] Read *lu* according to Tablet X?

[94] Writing is careless and crowded on tablet; I follow the reading of Tablet X.

[95] Or translate: With the tree of the Deep? On *tur-ra* = *apsû*, see Br. 10218 and 10220.

[96] With Col. 5 the text connects again with Tablet C, CT. XVI, pl. 31, line 10.

[97] Tablet C reads *tu-tu-e-ne*.

[98] Duplicate adds: *ib-ta-ê'*.

99 For *ê*=*ê'*, see Radau, Miscel. No. 8:7 *ê Keš*[ki] *azag-dib nun ê-a*="From the temple of Kesh, to which the holy enter(?) the Anunaki go forth." See also, Chiera, Lists of Personal Names from the Temple School of Nippur, PBS. XI, No. I, p. 31, note 2.

100 Barton's text commences with this line, see BMBI, p. 60 to 61.

101 Barton refers for this sign which I have read *uš* to OBW. 232. The reading of *uš*, which would be the adverbial suffix, is a mere conjecture.

102 Duplicate has the *dingir*-sign before *urta*.

103 Variant *bara(?)*

104 Text reads *bi*.

105 OBW. 239.

106 *me* omitted by scribe, according to duplicate text.

107 Barton's copy reads: *dingir-gar im-uš*.

108 Variant *aš*.

109 Or read with Barton *til-til?* The present text has, however, plainly *du* following the sign which I read *dim*.

110 *e* omitted.

111 *šuku dingir Ninni*=Kamânu, כַּוָּן, χαυῶνες. Cf. Jer. 44:19, עָשִׂינוּ לָהּ (לִמְלֶכֶת הַשָּׁמַיִם) כַּוָּנִים

112 See *Mittheilungen der Vorderasiatischen Gesellschaft*, Ninrag 369.

113 Read *la* instead of *sib*.

114 Barton emends in his transliteration *zi* into *zu*. Both texts, however, read *zi*.

115 Read *giš-ni* following Barton.

116 *ǵuš?* variant *ne*.

117 Duplicate adds *an*.

118 Variant reading *gi-gi-ri-a*.

119 Restore Barton's text to read *e* instead of *si-di*. The sign which Barton reads *di* is the *šuku*.

120 Line restored according to CT. XVI, pl. 1, line 36.

121 Restoration doubtful.

122 Cf. CT. XVI, pl. 9, Tablet IV, Col. I, lines 26–29; CT. XVI, pl. 12, Tablet V, Col. I, line 40; CT. XVI, pl. 34, line 2.

123 Conjectural restoration.

124 Probably nothing missing after *ki-a*.

125 Read *dim*.

126 *ina* omitted by scribe.

127 Was probably omitted by scribe for translation.

128 Cf. CT. XVII, pl. 31, Tablet T, line 31 for this and following line.

129 Cf. CT. XVII, pl. 39, Tablet "AA," lines 47–50.

130 Restored through the Semitic translation.

[131] Sic! This passage, in which the serpent-god is placed into the same position with the *Lilitum*, is very strange, when we consider that in the Caillou Michaux I:21 = I R. 70 and KB. IV 78 ff., the serpent-god is regarded of such importance that his name is mentioned in an oath side by side with the *ilâni rabûti*. Cf. also the *kud.* of Nebukadrezar I, Col. II:49 (IV R. 56). In this passage he is even called *ilu šupû*, i. e., "the excellent god." In CT. XXIV, 8 K. 4340 79-7-8, 294, Rev. Col. III, line 11 ff. he is named together with the protecting-deities *dingir Alad-šàg-ga, dingir Lama-šàg-ga, dingir Utug-šàg-ga,* etc. See also FRANK, *Studien zur babylonischen Religion*, pp. 250 ff. for a comprehensive presentation of this god.

[132] Probably nothing missing.

[133] Read *zaǵan* by emending *ǵar* to *ǵi?* or read *utuǵ-ǵar* with the text. Tablet reads plainly *ǵar*. The combination of *utuǵ-ǵar* seems to occur here for the first time.

[134] Restored according to CT. XVI, pl. 14, Tablet 5, Col. III, line 61.

[135] According to the few traces in line 30, this line probably must be restored to: *inim dingir En-ki-ge* .... *i-na (amât)* [ilu]*E-a* .... "By the command of *Ea*, ...

[136] For the restoration of this and the five following lines compare CT. XVI, pl. 11, Col. VI, Tablet 4, lines 33-37.

[137] The line following translated only part of "*ana qa-at dam-qa-a-tu ša ilâni*[meš] *lip-pa-qid.*"

[138] To *ur* without *ku* which occurs in this tablet a few times, compare POEBEL, *Die sumerischen Personennamen zur Zeit der Dynastie von Larsam und der ersten Dynastie von Babylon* (*Breslauer Habilitationsschrift* 1910) p. 33.

[139] The Semitic value of *tappu* for the Sumerian *an* is new. Or is the Semitic rendering simply a very free one for *dingir* in the sense of "protecting genius"? Compare with this, for instance, LUTZ, *Early Babylonian Letters from Larsa*, No. 15 l. 9 and note on p. 23. Here *ilu* in the sense of *tappu* seems to fit very well.

[140] *ni-gab* = *qepû*, see Br. 5352; *ni-gab* literally "the one who opens" *scil.* the door. It is probable that through this original meaning it came to be translated in Semitic into *qepû*, i. e., "one who is entrusted with something" not only in the specific meaning of a keeper of the door, but in a general sense, one who is entrusted with any kind of an office.

[141] *im-ri-a* = *kišit(t)u* is new.

[142] Should expect *te-ga*, text, however, reads twice *te-ta*, here and reverse line 22.

[143] On *ur-dur-ri*, see AJSL. 1918, p. 284.

[144] See AJSL. 1918, p. 284.

[145] It is characteristic of the second tablet of the series "*maqlu*," that each incantation ends with the phrase "Recite the incantation with a whisper-

ing voice," to which is always added that an image of either tallow, copper, honey, clay, bitumen, etc. be present.

146 *i-la-as-su-ma*, root *alaku*, to go; *i-la-ak-su*.

147 I read . . . *NIG*=*kalbati*, see DELITZSCH, *Sumerisches Glossar*, p. 200. Another possibility is to read *ki-el*, maiden.

148 Supply *nig-*[*ġul-dim-ma?*].

149 See FRANK, *Studien zur babylonischen Religion*, p. 18.

150 This text goes back to the time of the Ur dynasty.

151 *Sa* I take to be an abbreviation of *sa-gal-la*=rheumatism. See CT. XXIII, pl. 1 *inim-nim-ma sa-gal-la-kam*, "Incantation against rheumatism."

152 *ki* omitted by scribe.

153 *Nin-a-ḫa-kud-du* plays an important figure in the incantation texts, more so than would appear from the material here published, in which she is hardly mentioned. See particularly CT. XVI, pl. 46, Tablet "K," line 170, and IV R. pl. 56, Col. II, line 14 and line 20: $^{il\hat{a}t}$*Nin-a-ḫa-kud-du be-lit šipti*.

154 On *LI.DUR* see FRANK, SBR. p. 141, and ASSL. 30, 78.

155 Br. 9512; see also PBS. V, 136, 4, 8.

156 *dingir Lamga* according to Br. 11166=^{ilu}*Sin*. This line is interesting as well as important, as it states that evil spirits are the offsprings of the moon-god. We recall here that *Labartu* is called the daughter of *Anu*.

157 On the Greek **Γελλώ** (**Γελώ, Γιλλώ, Γιλώ, Γελοῦ, Γυλοῦ**) (Stephanus, Thes. Ling. Graec. II 252a: **Γελλὼ** Hesych. est **δαίμων, ἣν γυναῖκες τὰ νεογνὰ παιδία φασὶν ἁρπάζειν**)=*gallu*, cf. FRANK, *Zu babylonischen Beschwoeungstexten*, ZA. 24 (1910) pp. 161–165. pp. 333, 334.

158 Text reads *kur*, emend to *lù*.

159 For the restoration of four following lines compare CT. XVI, pl. 10, Col. 5, lines 34 and 36, and pl. 11, lines 37–46. It is possible that *ga-an-tu* has to be supplied instead of *u-šu-uš*. Notice that instead of *šeš* in *ga-ba-da-an-šeš* our text reads *šág*.

160 Text reads *ki*. Mistake of scribe?

161 Tablet reads erroneously *ša*.

162 A variant of *a-sag*=*asakku*.

163 Hebrew ריב.

164 Phonetic writing of *er*.

165 Restoration problematical.

166 *lu-ru-gù* hardly the one who is haughty.

167 *nu-um-ši-gi*=*nam-ši-gi*.

168 Compare with this text LANGDON, PBS. X, No. 2, text 18.

169 Restore PBS. X, 18:16.

170 Restore PBS. X, 18:17.

[171] The noun to be supplied here must be the name of a part of the human body. Perhaps *ṣillu* 'shadow' may be supplied here in view of the meaning of the verb employed in the sentence. I retain the reading of *idi-ia*, although the duplicate text seems to have only *mu*, assuming that the noun has been omitted by the scribe.

[172] Insert *pa-ni* in line 19 of Langdon's text.

[173] *uz-za-na-du*, II[2] of *zanadu*. Cf. the Arabic *zanada*.

[174] Restoration uncertain.

[175] Cf. PBS. X, 2, 18 Rev., line 3.

[176] Langdon reads here *dingir Lugal-dìg umun-nun* and translates "Oh divine lord of the dead, protector." *umun-nun* does, however, not mean protector at all! An *umun-nun* may just as well be a tyrant, an oppressor. A "divine lord of the dead" is also entirely out of place here, as well as for the context where it occurs in other passages. Compare f. i. Tablet 5 of the *maqlu*-series Col. 2, lines 23 and 24; to read here, "The fury of *Lugal-dìg*, the protector (!), which you have established for me, the fury of *Lugal-dìg*, the protector(!) may be placed upon yourself," would be a contradictio in adjecto. The reading of Langdon is therefore untenable.

[177] Duplicate passage, line 7 reads *ina bîti*.

[178] *pu-uḫ-pu-uḫ-tu*, see DHWB. p. 516 under *puḫu*, who refers to K. 247 Col. II 14: BAL. = *pu-uḫ-ḫu ša sinništi* (wahrscheinlich ein Weib vergewaltigen) *puḫpuḫtu* is probably used more generally to designate "oppression, act of violence."

[179] Restore parallel line in PBS. X, 2, 18: rev. 14.

[180] Here again *zab* with the value *nur* to which Langdon refers in Note 1, p. 198.

[181] Duplicate passage reads *rim*.

[182] The value of *NI.ŠE.SAG.UŠ* = *rapšu* is new.

[183] For restorations, see IV R. pl. 56 (63) Obv. Col. I.

[184] Duplicate passage reads *tap-par-ra-ma*. The emendation to *tap-par-ra-aš* by D. W. Myhrman, in ZA. 16, 154 proves to be correct.

[185] In IV R. 56: 10 follows a line which gives the ritual: "Upon a seal thou shalt write (it). Thou shalt place (it) on the neck of a child." The University Museum is in the possession of such a small seal, upon which is written in minute script, another short incantation text.

[186] Variant *ki*.

[187] Variant *ki*.

[188] Restore IV R. 56: 16, *ri-e-qi*, and not, with Myhrman, [*ši-tap-ri*]-*ši*. The horizontal wedge of *ši* must be separated from the preceding sign, which must represent the traces of *ki*, and read *ina*.

[189] Duplicate passage line 18 reads [ilat]*A-nu-ni-tum*, which must probably be emended to *Ṣar-pa-ni-tum*. Supply [ilu]*Marduk* instead of [ilat]*Ištar*.

[190] *ša silla anni-i taturrû-ma* is an addition in this text.

[191] Supplied according to IV R. 58 (65); Col. 2:61; see also Myhrman, ZA. 16, p. 176.

[192] IV. R. 58, Col. 2:61 reads *abu*. Read here *garaš*=*tibnu* (Delitzsch, Sum. Gl. p. 83) *ša UDU WARAD*.

[193] Restoration doubtful; cf. IV R. 58, Col. 2, line 63.

[194] Text follows from here on again the first part of the Labartu text in IV R. Col. 1, line 32 ff.

[195] Variant *ši*.

[196] Variant *an-qu-lum*.

[197] Variant *ti*.

[198] Variant *ti*.

[199] Variant *bi-na-a-ti*.

[200] Variant *ma-na-a-ni*.

[201] Duplicate passage inserts *a*.

[202] Variant reading: *a-na zumur pulani mâr pulani la sanaqi-ki ú-tam-me-ki*.

[203] Read *E-Gi-A*(?).

[204] Restoration doubtful.

[205] *šu*, addition of this text.

[206] Variant *kib-ra-a-ti*.

[207] Text connects here with IV R. pl. 58 (65), Col. I, line 6 ff.

[208] Restore *la* in duplicate passage, as surmised already by Myhrman, ZA. 16, p. 168, note 4.

[209] Text differs here from IV R. pl. 58, Col. I, lines 12 and 13, where after *ši-pir* that text inserts *limutti*.......... After *aš-šu* there is probably nothing missing.

[210] Restoration uncertain.

[211] Restore duplicate passage.

[212] Restore *ki-ma* in line 19.

[213] Restore *sik-ki-e la ta-ḫal-lu-pi ṣi-ra-ni-iš* in line 19.

[214] See Delitzsch, HWB. p. 603. Duplicate reads *ḫa-aṣ-bu ra-a-ti*.

[215] Restore line 21.

[216] Restore line 24.

[217] Restore line 25.

[218] Cf. IV R. 58, Col. II, lines 25 ff.

[219] In duplicate passage only *bu* preserved.

[220] Unfortunately both texts are nearly destroyed in the following few lines.

[221] Variant *ši*.

[222] Variant *ti*.

[223] Variant *ri*.

[224] Variant *ba*.

[225] Duplicate omits *mâr an-ni-i tanasaḫ*.

[226] Duplicate *ina kussi*.

[227] Variant *tu-uš-ša-bu*.

[228] Variant *ru*.

[229] Variant *mu-ra-a-ni-ki*.

[230] *KUR*=*napaḫu*, Br. 7395; Variant *i-nap-pa-ḫu*.

[231] *ǵad*=bright, splendid, brilliant; cf. *ǵad* ..*ê'* to go forth brilliantly, DSG., p. 209.

[232] *šupû ina ŠE.ḪAL-šu* omitted in IV R.

[233] For restoration compare IV R. 58, Col. II, lines 59–61.

[234] See IV R. 58, Col. III, lines 6–11.

[235] Variant *su-ta-a-ku*.

[236] Omitted in duplicate passage, *gi-iṣ-ṣa-ku*, root *qaṣaṣu*.

[237] Restores line 15.

[238] Restore *i-bak-ki* in line 18.

[239] Restore line 19.

[240] The restoration to *nu-ḫal-lak* is certain and line 20 in the duplicate can be restored accordingly.

[241] Supply *ša-a-ša* in IV R. pl. 58, Col. III, line 21.

[242] *ṣu* after *tam-tim* in duplicate passage? It is, however, more probable that also that text read *ša mâti idi-ma*.

[243] The present text has space for three or four signs left between *a-di* and *ru-ku-us-su*, which is defaced, but according to the duplicate it appears that there is nothing missing. Duplicate reads *e-di* instead of *a-di*.

[244] Restoration doubtful and improbable, according to the traces of the sign in the text. I have, however, retained the suggestive restoration of Myhrman, in ZA. 16, p. 178.

[245] *GA.DAGAL* probably to be transcribed by *šizbu gabšu*. The duplicate has had the phonetic reading of which only the beginning of *šizbu* is preserved. The mention of the milk-offering is interesting.

[246] The value *KUR-Ê'* for *kuṭru* is new. Literally, "that which goes forth from the mountain, or the land." Smoke is an indication of settled habitations for the traveler from the distance and it is well plausible why "smoke" could have the meaning "that which rises from settled habitation."

[247] *ana* omitted by scribe.

[248] Duplicate *šur-ba-ta*.

[249] Variant *rit-ta-a-ša*.

[250] Restore *kirimma-šu mu* in duplicate text.

[251] *nak-ki-lat* probably an addition of this text only. No space for it in duplicate.

[252] Variant *i-lap-pat lib-bu*.

253 Variant *i-šal-lup*.

254 Variant *ru*.

255 Variant *ú-še-naq*.

256 Duplicate is broken off at the same point. Restoration doubtful.

257 Variant *ziq-ziq-ku-um-ma*.

258 *Qu*=excrements, vomit, Hebrew קיא. Restoration, however, doubtful.

259 Variant *ša*.

260 Variant *ma-ri*.

261 See IV R. 58, Col. IV, line 7 following.

262 Variant *ra*.

263 Variant *gim*.

264 Text reads *ki;* mistake of scribe?

265 Here the verb is in the plural. Notice also that below, Labartu has the plural sign.

266 Read *ga* instead of *igi*, which is a mistake of the copy

267 Or is *Lù-gi-na* to be taken as a personal name?

268 II[1] of *wagû*=*iagû*, UNGNAD, *Babylonische Briefe*, 309. The root is entered in DELITZSCH, HWB. 16 and MUSS-ARNOLT, *Lexicon*, p. 13, but its etymology was not understood at that time. *Waw* and *jodh* interchange in this root.

269 Restoration doubtful.

270 *libbu*, literally, "the heart," "the contents."

271 Supply [*amâtam*] *annîtam*.

272 For the reading *PA.PA*=*dekû*, see UNGNAD, *Babylonische Briefe*, p. 288, and BA. VI, pt. 5, p. 47. Literally, "the summoner."

273 Text has *za!*

274 *ma* is repeated by error of the scribe.

275 *qu-um* probably construct of *qummû*, *qumû*, literally, "thirst;" here, however, used metaphorically.

276 Restoration is doubtful.

277 Or "supreme-judge?"

278 Or read *NU-KI*^{ki}? this would give the meaning: "the men of nowheres," i. e., the men of the quartermaster-corps, who might have been called thus on account of their special work, which called them from place to place. This reading has been adopted in the translation.

279 ^{gi}*GUR.DA* represents an article made of cane. See CT. 4:30 Al; Rm. 2, 27, li. 2; and Meissner SAI. 1519; it occurs also in the Buffalo tablets published by MISS HUSSEY, No. 2, Rev. 31; a reed rack for the transportation of grain.

280 On *Ê-DUB-BA* as a title of an officer, see Amherst, 42, Obverse 5; also RTC. 287 and DELAPORTE, 108; record-keeper. As the name of a place *Ê-DUB-BA* is mentioned in CT. VIII, 25 b, li. 1=1 *gan eqlim i-na Ê-DUB-BA*.

[281] *ašar ka-ti*, "in thy stead?"

[282] *GIŠ-A-Am* equals *adaru* and *ildaqqu;* vide, MEISSNER, *Suppl.* 23 Rev. 23 and 24; both words occur also together in CT. XII, 18 B. 40 ff. STRASSMEIER, NERIGLISSAR 28:29, a bed is made of *adaru*-wood. In LEGRAIN'S *Drehem Texts* N. 303 a bed is made of *adaru*-wood and bronze. The interpretation in MUSS-ARNOLT of *ildaqqu*, as meaning "young shoot, sprout" is wrong.

[283] *KI kam-ri=ašar kamri*, literally, the place of a heap, the place of heaping up, whence probably also place of storage.

[284] *še-e-ta*, something woven, a sling, a net. As it is here named as a utensil which is used for traveling, and kept when not in use in the house where the implements of the journey were deposited, it may have been the hammock.

[285] The tablet reads *du*, which is a mistake of the scribe for *ra*.

[286] The tablet plainly reads *uš-tu*, which also not incorrect for *ultu*, can hardly have been in use during the Cassite period, where the tendency prevailed to change the sibilants into labials. If, however, this is not to be taken as a scribal error, then it stands as a rare example of the original form of *ultu*.

[287] Note the writing of *ú-še-bi-al-ku*, which must be intentional as it occurs twice on the tablet.

[288] Read *GIŠ-NER-DU*, an abbreviation of Br. 9208; Meissner, SAI. 6941; *gištabbu* and *qirṣapu;* see also KNUDTZON, *Die El-Amarna Tafeln, Glossar*, p. 1411.

[289] *tilû*, pot, vessel. Cf. CLAY, BE. XIV, 123, 7 *ti-li-e šamni rabûti*, "great jars of oil." *Tilû* is undoubtedly a loanword from Sumerian *dil*, a variant of *dal*. Note *duk-dal=tallu, duk-dal-maǵ=talmaḫḫu*, Br. 2579; 2587. Also AO. 2162 II:13 *duk* (*da-al*) *RI=tal-lu*. Perhaps the same word is to be found in *ub=têlu, têltu*, SAI. 4101 f., and *úb=tultu*, SAI. 7811. Cf. Nos. 4104 and 4106 f. (!) Note DELITZSCH, *Sum. Glossar*, p. 40 *ub-ag-a=telum*, which probably had the original meaning "to make a cavity, or a hole." *Ti-il-li-šu-nu ša kaspi* cited by MUSS-ARNOLT, *Lexicon*, p. 1160 is probably the same word. The reading *til-lu-ú* in line 18 is uncertain; perhaps read *be-lu-ú*(?).

[290] *li-kar-ru*. The translation is suggested by the context, and the expression *ikku kuri* for "fasting"; see KUECHLER, *Medizin* 122 *ik-ka-šu ik-ta-nir-ru*, "his gum is dried up."

[291] Reading doubtful.

[292] On *adinu, adinnu*, until now, with *la*, not yet, see ZDMG. 69, 503. Cf. *udina la*, LSS. V 6, 56 f.

[293] The reader will observe that this letter excludes the possibility of identifying *beli-ia* "my lord" with the king himself. This throws considerable doubt on the proposition of RADAU (BE. XVII, Introduction) that these

Cassite letters, addressed "*ana belia,*" are invariably destined for the king. Not less than forty letters are contained in this volume which are addressed "*ana belia,*" but it is absolutely impossible to surmise from their contents that they are addressed to the king himself, although in some instances this may be possible.

[294] From the material published in previous volumes of the University Museum we learn that the king mentioned in this letter is to be identified with *Shagarakti-Shuriash*. The addressee *Amêl-Marduk* was a *GU.EN.NA* officer, that is probably the royal chief sheriff of that king. This identification of the addressee with the *GU.EN.NA* officer mentioned in Vols. XIV, XV and XVII, affords the means of interpreting this short letter. *Amêl-Marduk* receives the royal summons to bring in his official capacity as chief sheriff *Apil-shadû-rubùa*, a person under indictment, to the capital.

[295] *kulda*, from *kašâdu;* imperative *kušdu>kuldu>kulda*, the sibilant as usual in the Cassite period passing into a labial. The "*a*" in *kulda* denotes the energetic form; cf. Creation II, 136 *šukna* for *šuknu*.

[296] The tablet reads *šàg*, which is a mistake of the scribe for *ba*.

[297] The sign which looks more like *bu* on the tablet is probably intended for *li*.

[298] *ù-lu* for *ù-la*.

[299] Sic! *mîtum*, not *mîtûti*.

[300] On the phrase and restoration of line 22, see ThD., *Sargon*, 252.

[301] Restoration doubtful.

[302] Restoration doubtful.

[303] Restoration doubtful.

[304] See CRAIG, *Religious Texts*, 57, 24.

[305] *ḫi-il-ti* is probably a colloquialism of *ḫiritu; ḫirtu>ḫiltu*.

[306] L. DENNEFELD, *Babylonisch-Assyrische Geburts-Omina*, p. 28, e, 11 translates *e-dir-ti* by Not, Bedraengniss; the passage reads "*šumma amêlu šinâta-šu iš-tin qibit e-dir-ti*.. If a man urinates, command of affliction."

[307] On *zu-ú-tu* "sweat," Hebrew זֵעָה, see H. HOLMA, *Koerperteile*, p. 8. Cf. also HARPER, *Letters*, 391, R. 14: *issuru zu-ú-tu šarri iqarrara*, "as soon as the sweat of the king dries up"; HL. 363:6 *zu-ú-tu ina libbi liqrura*, "sweat therein may dry up"; II R. 61, a50, *niqilpu ša zu-ú-tu*, "falling of the sweat."

[308] The restorations of this letter have been made by means of three other letters which were published by RADAU in Vol. XVII, Part I, of the BE. series, letters 31, 32 and 33. Letter 31 is particularly interesting as there appear, besides the name of the physician, who reported on the condition of certain ladies connected probably with the temple at Nippur, to his lord, all the names mentioned in this letter. By the help of that letter both names of the lady *Lata* and of the daughter of the *Ahlamite* have been restored here.

That these were mentioned in this letter is probably indicated by the number eight in line 31.

[309] On 2 (*išâtu* omitted) see RADAU, BE. XVII, part I, p. 36, note 7.

[310] The uncertainty of the name in BE. XVII, 31:27, which is there read *Ush(? or BA?)-ba (? or ka)-....*, is removed here. The name is to be read *Ba-ba-ti*.

[311] Restoration uncertain.

[312] *kamma* ša for kima ša (?), cf. THUREAU-DANGIN, *Sargon* 90.

[313] *a-na li-it* "into the presence of," see JENSEN, KB. VI, 403. ***Lîtu*** is probably identical with the word *lîtu, lêtu*, cheek. If this word really is ***lîtu***, cheek, and not *lîtu*, strength, then the meaning of *lîtu* as a part of the body points at least to some part of the face, but certainly not to the "*back*," since the phrase means "into the presence of." For parts of the body used as prepositions see HOLMA, *Koerperteile*, p. IX.

[314] Read *liš*, which is carelessly written on tablet.

[315] On *ẓi-ri-im* compare CT. VI 23a:21 and K. 48:11, written here *ẓi-ir-mi-(ma)*.

[316] *liš-ša-ar-an-ni* for *li-(iš)-ši-ir-an-ni;* "*i*" under the influence of the following "*a*" changed to "*a*."

[317] This grammatical monstrosity doubtless stands for the form *i-ta-ba-tum* (=*tu-ma*).

[318] The total excludes the old grain in both instances.

[319] The tablet reads *NIG-KUR-DA;* is this a mistake for *NIG-KUD-DA?*

[320] Or *šîbê*. Written *AB-BA*.

[321] *al-ta*, probably a verb form. The text does not seem to be in order.

[322] For *šipirti* cf. also *našpartu*>*našpaštu*, BE. IX, 73:5.

[323] Restoration doubtful.

[324] See HAV. p. 424.

[325] The transliteration and translation of this line is doubtful. It might also be transliterated by: *KAB-DUK lu-ú ša šamnim ḫa-?* The reading of *iṭ* in *ḫa-iṭ* is a mere conjecture. Perhaps read *ṭe* for *ṭu*=*ḫa-ṭu*, transparent, clear.

LISTS OF NAMES

A. Personal Names

B. Geographical Names

Names of Countries, Cities and Villages

Names of Rivers and Canals

C. Names of Gods[17]

NOTES TO LISTS OF NAMES

[1] Ilâni omitted by scribe.

[2] Cf. *Bel-ana-kala-*^{ilu}Marduk, BE. XIV, 136:9.

[3] Cf. BE. XIV, 33:7.

[4] Cf. *E-ri-en-šu-ti*, BE. II, 2; 106:18; 98:8.

[5] Cf. *Ḫu-un-ni*, BE. II, 2; 53:36.

[6] See Clay, CPN. p. 88.

[7] Cf. Clay, CPN. p. 93: *Iš-bi-ú-la*.

[8] Written *KI-ia* in BE. XV, 149:34.

[9] For *mu-kal-lim*.

[10] Cf. BE. XIV, 46a:2; BE. XV, 178:15.

[11] See Lutz, EBL. p. 33, note.

[12] Comp. BE. XV, 185:23.

[13] See BE. XVII, 66:3; 67:3; compare also BE. XIV, 18:4; 31:11: *E-mu-qat-Nippuru*^{ki}.

[14] Cf. BE. XVII, 99:6: ^{âlu}*Lu-ub-di-ša*^{ki}.

[15] See BE. XIV, 66:3.

[16] BE. XVII, 27:4 read *Ši-i-tu-la*^{ki}; the emendation to ^{âlu}*Ši-i-tu-na*(?)[*-li*^{ki}] is wrong.

[17] Only the divine names occurring in the letters have been catalogued.

LIST OF TABLETS

Text	Museum Number	Description and Contents
1	4711	Black; envelope preserved, containing seal-impression. See Ungnad, PBS. VII, pl. 1, No. 1 and pl. XCVII, for photographic reproduction of envelope. Insc. 7 (Obv.) 1 (Lo. E.) 9 (Rev.) 1 (U. E.) 2 (L. S.) = 20 li. Letter to Gimil-ili from Ibi-ilum.
2	7124	Meas. 61×40×23; sun-dried; light brown. Insc. 8 (Obv.) 1 (Rev.) = 9 li. Letter to Ibiq-Ištar from ^{ilu}Enlil-lù-šag.
3	7127	Meas. 91×48×19; Obv. defaced; envelope preserved, containing seal-impression; light brown; slightly baked. Insc. 19 (Obv.) 7 (Rev.) = 26 li. Letter to Lugâ.
4	7040	Meas. 93×44×22; light brown; sun-dried. Insc. 22 (Obv.) 1 (Rev.) = 23 li. Letter of Sin-magir.
5	7182	Meas. 65×43×21; upper two lines of Rev. broken away, otherwise well preserved; baked; light brown. Insc. 9 (Obv.) 1 (Lo. E.) 7 (Rev.) = 17 li. Letter to Iltani from Šamuḫtum.
6	7046	Meas. 88×42×21; gray; badly preserved; sun-dried. Insc. 17 (Obv.) 5 (Rev.) = 22 li. Letter to Sin-magir from Belti-ṣululšu.
7	7126	Meas. 91×49×24; well preserved; light brown; sun-dried. Insc. 17 (Obv.) 3 (Rev.) = 20 li. Letter to Lugâ from Ḫammurabi-ili.
8	7169	Meas. 57×45×20; light brown; sun-dried. Insc. 10 (Obv.) 2 (Lo. E.) 11 (Rev.) 1 (L. S.) = 24 li. A letter.
9	1236	Meas. 80×59×28; upper part of tablet, covering about three lines each on the Obv. and the Rev. is broken away; baked; yellow with black and reddish spots. Insc. 15 (Obv.) 1 (Lo. E.) 14 (Rev.) = 30 li. A letter.
10	7125	Meas. 71×46×23; light brown; slightly baked. Insc. 11 (Obv.) 2 (Lo. E.) 9 (Rev.) 2 (U. E.) = 24 li. Letter to the "abbini dajanê ša Nippuru^{ki} from the rabianum ù šibû abbini dajanu."
11	7183	Meas. 10×52×23; broken into two parts, glued together. Insc. chipped off along the line of the break, otherwise

Text	Museum Number	Description and Contents
		well preserved. Slightly baked; light brown. Parts of envelope preserved, containing seal-impressions. Insc. 22 (Obv.) 12 (Rev.) = 34 li. Letter to Amêl-^{ilu}Ninib from Kurum.
12	7217	Meas. 105×54×25; brown; slightly baked. Insc. 17 (Obv.) 2 (Lo. E.) 15 (Rev.) = 34 li. Letter of Samsu-iluna, the king and successor of Ḫammurabi, to the "bêl teritim ù šatamme."
13	7216	Meas. 91×49×24; well preserved; slightly baked; Rev. uninscribed; gray. Insc. 11 (Obv.) = 11 li. Letter of king Samsu-iluna to the "bêl teritim ù dajanê ša Nippuru^{ki}."
14	7042	Meas. 83×46×18; Rev. not inscribed; slightly baked; light brown. Insc. 15 (Obv.) = 15 li. Letter of Abililišu to Sin-ma ....
15	14129	Meas. 44×57×25; fragment; brown. Insc. 8 (Obv.) 9 (Rev.) = 17 li. Letter of Kišaḫbut to his lord.
16	4756	Meas. 96×59×23; badly preserved; sun-dried; brown. Insc. 22 (Obv.) 19 (Rev.) = 41 li. Letter of Kuduranu to his lord.
17	4752	Meas. 48×44×21; upper third of tablet broken away; sun-dried; brown. Insc. 7 (Obv.) 4 (Rev.) = 11 li. A letter.
18	4747	Meas. 36×52×20; fragment; baked; light brown with black spots. Insc. 9 (Obv.) 7 (Rev.) = 16 li. Letter of ^{ilu}Nin-ib-riṣušu to his lord.
19	4736	Meas. 62×44×23; black; slightly baked. Insc. 10 (Obv.) 10 (Rev.) = 20 li. A letter.
20	9265	Meas. 94×55×20; white with reddish spots; surface of Rev. defaced. Insc. 20 (Obv.) 2 (Lo. E.) 19 (Rev.) 2 (U. E.) = 43 li. Letter of Etelpu to his lord.
21	1307	Meas. 51×40×21; damaged on the upper right side, otherwise well preserved; brown. Insc. 10 (Obv.) 2 (Lo. E.) 9 (Rev.) 2 (U. E.) 3 (L. E.) = 26 li. Letter of ^{sal}Ri-šat-^{ilu} ...... to Ḫunna.
22	3873	Meas. 68×47×20; brown with reddish and black spots; right edge of Obv. and lower part of right side of Rev. broken away; baked. Insc. 15 (Obv.) 1 (Lo. E.) 15 (Rev.) 2 (U. E.) = 33 li. Letter of Barmu to his lord.
23	4763	Meas. 70×43×22; light brown; Rev. not inscribed; sun-dried. Insc. 10 (Obv.) = 10 li. Letter of ^{ilu}Enlil-alšag to ^{ilu}Amurru-karabi-išme.

Text	Museum Number	Description and Contents
24	1398	Meas. 50×39×16; dark brown; sun-dried; well preserved. Insc. 7 (Obv.) 2 (Rev.)=9 li. Letter of a king to Amêl-^{ilu}Marduk.
25	4791	Meas. 44×33×16; white; baked. Insc. 9 (Obv.) 10 (Rev.) 1 (U. E.)=20 li. Letter of Kišaḫbut to his lord.
26	7747	Meas. 61×57×21; fragment; grayish-brown; sun-dried. Insc. 13 (Obv.) 10 (Rev.) 3 (U. E.) 2 (L. S.)=28 li. Letter of Ilu-ippašra to his lord.
27	4749	Meas. 37×56×23; fragment; Rev. badly preserved; black. Insc. 8 (Obv.) 9 (Rev.) 3 (U. E.) 2 (L. S.)=22 li. Letter of Taribu to his lord.
28	4759	Meas. 62×63×25; fragment; brown; sun-dried. Obv. weathered to such an extent that only a few signs can be recognized. Insc. 14 (Rev.)=14 li. A letter.
29	4882	Meas. 65×43×18; slightly baked; black. Insc. 13 (Obv.) 10 (Rev.)=23 li. A letter.
30	4760	Meas. 51×55×24; fragmentary; brown with black spots; sun-dried. Insc. 9 (Obv.) 10 (Rev.)=19 li. Letter of Izkur-^{ilu}Marduk to Amêlia.
31	4746	Meas. 57×39×18; dark brown; baked. Insc. 11 (Obv.) 8 (Rev.)=19 li. A letter.
32	4883	Meas. 59×41×19; fragmentary; light brown; sun-dried. Insc. 9 (Obv.) 4 (Rev.)=13 li. Letter of Kimaḫdi-^{ilu}Uraš to Ḫambi.
33	4755	Meas. 56×53×21; sun-dried; light brown; fragmentary. Obv. defaced. Insc. Rev. 12 li. A letter.
34	9247	Meas. 74×50×21; not baked; brown. Insc. 11 (Obv.) 6 (Rev.)=17 li. Letter of ^{ilu}Adad-šar-ilâni to Ukintuša.
35	7045	Meas. 76×48×21; not baked; light brown. Insc. 14 (Obv.) 1 (Lo. E.) 9 (Rev.)=24 li. Letter of Aarum.
36	4751	Meas. 66×42×17; brown with black spots; slightly baked. Insc. 15 (Obv.) 11 (Rev.)=26 li. Letter of Úsat^{ilu}Marduk to Amêlia.
37	4766	Meas. 58×39×25; fragmentary; gray; sun-dried. Insc. 10 (Obv.) 3 (Rev.)=13 li. A letter.
38	4744	Meas. 43×40×15; fragment; baked; black. Insc. 7 (Obv.)=7 li. Letter of Šadû-rabû-naṣir.
39	4728	Meas. 30×38×14; fragment; slightly baked; light brown. Rev. completely destroyed. Insc. 6 li. A letter.
40	13874	Meas. 81×61×22; light brown; fragmentary. Insc. 15 (Obv.) 15 (Rev.)=30 li. A letter.

Text	Museum Number	Description and Contents
41	7043	Meas. 91×61×23; slightly baked; brown. Insc. 14 (Obv.) 17 (Rev.) 2 (U. E.)=33 li. Letter of Imgurum to his lord.
42	4738	Meas. 55×64×29; fragment; brown. Insc. 12 (Obv.) 11 (Rev.) 3 (U. E.)=26 li. Letter of X-šar-aḫê to his lord.
43	4775	Meas. 81×53×21; reddish-yellow; baked. Insc. 17 (Obv.) 18 (Rev.) 1 (U. E.)=36 li. Letter of ^{ilu}Nusku-teṣlitam-išme to his lord.
44	4778	Meas. 105×64×26; baked; white with red spots. Rev. not inscribed. Insc. 18 li. A letter.
45	4758	Meas. 64×48×19; sun-dried; brown. Insc. 9 (Obv.) 1 (Lo. E.) 5 (Rev.)=15 li. Letter of Katar-SAḪ to Amêlia.
46	11690	Meas. 29×39×17; fragment; brown. Insc. 4 (Obv.) 5 (Rev.)=9 li. A letter.
47	4729	Meas. 62×45×22; sun-dried; dark brown. Insc. 13 (Obv.) 13 (Rev.) 4 (U. E.) (2 L. S.)=32 li. Letter of Etelpu to his lord.
48	4733	Meas. 61×41×19; sun-dried; dark brown. Insc. 10 (Obv.) 2 (Lo. E.) 7 (Rev.)=19 li. Letter of ^{ilu}Ninib-kabti-aḫišu to his lord.
49	4786	Meas. 52×51×22; fragment; baked; white with red spots. Insc. 15 (Obv.) 14 (Rev.) 2 (L. S.)=31 li. A letter.
50	4757	Meas. 149×80×31; slightly baked; dark brown. Insc. 32 (Obv.) 32 (Rev.) 1 (L. S.)=65 li. A letter.
51	4781	Meas. 52×53×24; upper half of tablet missing; baked; white with red spots. Insc. 12 (Obv.) 3 (Lo. E.) 12 (Rev.) 1 (L. S.)=28 li. A letter.
52	4734	Meas. 42×35×17; not baked; light brown. Insc. 11 (Obv.) 2 (Lo. E.) 10 (Rev.) 1 (U. E.)=24 li. A letter of Etel-pû-^{ilu}Ninib to his lord.
53	4884	Meas. 59×44×19; not baked; dark brown. Insc. 12 (Obv.) 2 (Lo. E.) 12 (Rev.) 3 (U. E.)=29 li. Letter of Ikuna to his lord.
54	12526	Meas. 71×53×24; baked; white with red spots. Insc. 16 (Obv.) 2 (Lo. E.) 17 (Rev.) 2 (L. S.)=37 li. A letter.
55	9245	Meas. 69×73×33; fragment; slightly baked; brown. Insc. 11 (Obv.) 8 (Rev.) = 19 li. A letter of Amêl-^{ilu}Marduk to his lord.

Text	Museum Number	Description and Contents
56	4881	Meas. 66×48×19; not baked; grayish-brown. Insc. 13 (Obv.) 13 (Rev.) = 26 li. A letter to someone's lord.
57	9818	Meas. 84×52×24; brown; sun-dried. Insc. 21 (Obv.) 3 (Lo. E.) 16 (Rev.) = 40 li. A letter.
58	9259	Meas. 71×47×18; slightly baked; brown; lower right part of Obv. defaced. Insc. 14 (Obv.) 10 (Rev.) = 24 li. Letter of Eriba-[ilu]Marduk to his lord.
59	13087	Meas. 48×58×22; fragment; slightly baked; brown with black spots. Insc. 9 (Obv.) 7 (Rev.) 2 (U. E.) 3 (L. S.) = 21 li. Letter of Idi-[ilu]Marduk to his lord.
60	3666	Meas. 42×59×20; fragment; baked; white. Insc. 6 (Obv.) 2 (Lo. E.) 7 (Rev.) = 15 li. A letter.
61	13086	Meas. 73×48×22; slightly baked; brown. Insc. 16 (Obv.) 1 (Lo. E.) 7 (Rev.) = 24 li. A letter.
62	4785	Meas. 97×54×19; baked; white. Insc. 19 (Obv.) 20 (Rev.) 1 (U. E.) = 40 li. Letter of [ilu]Ninib-kabti-aḫišu to his lord.
63	9190	Meas. 167×110×18; baked; white. Rev. broken away. Insc. 33 li. A letter.
64	9239	Meas. 113×72×31; brown; surface of Obv. badly damaged. Insc. 16 (Obv.) 6 (Rev.) = 22 li. Letter of [ilu]Enlil-tukulti to his lord.
65	4726	Meas. 37×34×22; fragment; not baked; brown. Insc. 7 (Obv.) 6 (Rev.) = 13 li. Letter of [ilu]Ninib-kabti-aḫi-šu to his lord. Cf. letter No. 62 for same address.
66	4741	Meas. 54×38×25; fragment; light brown; sun-dried. Insc. 4 (Obv.) 5 (Rev.) = 9 li. A letter.
67	7745	Meas. 70×47×16; well preserved; baked; brown with black spots. Insc. 15 (Obv.) 3 (Lo. E.) 14 (Rev.) = 32 li. Letter of [ilu]Marduk-mušalim to Amêlia.
68	7044	Meas. 92×56×23; brown; sun-dried. Insc. 13 (Obv.) 5 (Rev.) = 18 li. Letter of Idin-[ilu]Adad to his lord.
69	4762	Meas. 73×41×21; Obv. defaced; sun-dried; light brown. Insc. 12 (Obv.) 12 (Rev.) = 24 li. Letter of Luṣi-ana-nûr-[ilu]Enlil to Idin-[ilu]Marduk.
70	7746	Meas. 61×48×18; dark brown; sun-dried. Insc. 13 (Obv.) 5 (Rev.) = 18 li. Letter of Muli-[[ilu]Šamaš(?)] to his lord.
71	9810	Meas. 117×62×26; two fragments joined together; brown. Insc. 16 (Obv.) 15 (Rev.) = 31 li. Letter of the physician Mukallim to his lord.

Text	Museum Number	Description and Contents
72	12930	Meas. 98×55×24; baked; white. Insc. 20 (Obv.) 3 (Lo. E.) 22 (Rev.)=45 li. A letter to someone's lord.
73	13920	Meas. 136×71×27; slightly baked; grayish-brown. Insc. 23 (Obv.) 16 (Rev.)=39 li. Letter of [ilu]Ninib-ašarid to his lord.
74	4732	Meas. 49×39×4; fragment; Rev. completely destroyed; baked; light brown. Insc. 12 (Obv.)=12 li. Letter of [ilu]Nannar-iddina to Iddia.
75	13294	Meas. 45×35×28; fragment; sun-dried; brown. Insc. 10 (Obv.) 2 (Lo. E.) 8 (Rev.) 2 (L. S.)=22 li. A letter.
76	4754	Meas. 33×33×17; well preserved; brown with black spots. Insc. 6 (Obv.) 1 (Lo. E.) 3 (Rev.)=10 li. Letter of a king to [ilu]Ninib-nadin-aḫê.
77	4790	Meas. 46×42×20; fragmentary; white. Insc. 8 (Obv.) 3 (Lo. E.) 10 (Rev.)=21 li. A letter.
78	4745	Meas. 31×54×21; fragment. Insc. 5 (Obv.) 6 (Rev.)= 11 li. A letter.
79	4750	Meas. 53×38×17; brown. Insc. 8 (Obv.) 3 (Lo. E.) 12 (Rev.)=23 li. A letter.
80	4737	Meas. 52×41×19; black; well preserved. Insc. 9 (Obv.) 5 (Rev.)=14 li. Lettei of Ikišam to his lord.
81	4789	Meas. 53×42×19; fragmentary; white with red and black spots on Obv. Insc. 10 (Obv.) 10 (Rev.)=20 li. Letter of [ilu]Šamaš-mušalim to his lord.
82	7047	Meas. 77×51×23; light brown; sun-dried. Rev. nearly destroyed. Insc. 12 (Obv.) 4 (Rev.)=16 li. Letter of [ilu]Enlil-kidini to Mukallim.
83	4743	Meas. 57×46×22; fragmentary; light brown; sun-dried. Insc. 8 (Obv.) 7 (Rev.) 3 (U. E.)=18 li. Letter of Belanum to his lord.
84	10631	Meas. 42×50×27; fragment. Insc. 7 (Obv.) 5 (Rev.)= 12 li. Letter of Rabâša-[ilu]Enlil to his lord.
85	4761	Meas. 50×60×27; fragment; brown; sun-dried. Insc. 10 (Obv.) 3 (Rev.)=13 li. Letter of Kišaḫbut to his lord.
86	4783	Meas. 81×55×24; baked; white with red spots on Obv. Insc. 11 (Obv.) 2 (Lo. E.) 12 (Rev.) 2 (U. E.)=27 li. A letter.
87	3631	Meas. 49×27×15; slightly baked; light brown; a small corner on the upper left edge chipped off, otherwise well

Text	Museum Number	Description and Contents
		preserved. Insc. 11 (Obv.) 11 (Rev.) 2 (U. E.) = 24 li. Letter of Sallaia to ^{ilu}Ninib-aḫ-iddina.
88	3626	Meas. 27×38×16; brown; sun-dried; writing weathered. Insc. 4 (Obv.) 1 (Lo. E.) 1 (Rev.) = 6 li. A letter.
89	3632	Meas. 46×27×15; light brown; sun-dried. Rev. not inscribed. Insc. 10 li. Letter of Širiqtum-^{ilu}Ninib to Gimillu.
90	326	Meas. 54×28×13; slightly baked; reddish-brown; well preserved. Rev. not inscribed. Insc. 10 li. Letter of ^{ilu}Marduk-zêr-ibni to Bel-ittia.
91	14000	Meas. 89×61×32; light brown; well preserved; partly baked. A Sumerian letter.
92	19794	Meas. 88×62×32; brown; sun-dried; well preserved. A Sumerian letter.
93	14116	Meas. 78×53×26; baked; brown with black spots. A Sumerian letter.
94	14117	Meas. 86×67×34; light brown; unbaked. Rev. not inscribed. A Sumerian letter.
95	14118	Meas. 84×64×32; light brown; upper lines of tablet completely destroyed; sun-dried. Rev. not inscribed. A Sumerian letter.
96	14045	Meas. 102×69×33; light-colored; slightly baked. Rev. defaced. A Sumerian Code of Laws.
97	8425	Meas. 56×42×18; a small two column Ur-dynasty tablet; light brown; sun-dried. Contents historical(?).
98	4573	Meas. 62×65×29; lower half of a brown, half-baked tablet. Cf. PBS. Vol. XII, pl. 40 which is a poor copy of the text. A Sumerian Code of Laws.
99	14089	Meas. 96×74×32; light brown; badly preserved two column tablet. Fragment of a Semitic Code of Laws.
100	13632 } 13647 }	Meas. 88×65×36; two fragments joined together; light brown; sun-dried. A Sumerian Code of Laws.
101	8284	Meas. 112×67×38; light brown; well preserved double column tablet. Duplicate of No. 100. A Sumerian Code of Laws.
102	8326	Meas. 131×72×36; a light brown, sun-dried double column tablet. Rev. nearly destroyed. A Sumerian Code of Laws.
103	14085	Meas. 88×64×32; single column tablet; light brown; sun-dried; upper four lines of Obv. destroyed. Lower

Text	Museum Number	Description and Contents
		right edge of tablet chipped off. A Sumerian Code of Laws.
104	14097	Meas. 90×78×34; light brown; baked; upper right corner of Obv. broken away, otherwise well preserved. A Prayer of an Incantation Priest.
105	14067	Meas. 114×72×33; complete light brown single column tablet; sun-dried; cracked. A Sumerian Hymn to Ea.
106	1516	Meas. 122×64×22; reddish-brown; baked. Obv. defaced. Prayers in Semitic to Ea, Shamash and Marduk, and Shamash and Sin.
107	8231	Meas. 58×44×19; small dark tablet; lower part destroyed. Single column. Ur or Isin period. A Sumerian Incantation.
108	1701	Meas. 111×96×34; grayish, baked tablet. Neo-Babylonian. Semitic Hymn to Marduk of the Series "The lifting up of the hand."
109	14069	Meas. 56×75×27; complete dark, small tablet; partly baked. Isin or Ur Period.
110	1693	Meas. 58×51×29; fragment; dark brown; baked. Prayer of Shamash-shum-ukin to ^{mul}Kak-si-di.
111	14173	Meas. 48×79×23; light brown; partly baked; lines running from Obv. over the complete length of Rev. A small medical tablet.
112	590	Meas. 168×126×34; three fragments of an unbaked tablet joined. Obv. partly defaced. Neo-Babylonian. A Sumerian Exorcism.
113	13939	Meas. 117×99×30; light brown, sun-dried, double column tablet. Upper and lower parts destroyed. A series of incantations in Semitic against the female demon of plague, Labartu.
114	14152	Meas. 102×67×31; a well-preserved sun-dried tablet; ruled; grayish-brown. A Sumerian Hymn and Exorcism to Enlil.
115	13858	Meas. 124×76×32; three fragments; reddish-brown; partly baked. An Interlinear Incantation.
116	4507	Meas. 100×62×24; reddish-brown; slightly baked. Bilingual Exorcism.
117	14078	Meas. 95×71×26; complete, reddish-brown, single column tablet. Ur or Isin Period. A Sumerian Hymn.
118	589	Meas. 165×120×23; dark brown, two column tablet; baked; three fragments joined. Obv. nearly completely

Text	Museum Number	Description and Contents
		destroyed. With this text compare MN. 587, which is an unpublished duplicate of this text. A Sumerian Hymn to Shamash.
119	1209	Meas. 113×73×31; dark brown; baked. Neo-Babylonian. A Prayer to Nergal.
120	1505	Meas. 100×64×23; light brown; baked; lower right half of Obv. destroyed. Incantation against Witchcraft.
121	1543	Meas. 73×55×24; four parts of tablet joined; reddish-brown with black spots. Neo-Babylonian Exorcism.
122	332	Meas. 159×72×31; reddish color; baked. Upper and lower right part of tablet broken away. On Rev. writing is chipped off. Partly interlinear incantation tablet.
123	8380	Meas. 58×46×21; dark gray; sun-dried; well preserved. Ur or Isin period. Incantation Ê-nu-šub.
124	1572	Meas. 63×72×33; dark brown; baked; fragmentary. Semitic incantation for the building of house and city.
125	36	Meas. 98×56×22; reddish-brown; baked; only center part of tablet preserved. Rev. destroyed. Litany-Bilingual Hymn.
126	1556	Meas. 105×65×29; dark gray; baked; fragment. Two parts joined. Bilingual Hymn to Shamash.
127	591	Meas. 154×117×32; dark brown, three column tablet; baked; fairly well preserved. I. Dyn. Period. A Sumerian Exorcism.
128	1532	Meas. 114×120×33; dark brown, three column tablet; baked. I. Dyn. Period. A Sumerian Exorcism.
129	458	Meas. 114×87×36; fragment, grayish-brown. Rev. destroyed. Semitic Incantation.
130	8371	Meas. 74×48×20; brown; sun-dried; lower left edge of Obv. and right upper edge of Rev. destroyed. Ur Period. An Incantation. Notice that the name of Sippar is mentioned in place of the usual Eridu.
131	8230	Meas. 83×53×22; dark brown; sun-dried; upper three lines of tablet destroyed. Ur Period. Sumerian Incantation.
132	1636	Meas. 72×48×23; light brown; two parts joined. Obv. defaced. I Dyn. Period. A Sumerian Exorcism.
133	334	Meas. 122×94×38; reddish-brown; baked. Semitic Incantations and Prayers against Witchcraft.

Text	Museum Number	Description and Contents
134	14046	Meas. 114×64×29; nearly complete, light brown tablet; sun-dried; top broken away. Sumerian Historical and Religious Dedication.
135	1596	Meas. 113×72×31; white with red spots; baked; fragmentary. A bilingual school exercise of disconnected sentences.
136	6498	Meas. 58×84×23; light-colored; sun-dried. Rev. not inscribed. School-text.
137	5879	Meas. 103×101×35; brown, sun-dried, round tablet. Rev. not inscribed. School-text.
138	6501	Meas. 70×70×27; light-colored; sun-dried, round tablet. Rev. not inscribed. School-text.
139	6551	Meas. 98×98×32; light brown, sun-dried, round tablet. Rev. not inscribed. School-text.

INDEX OF TABLETS

Museum Number	Text Number	Museum Number	Text Number	Museum Number	Text Number
36	125	4733	48	4791	25
326	90	4734	52	4881	56
332	122	4736	19	4882	29
334	133	4737	80	4883	32
458	129	4738	42	4884	53
589	118	4741	66	5879	137
590	112	4743	83	6498	136
591	127	4744	38	6501	138
1209	119	4745	78	6551	139
1236	9	4746	31	7040	4
1307	21	4747	18	7042	14
1398	24	4749	27	7043	41
1505	120	4750	79	7044	68
1516	106	4751	36	7045	35
1532	128	4752	17	7046	6
1543	121	4754	76	7047	82
1556	126	4755	33	7124	2
1572	124	4756	16	7125	10
1596	135	4757	50	7126	7
1636	132	4758	45	7127	3
1693	110	4759	28	7169	8
1701	108	4760	30	7182	5
3626	88	4761	85	7183	11
3631	87	4762	69	7216	13
3632	89	4763	23	7217	12
3666	60	4766	37	7745	67
3873	22	4775	43	7746	70
4507	116	4778	44	7747	26
4573	98	4781	51	8230	131
4711	1	4783	86	8231	107
4726	65	4785	62	8284	101
4728	39	4786	49	8326	102
4729	47	4789	81	8371	130
4732	74	4790	77	8380	123

INDEX OF TABLETS—*Continued.*

Museum Number	Text Number	Museum Number	Text Number	Museum Number	Text Number
8425	97	13086	61	14069	109
9190	63	13087	59	14078	117
9239	64	13294	75	14085	103
9245	55	13632	100	14089	99
9247	34	13647	100	14097	104
9259	58	13858	115	14116	93
9265	20	13874	40	14117	94
9810	71	13920	73	14118	95
9818	57	13939	113	14129	15
10631	84	14000	91	14152	114
11690	46	14045	96	14173	111
12526	54	14046	134	19794	92
12930	72	14067	105		

AUTOGRAPHED TEXTS

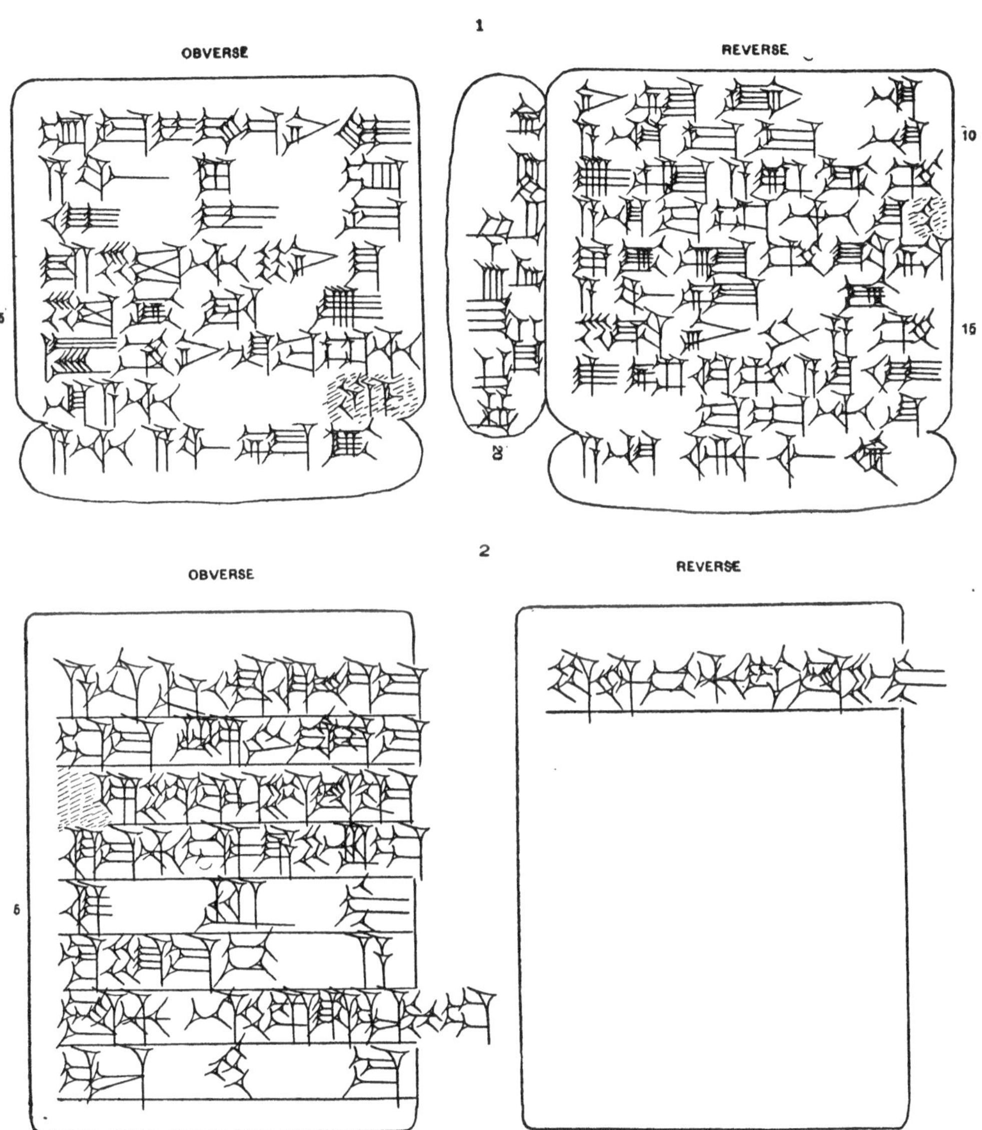
1
OBVERSE
REVERSE
2
OBVERSE
REVERSE

3

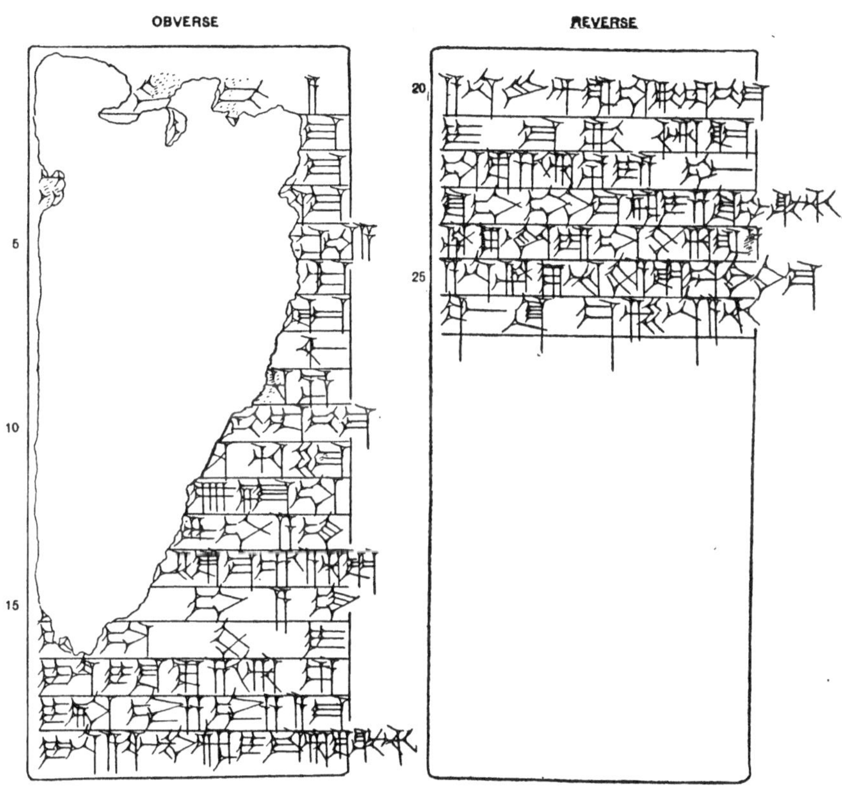

4

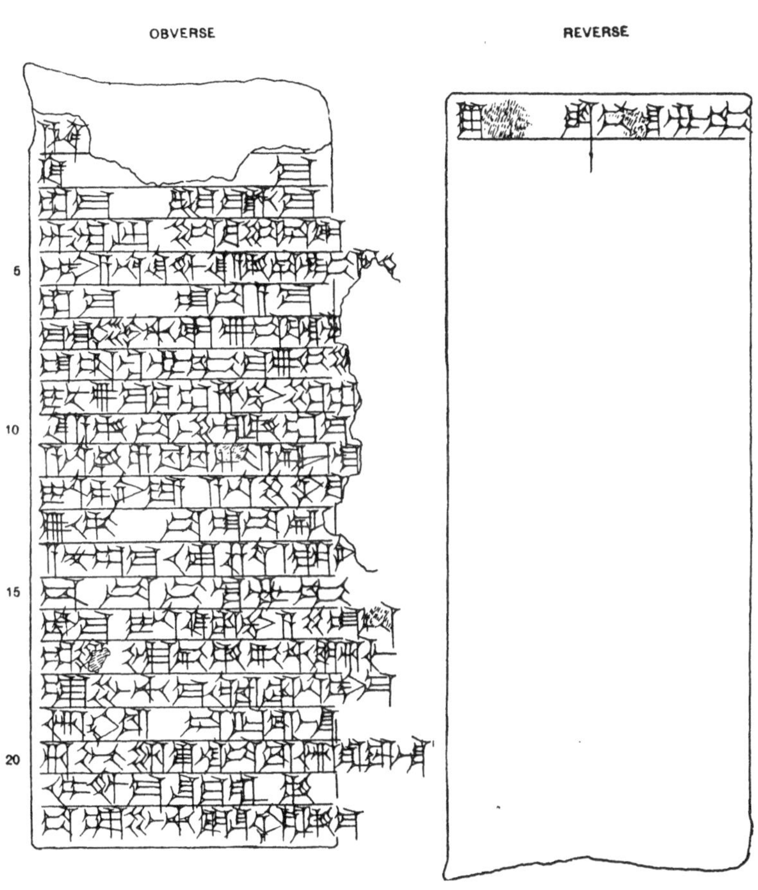

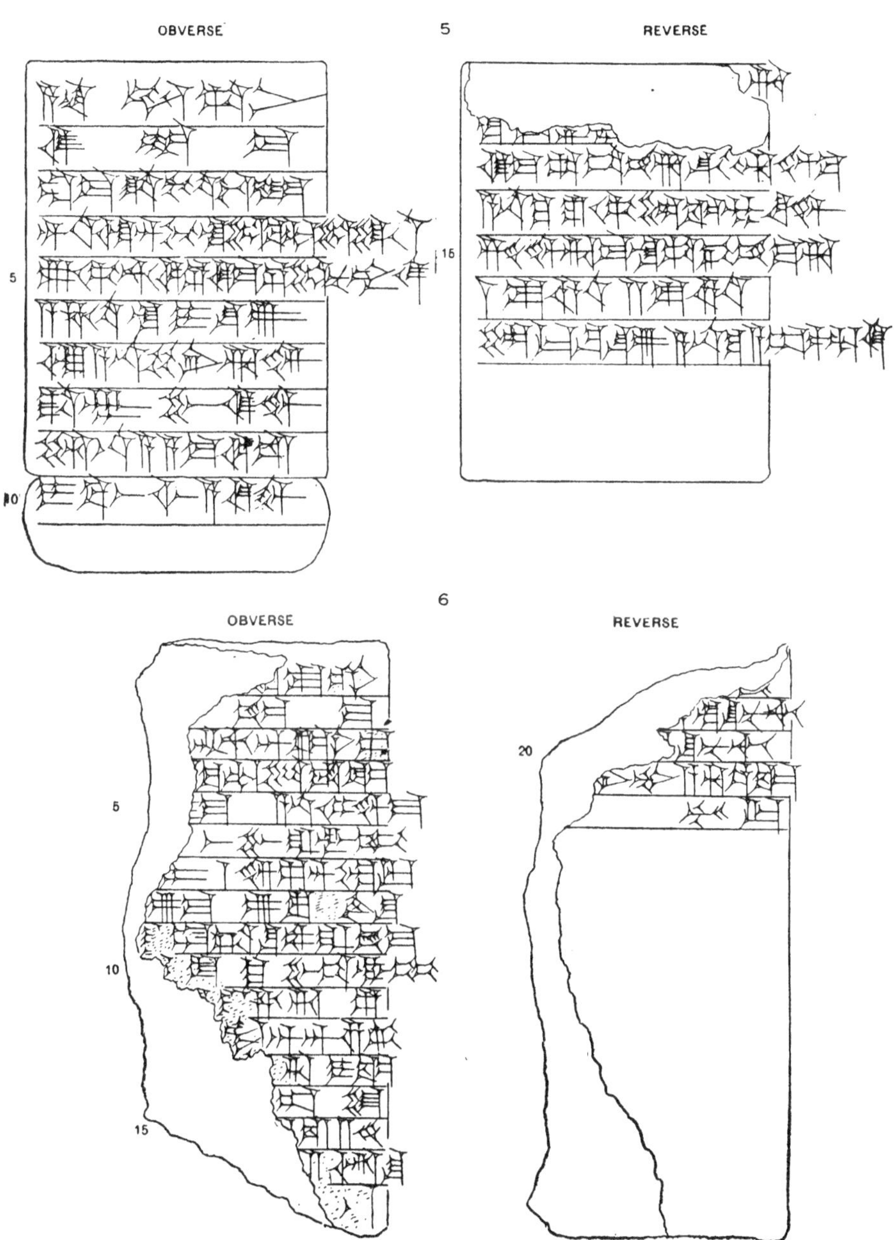

5
OBVERSE
REVERSE
6
OBVERSE
REVERSE

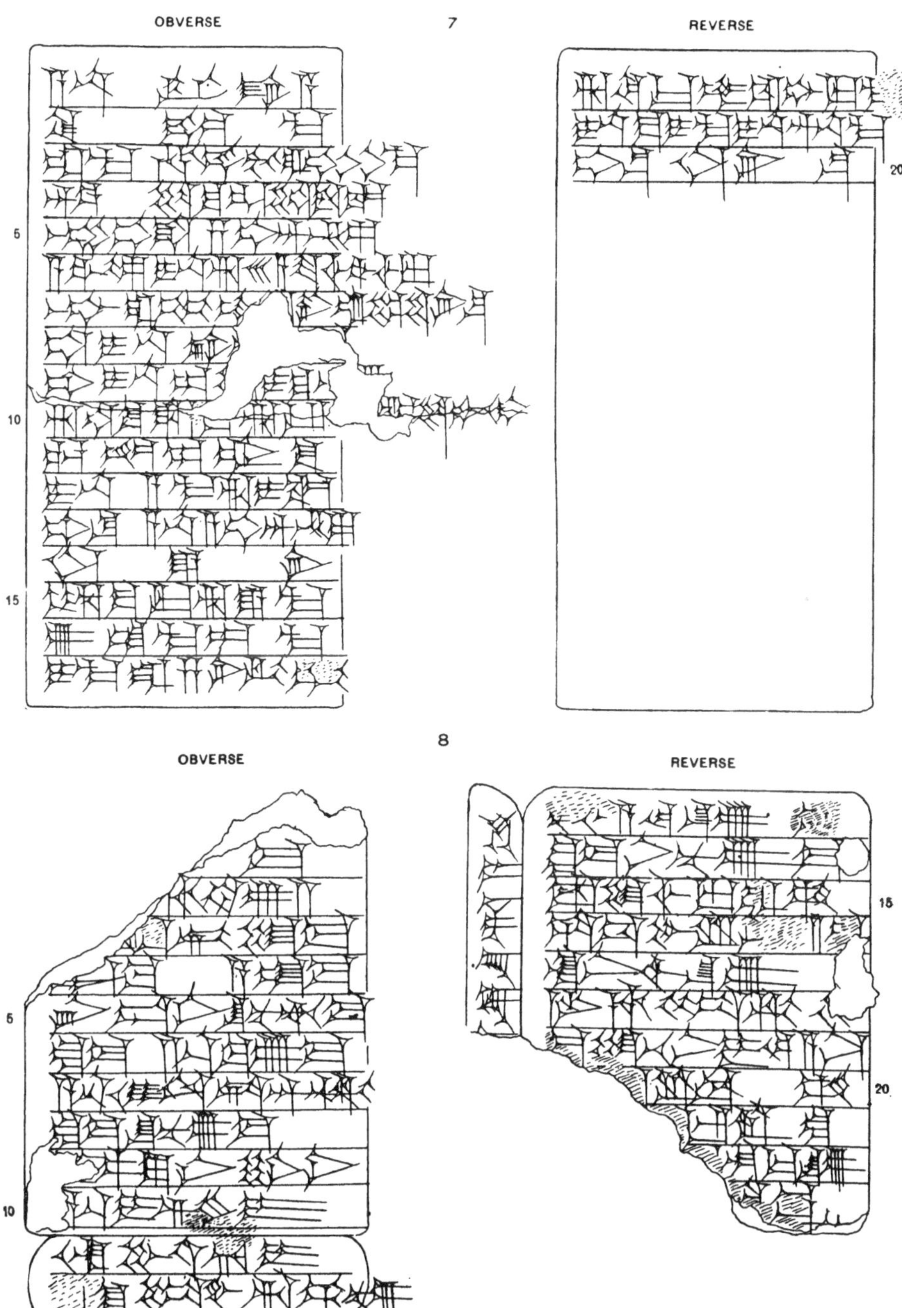
OBVERSE
7
REVERSE
8
OBVERSE
REVERSE

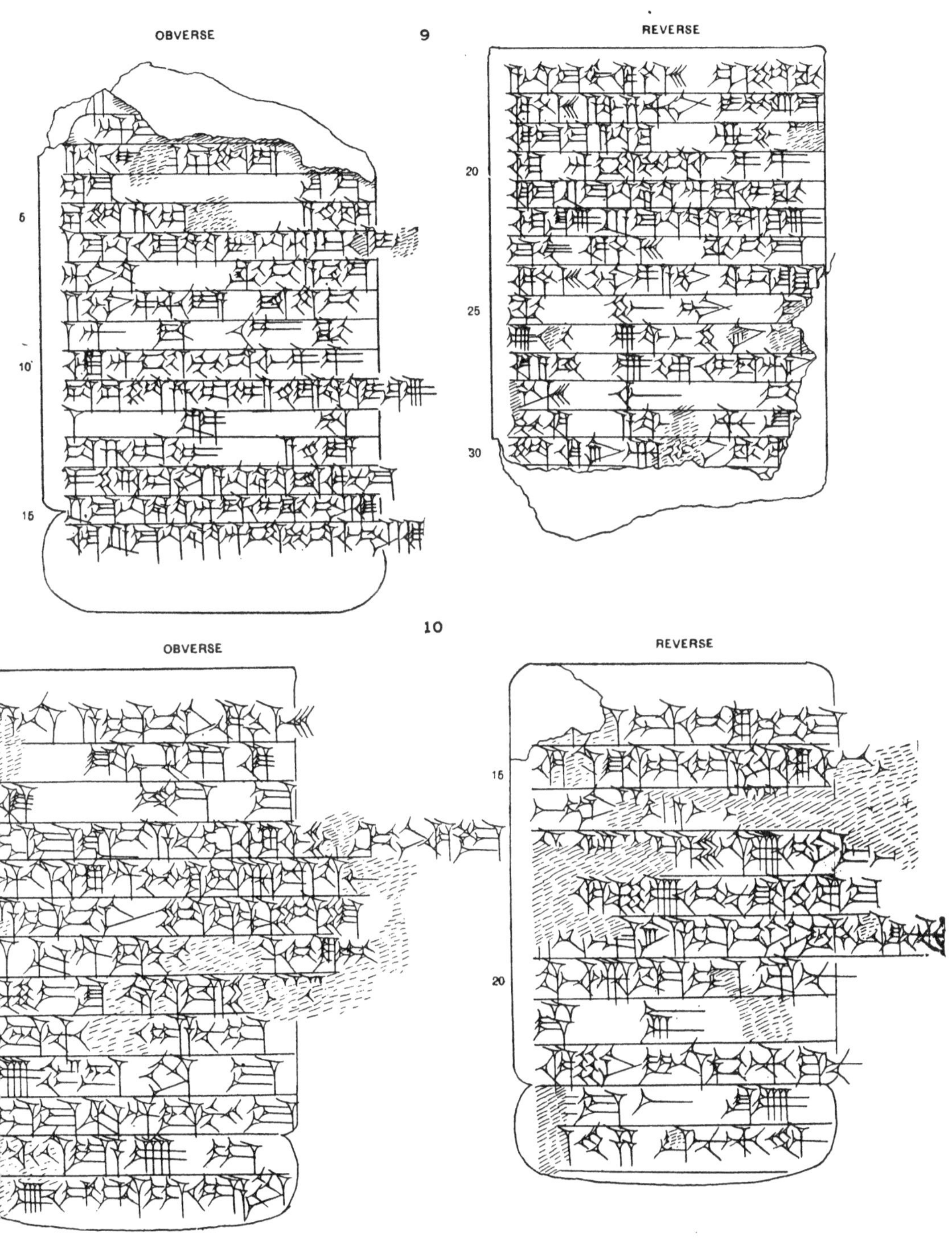
OBVERSE
9
REVERSE
10
OBVERSE
REVERSE

11

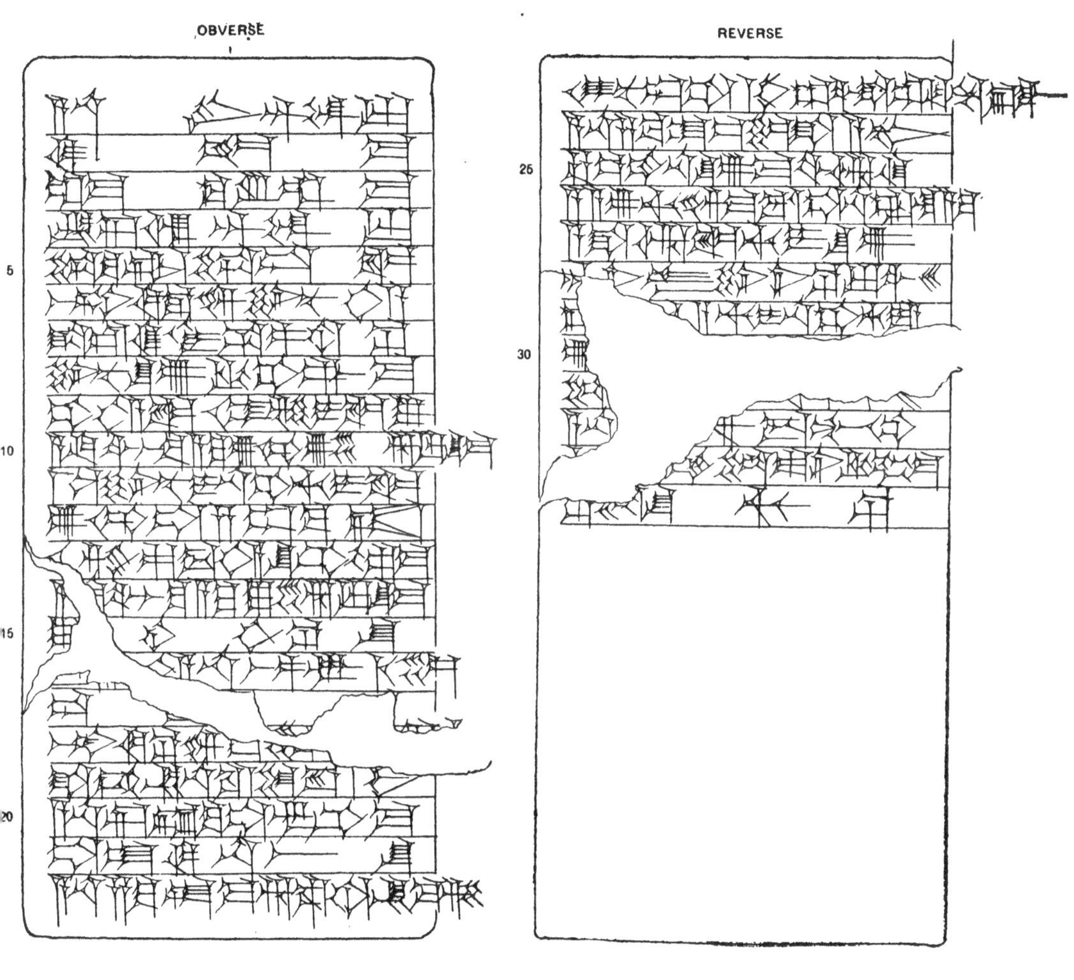

12

OBVERSE

REVERSE

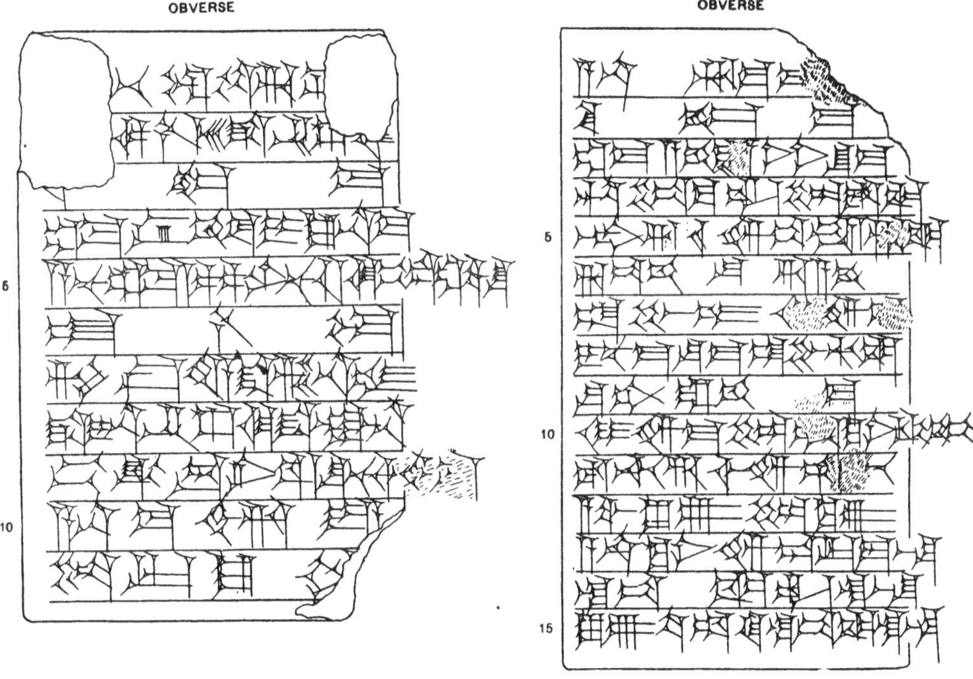
13
OBVERSE
14
OBVERSE
REVERSE UNINSCRIBED

15

OBVERSE

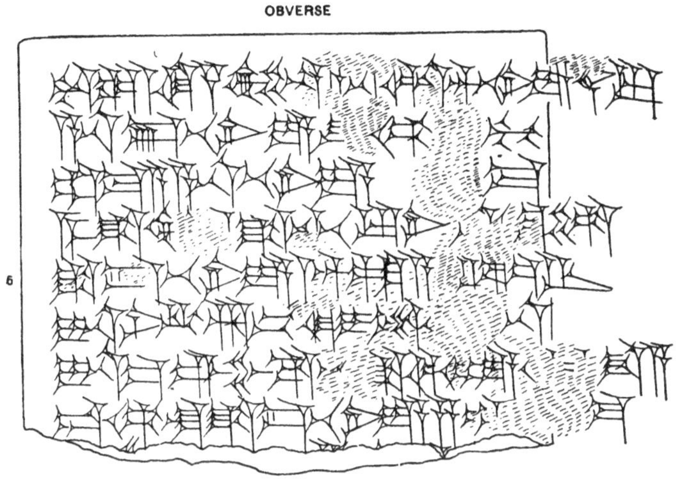

REVERSE

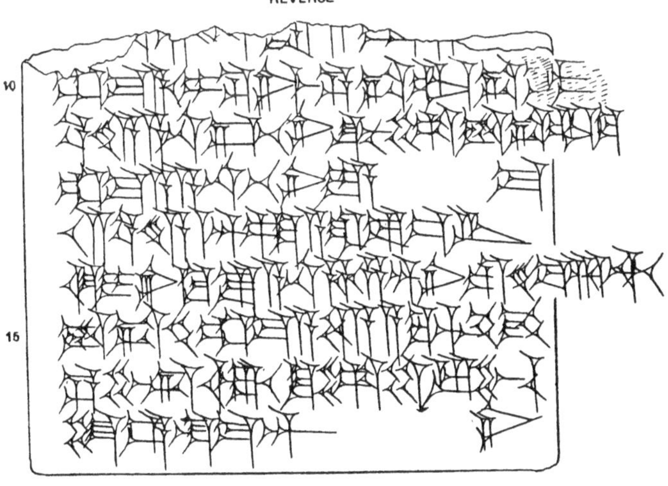

16

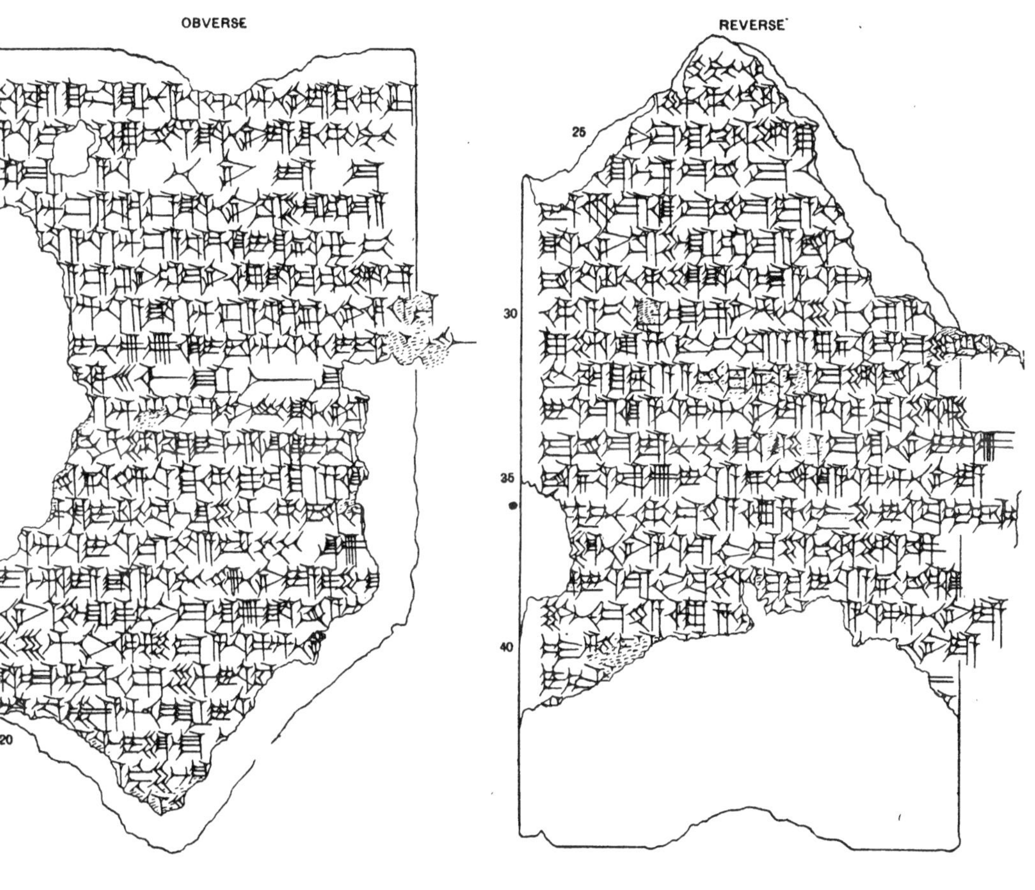

17

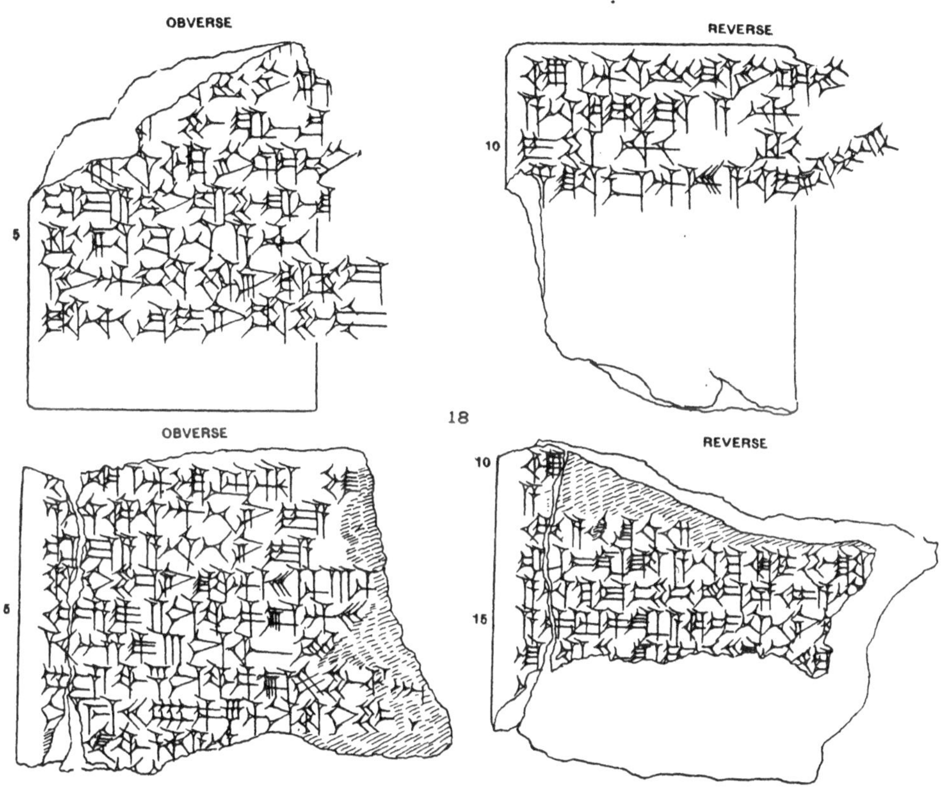

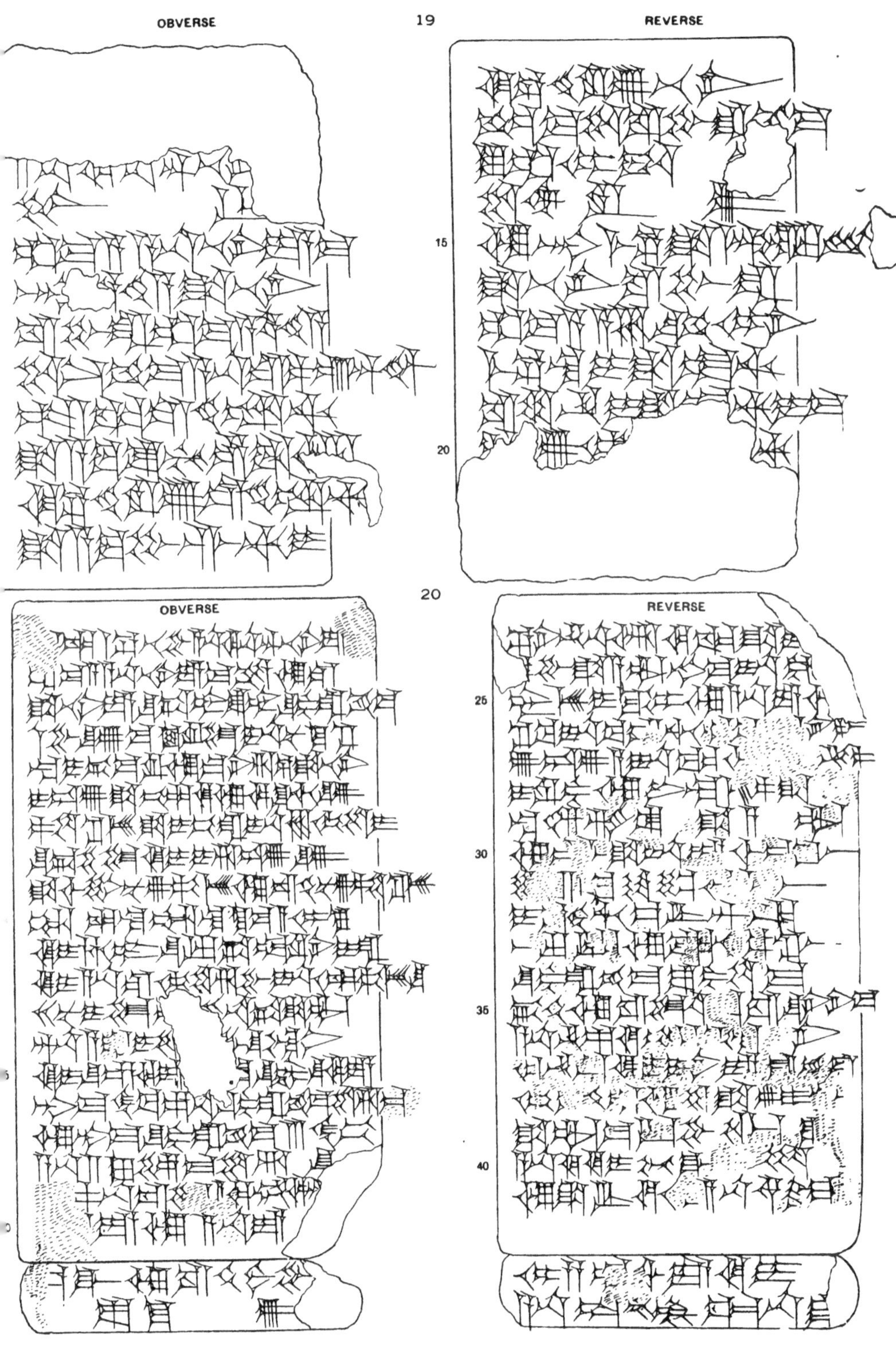
19
OBVERSE
REVERSE
20
OBVERSE
REVERSE

21

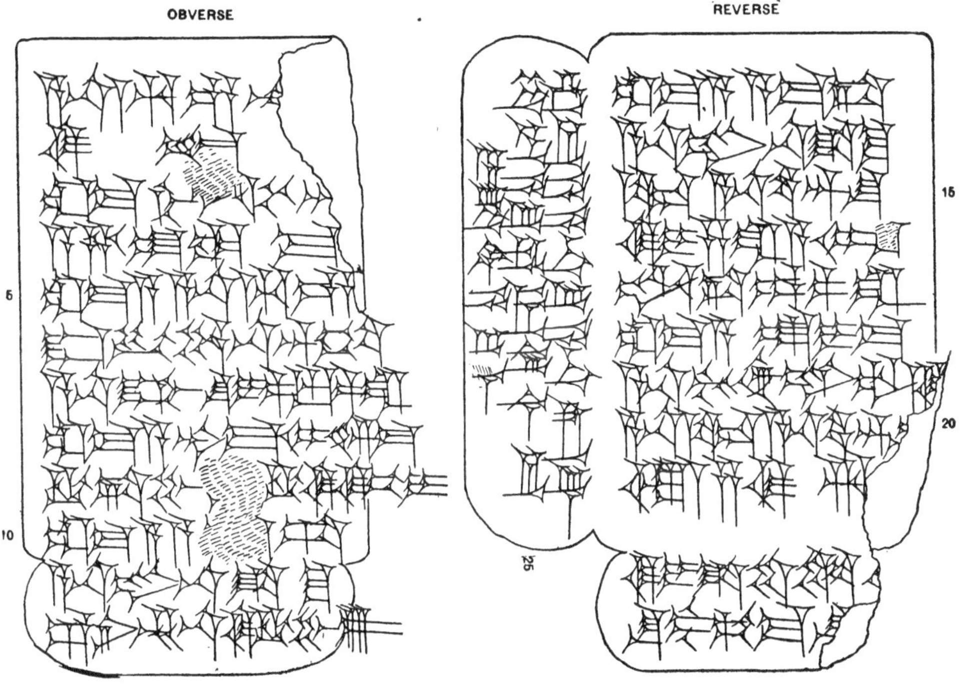

22

OBVERSE

REVERSE

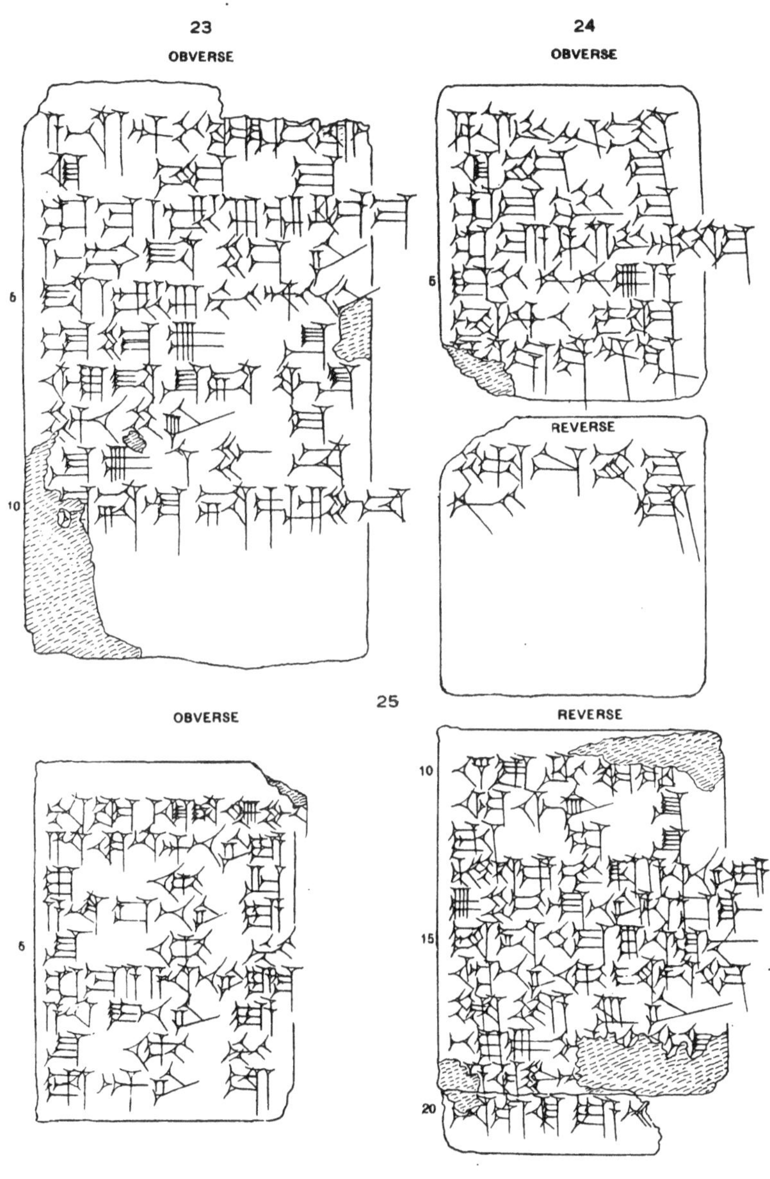
23
OBVERSE
24
OBVERSE
REVERSE
25
OBVERSE
REVERSE

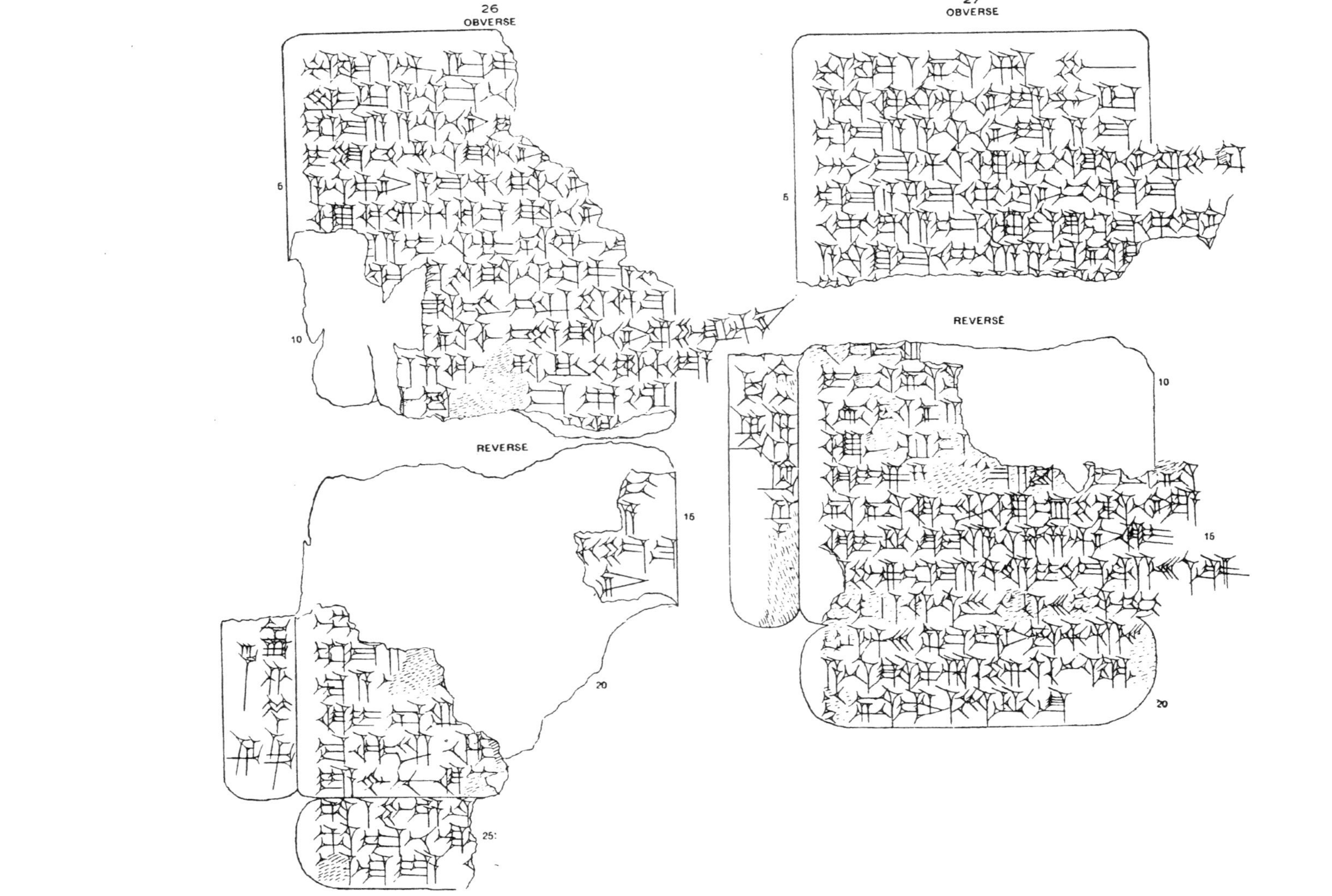
26
OBVERSE
REVERSE
27
OBVERSE
REVERSE

28

REVERSE

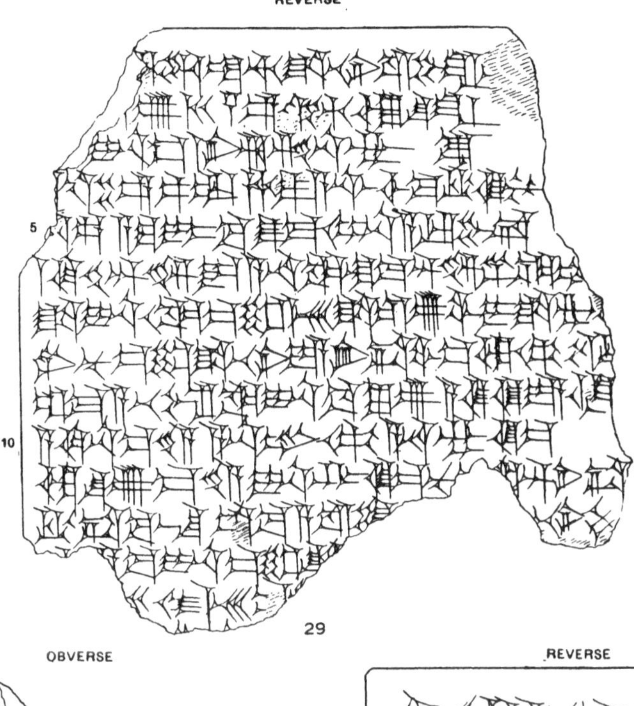

29

OBVERSE

REVERSE

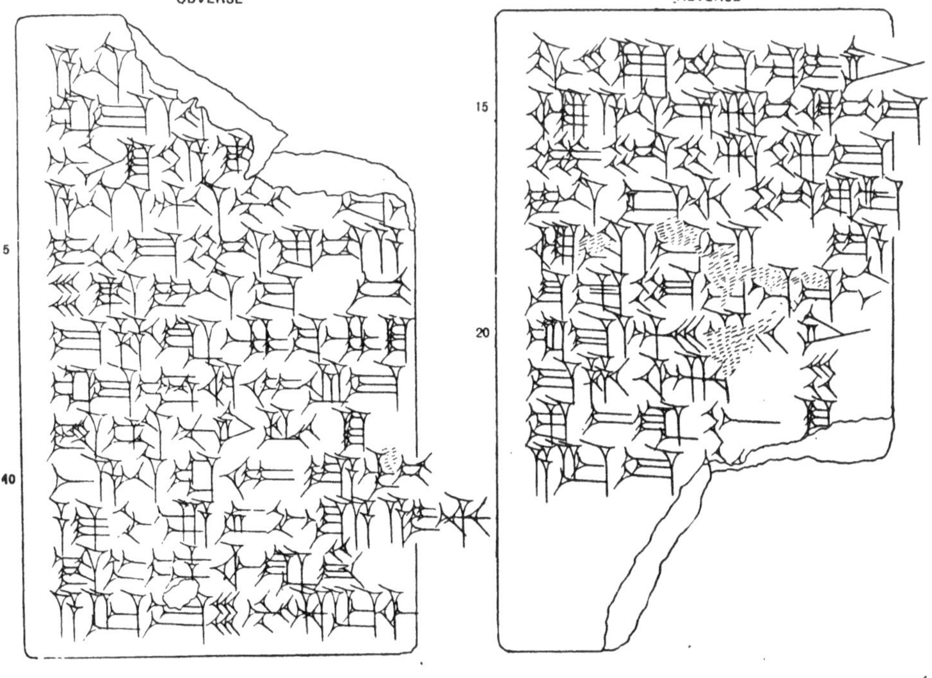

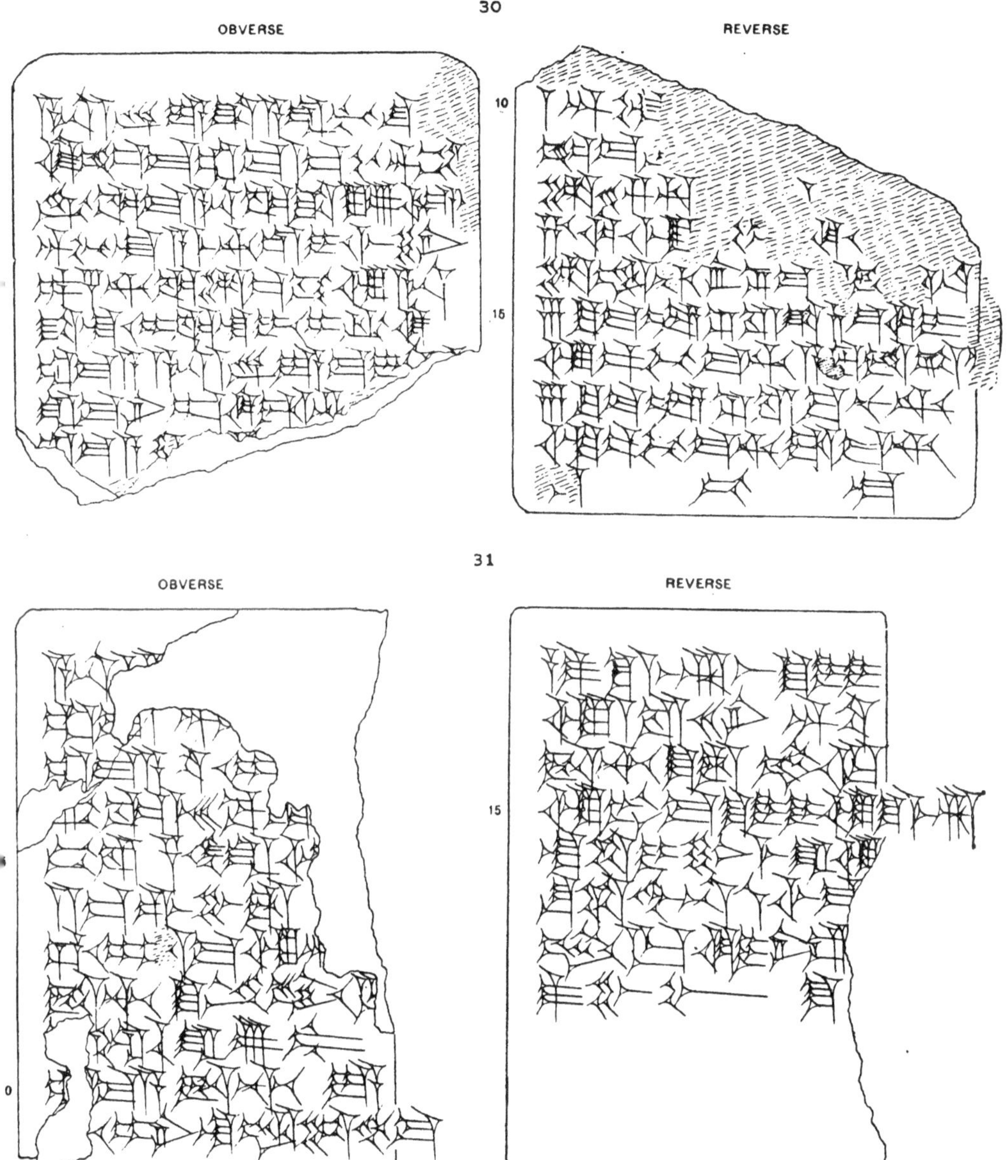
30
OBVERSE
REVERSE
31
OBVERSE
REVERSE

32

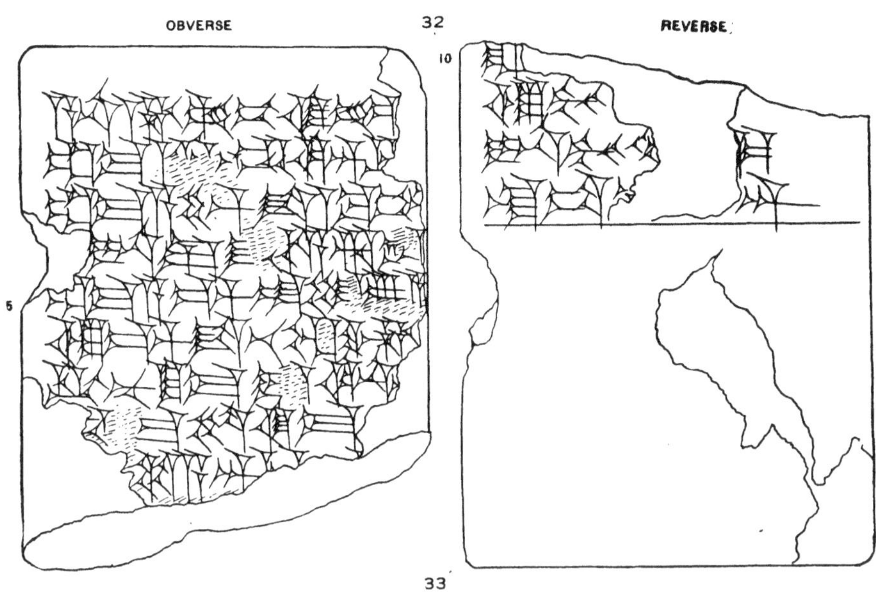

33

REVERSE

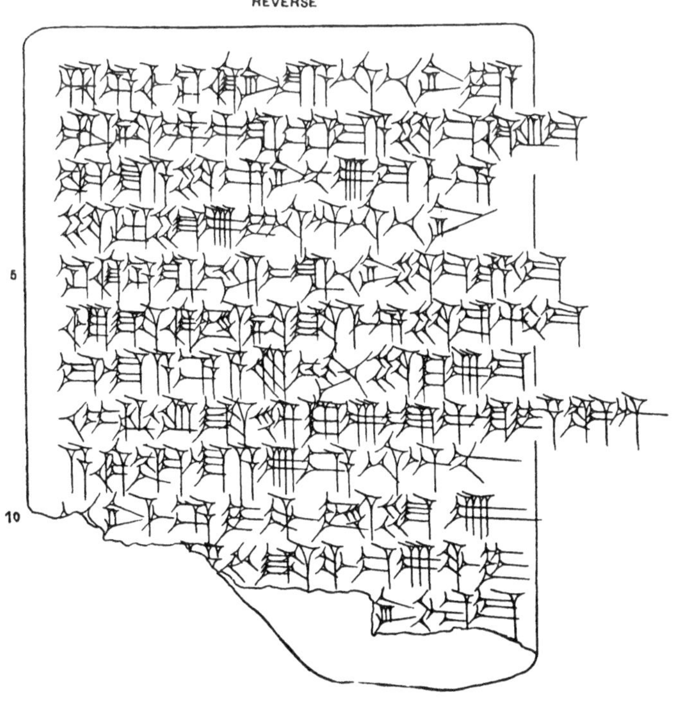

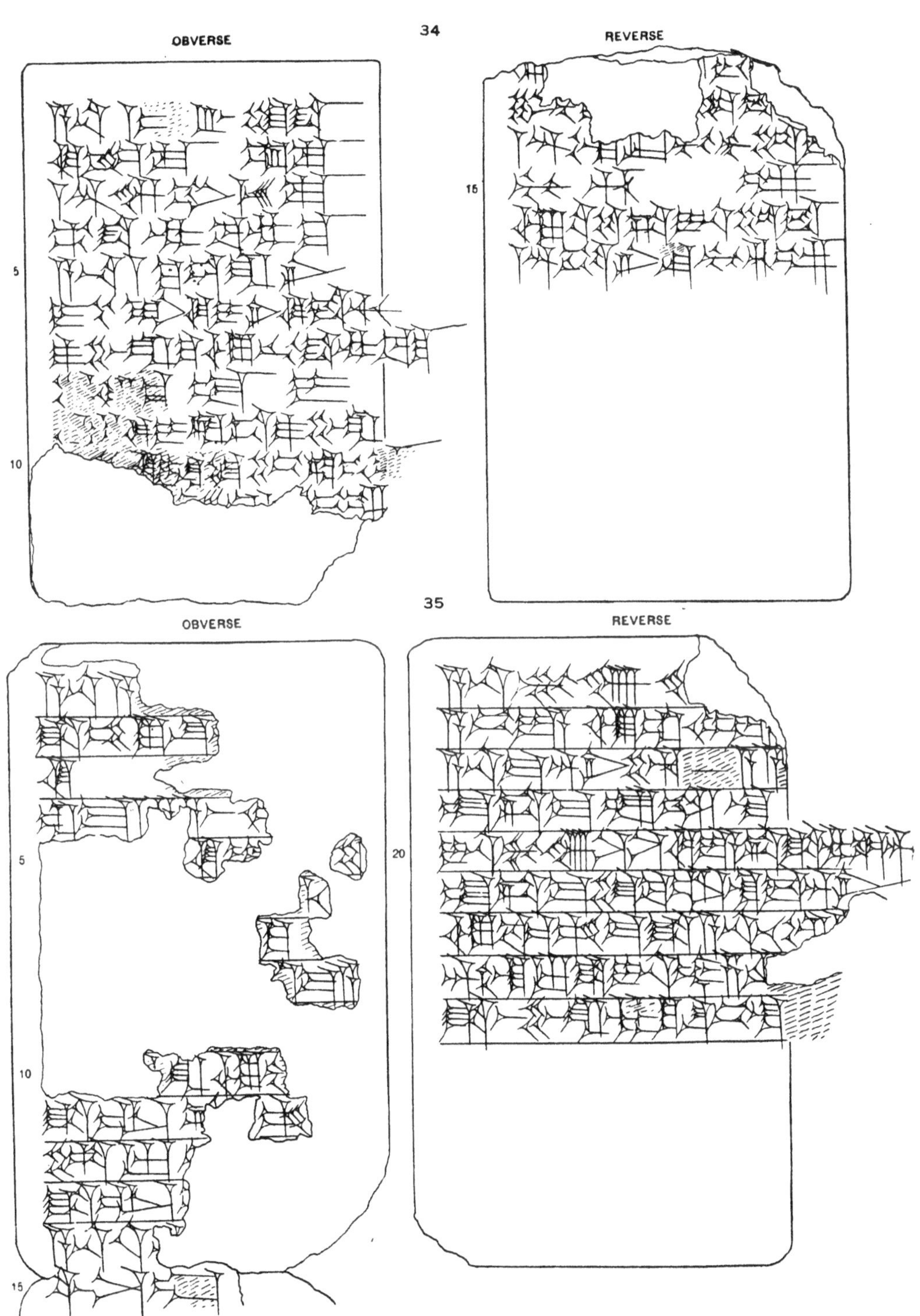
34
OBVERSE
REVERSE
35
OBVERSE
REVERSE

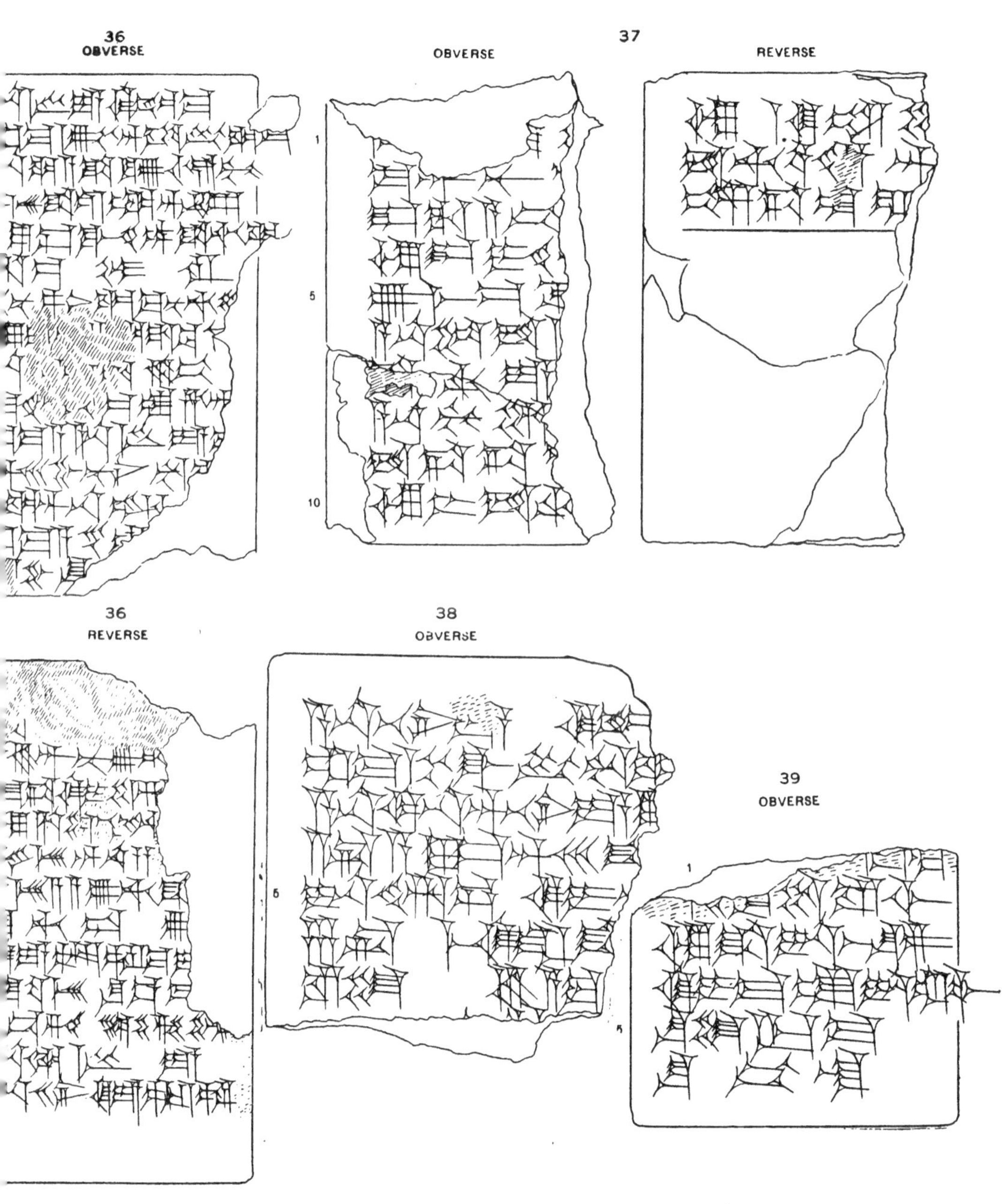
36
OBVERSE
37
OBVERSE
REVERSE
36
REVERSE
38
OBVERSE
39
OBVERSE

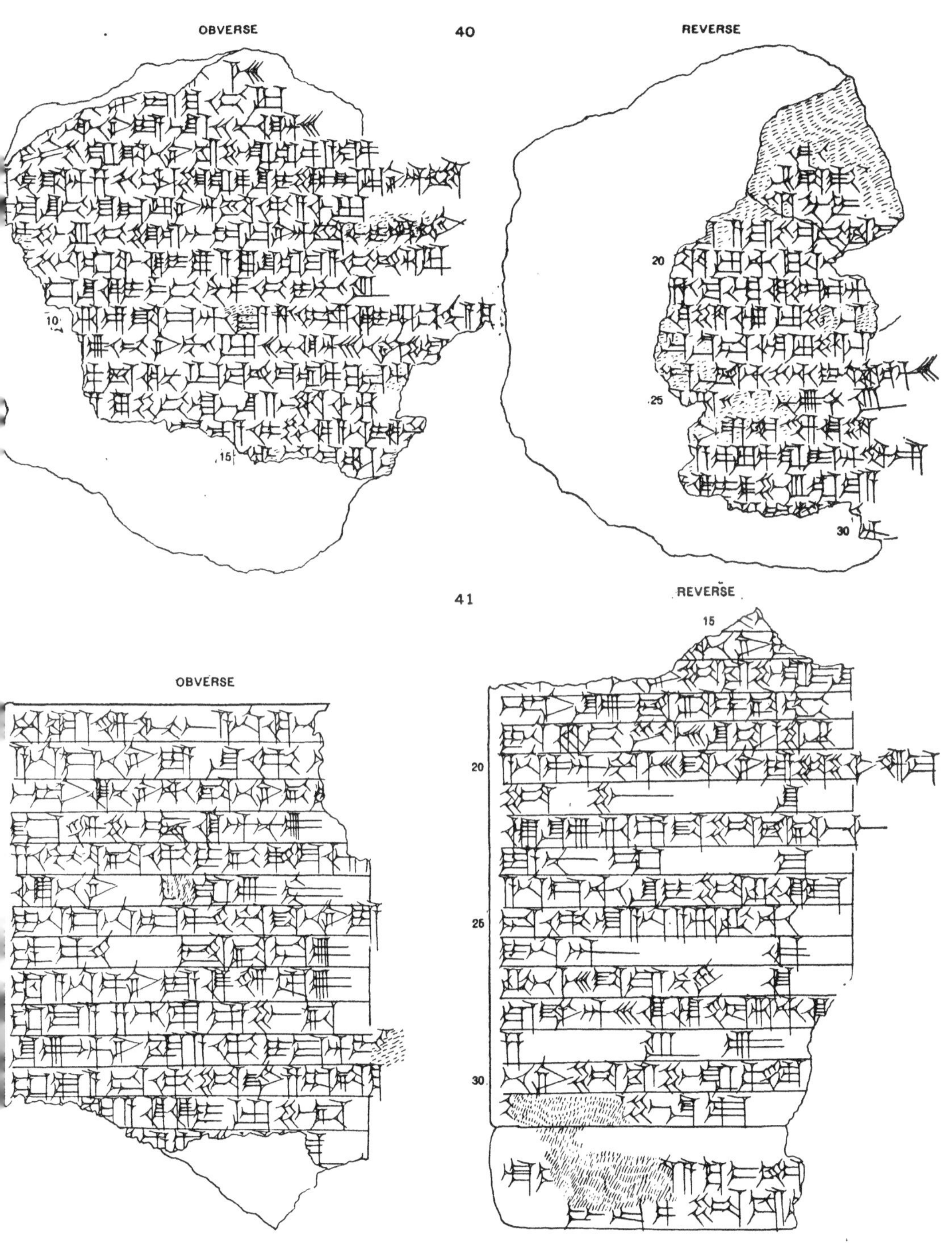
OBVERSE
40
REVERSE
41
REVERSE
OBVERSE

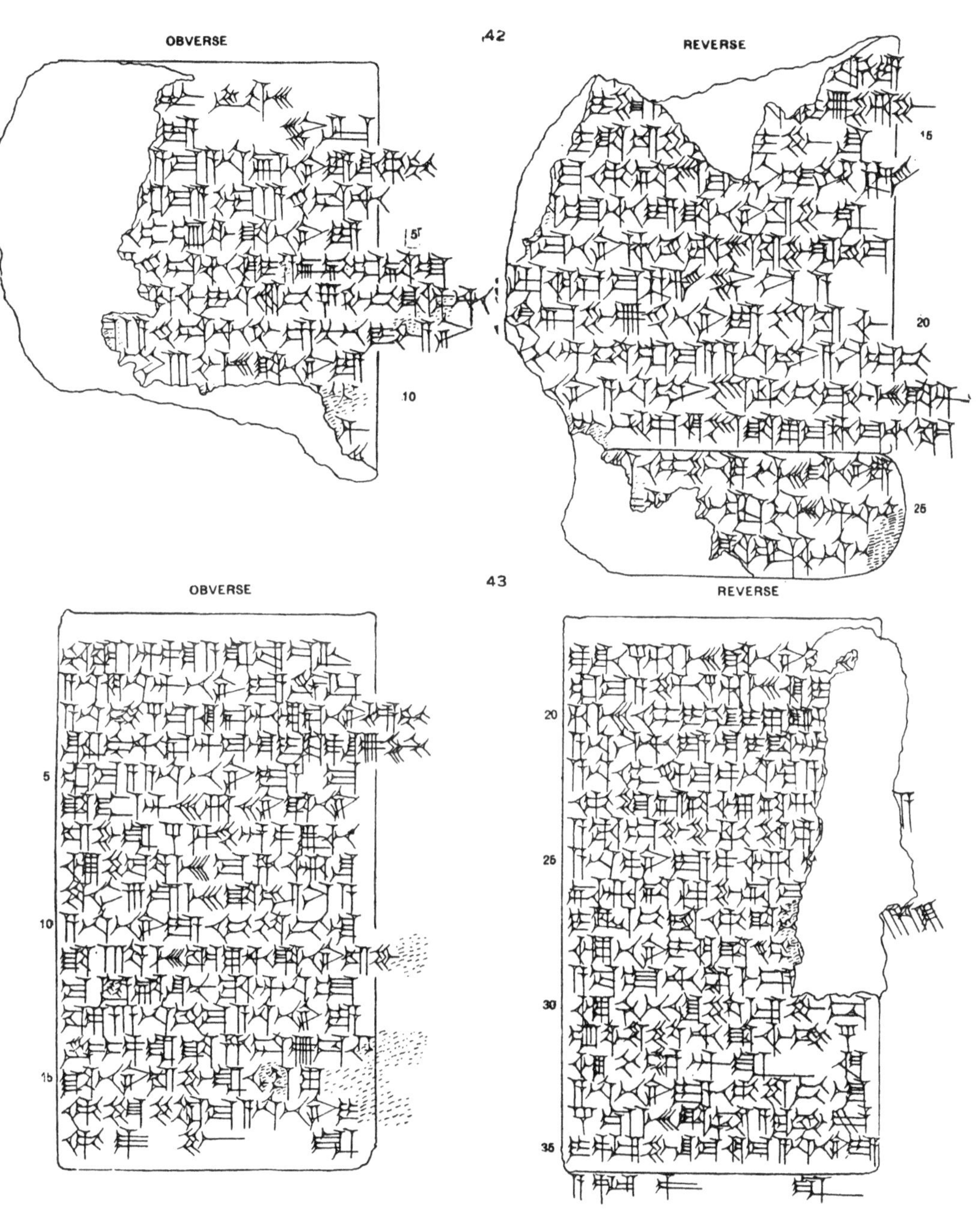
42
OBVERSE
REVERSE
43
OBVERSE
REVERSE

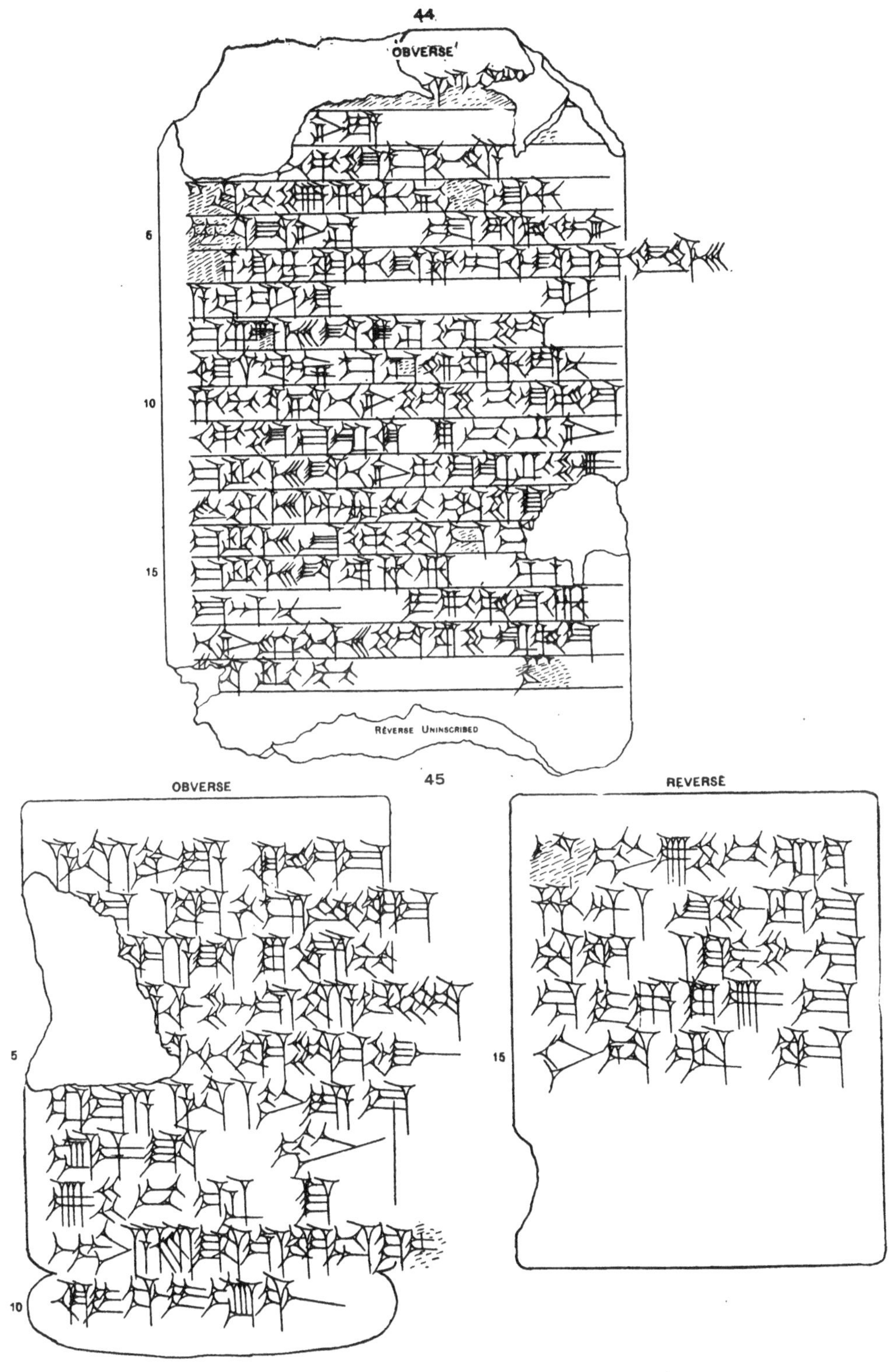
44
OBVERSE
RÉVERSE UNINSCRIBED
45
OBVERSE
REVERSE

46

OBVERSE

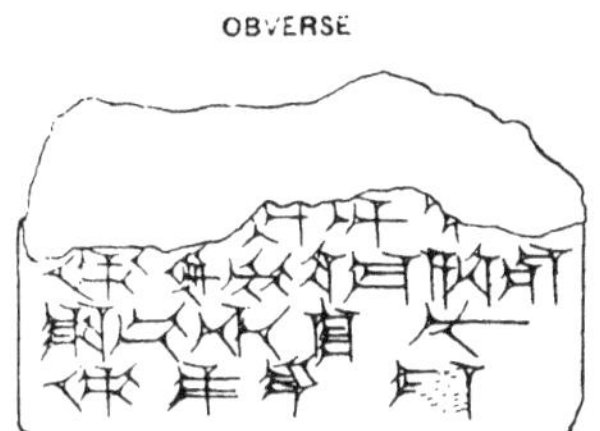

REVERSE

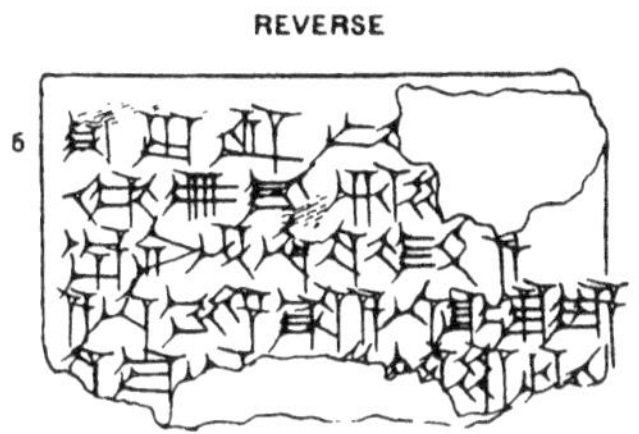

47

OBVERSE REVERSE

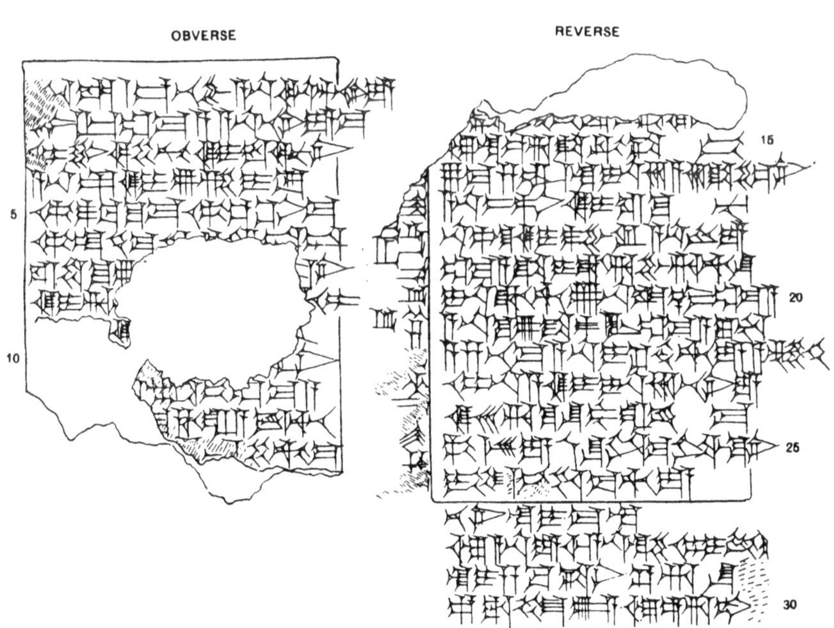

48

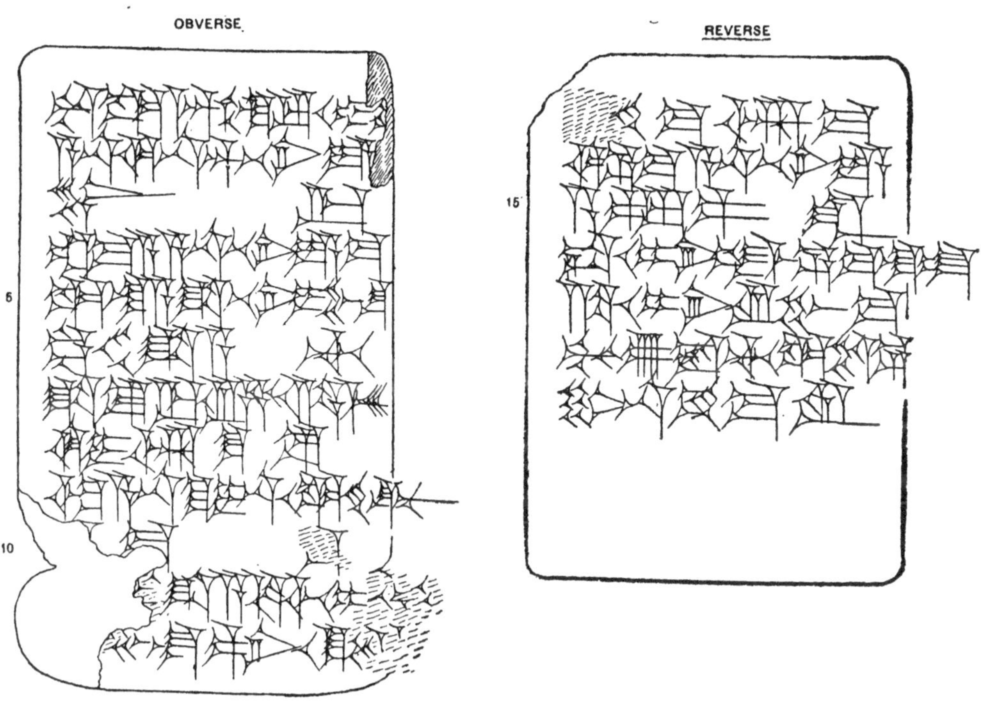

49

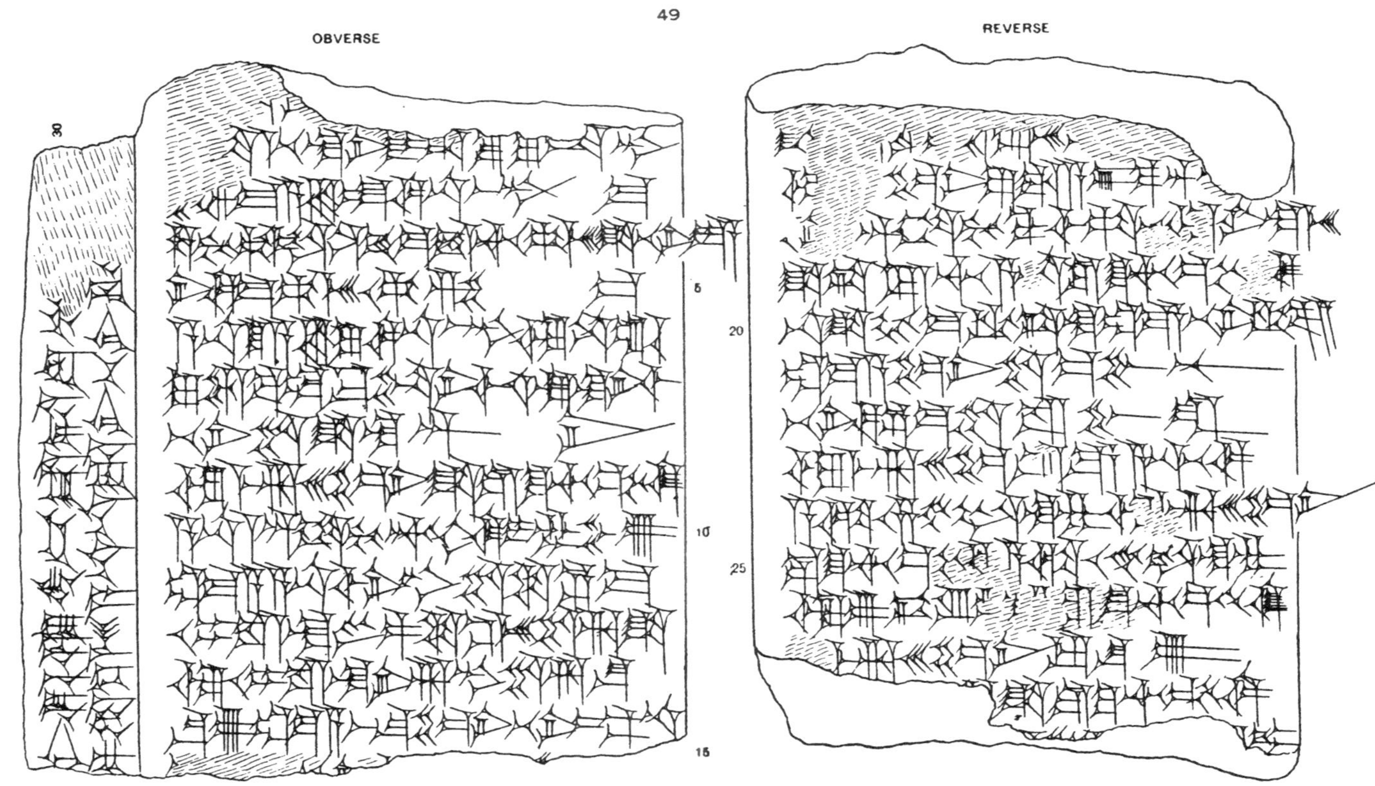

50

OBVERSE

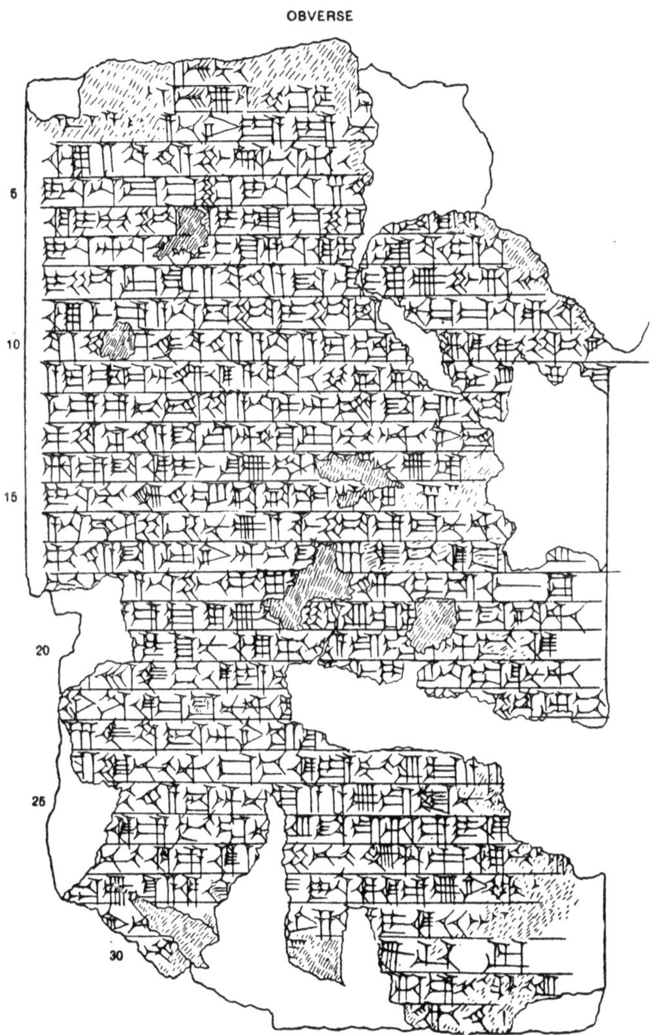

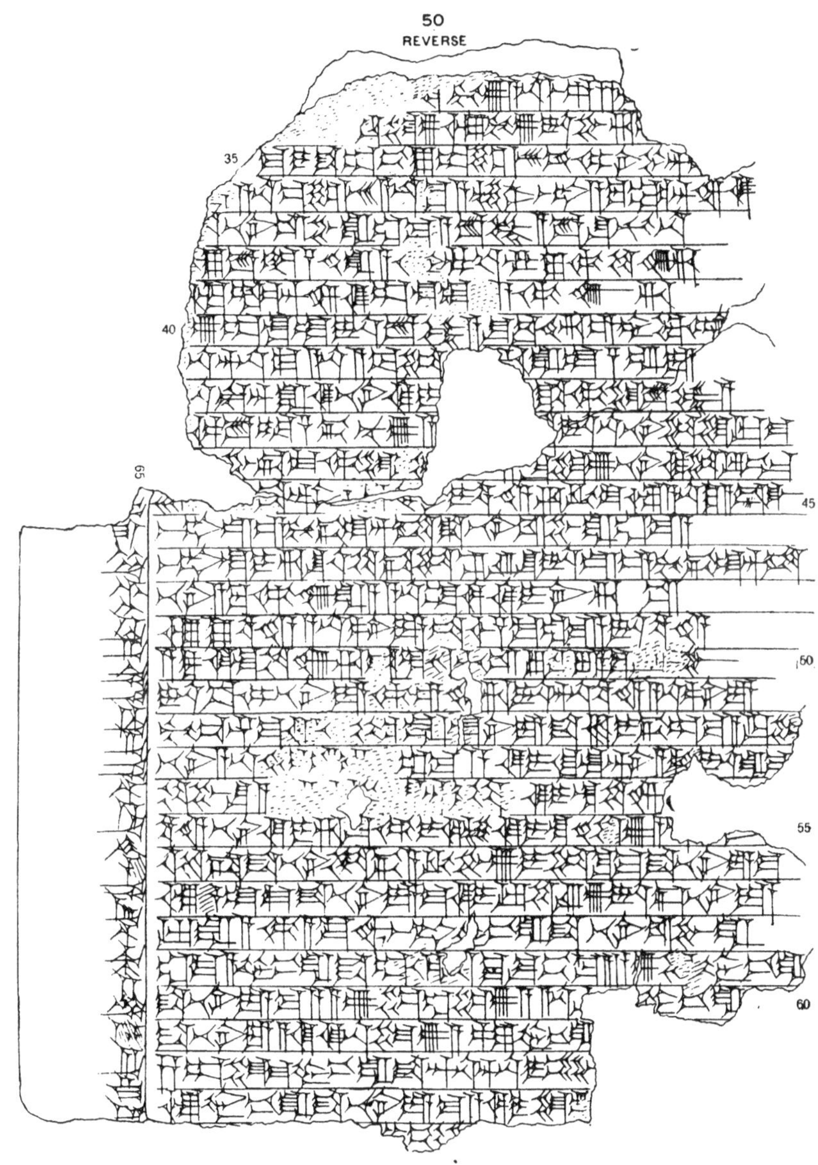
50
REVERSE

51

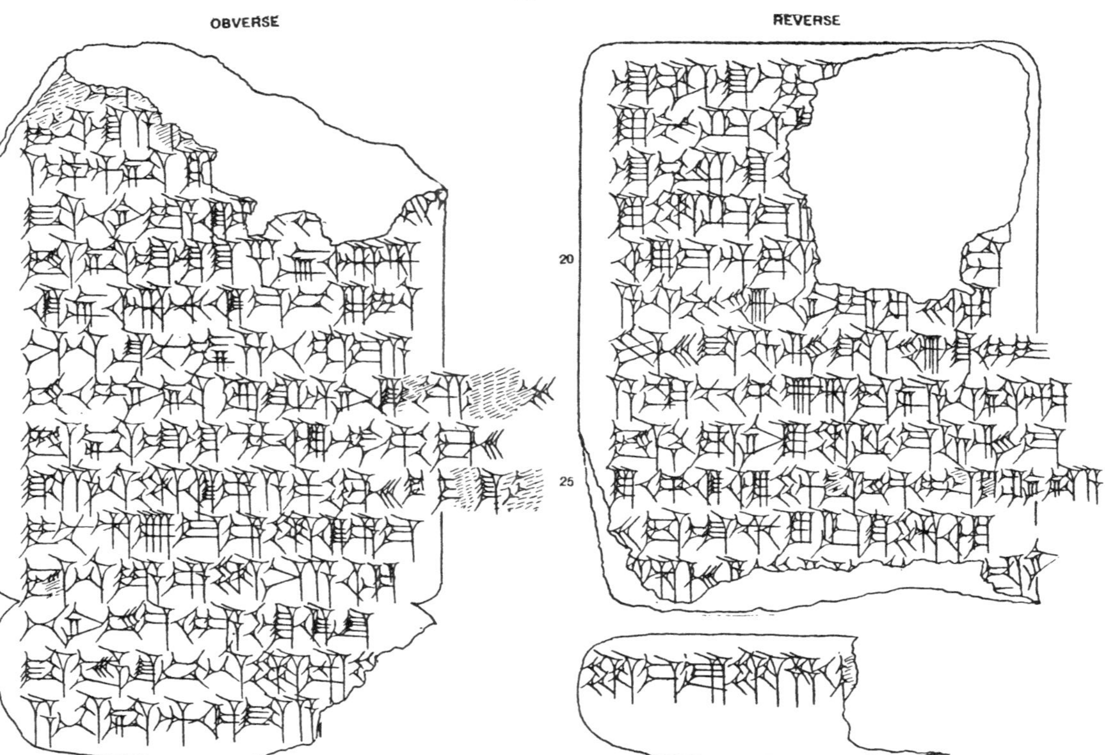

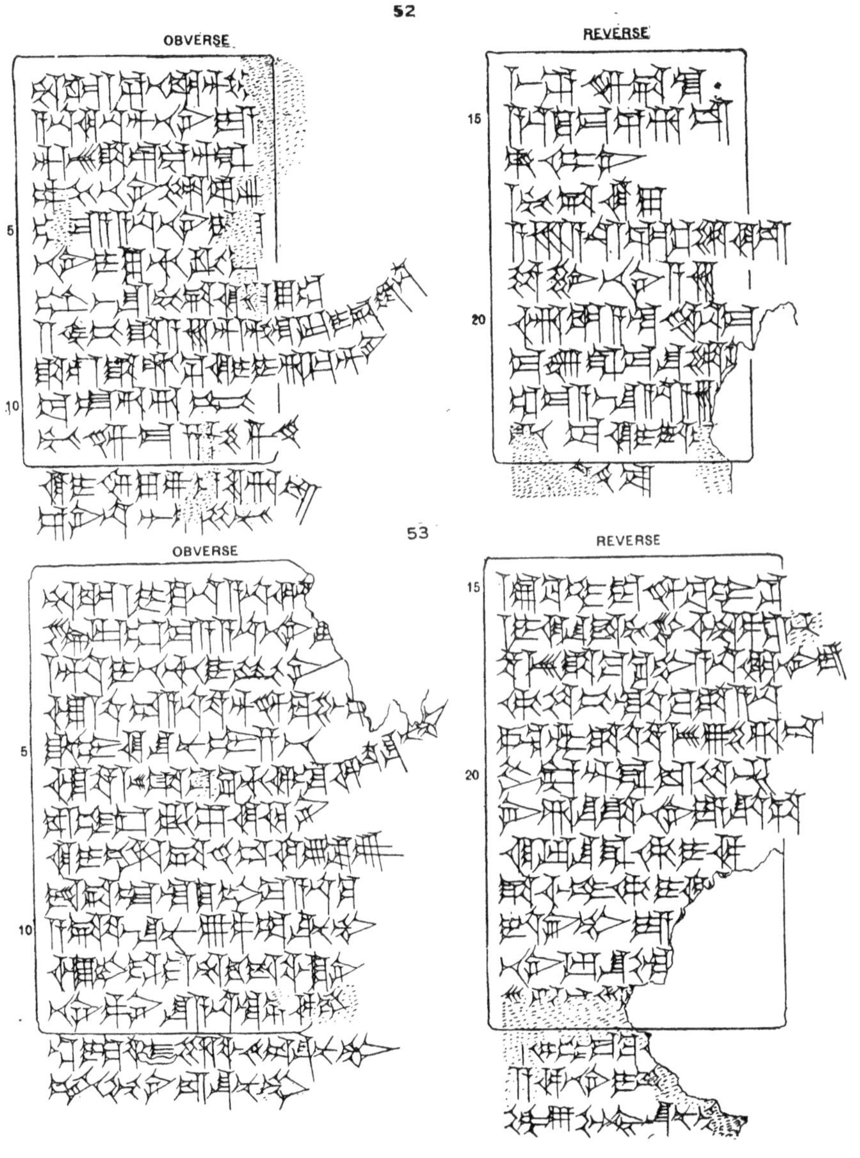
52
OBVERSE
REVERSE
53
OBVERSE
REVERSE

54

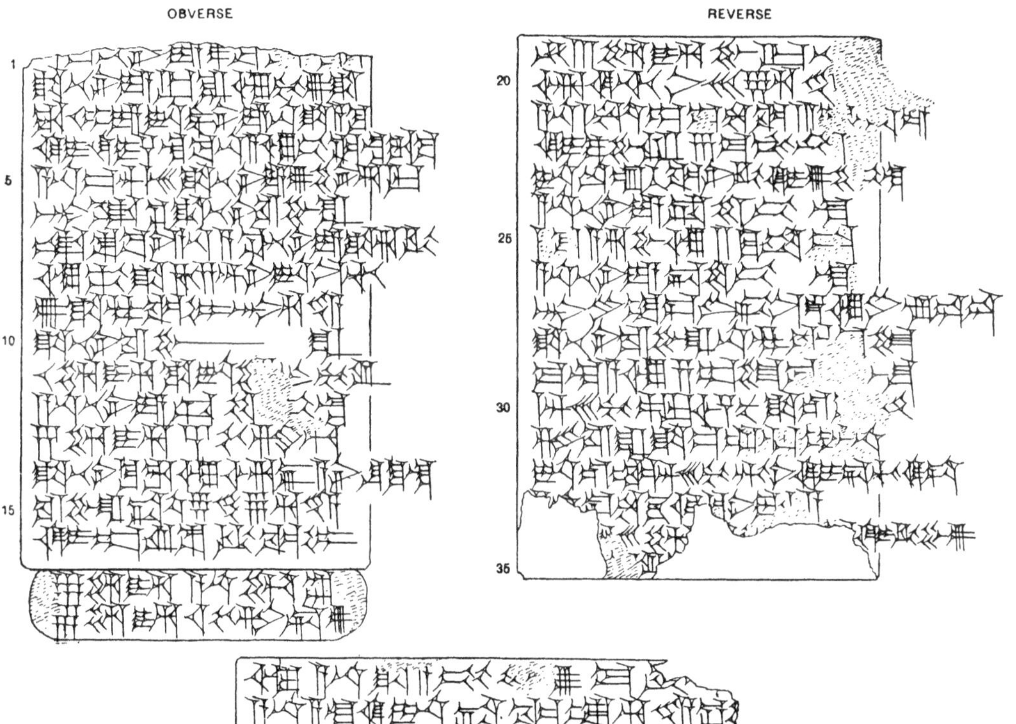

55

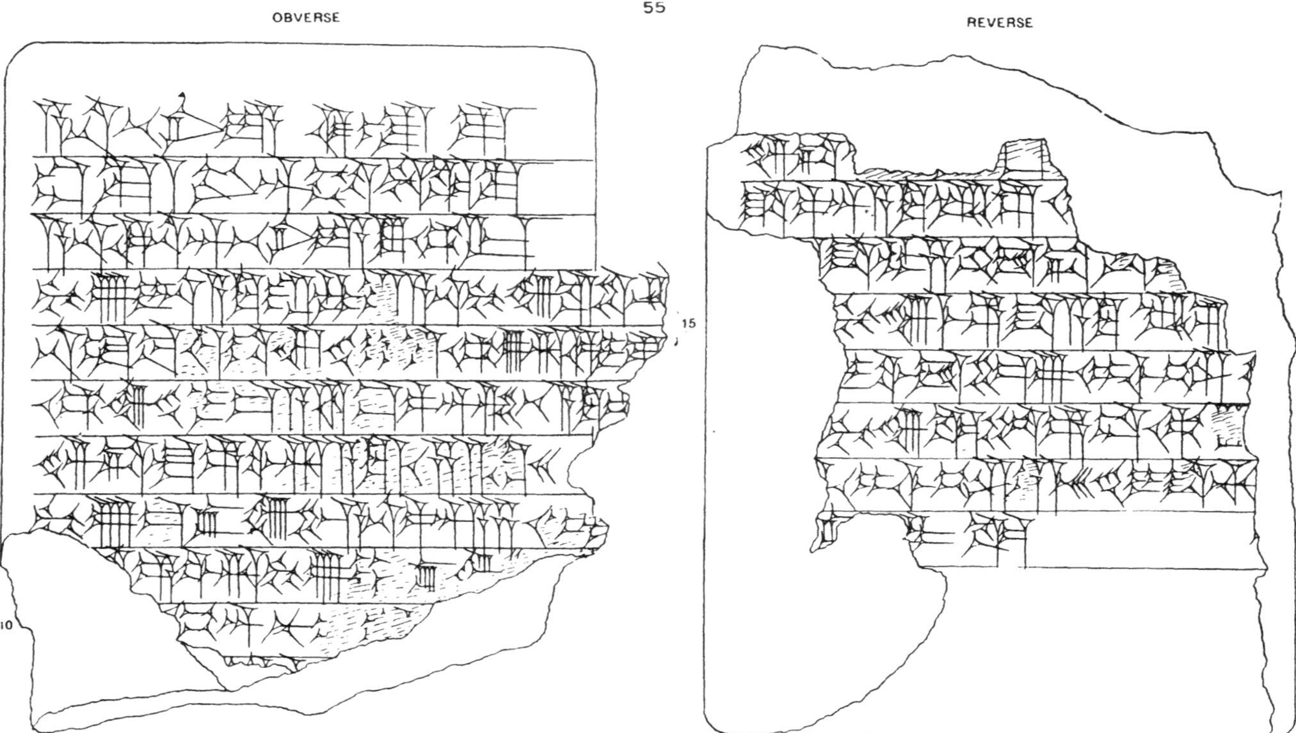

56

OBVERSE

REVERSE

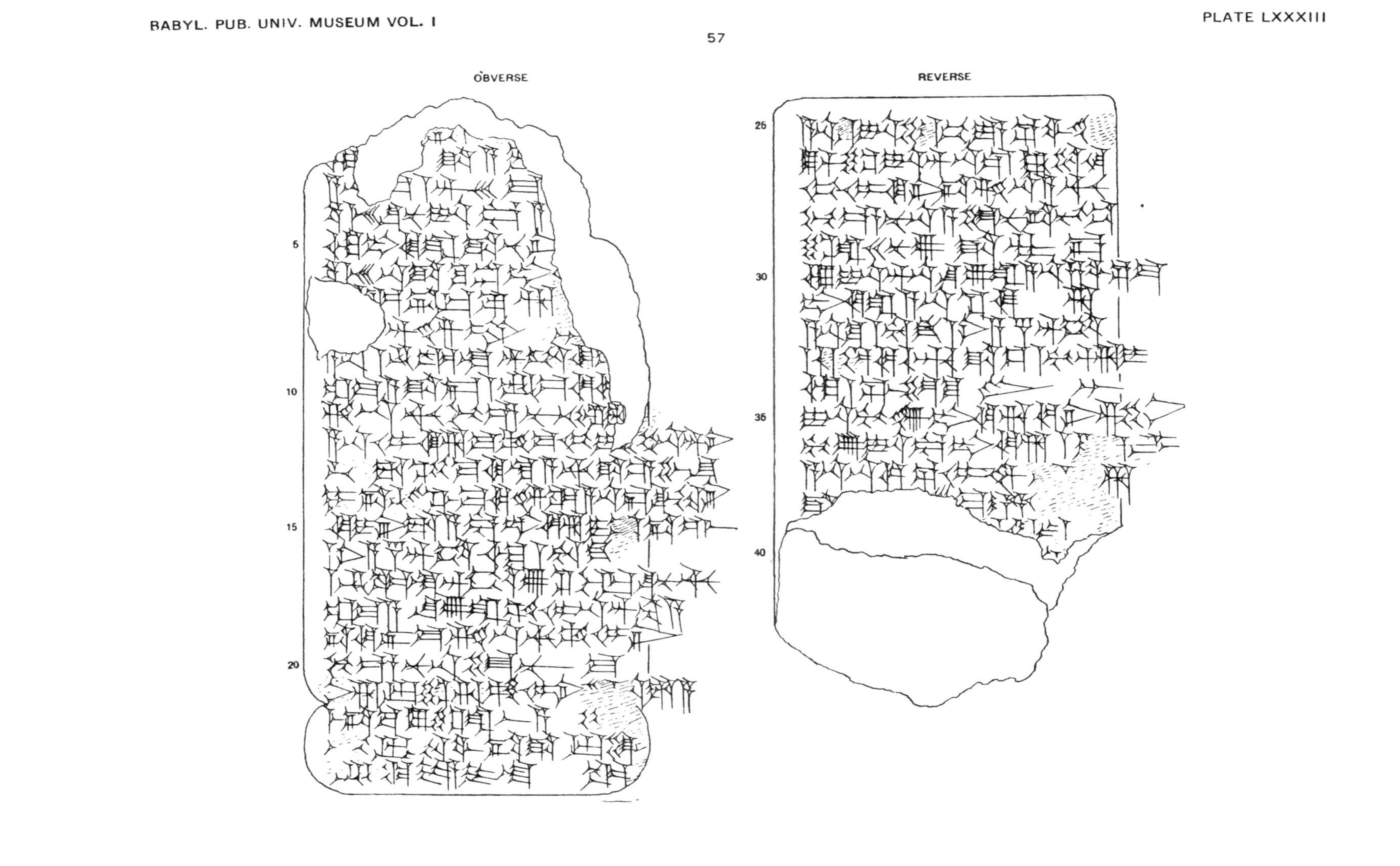

OBVERSE

REVERSE

58

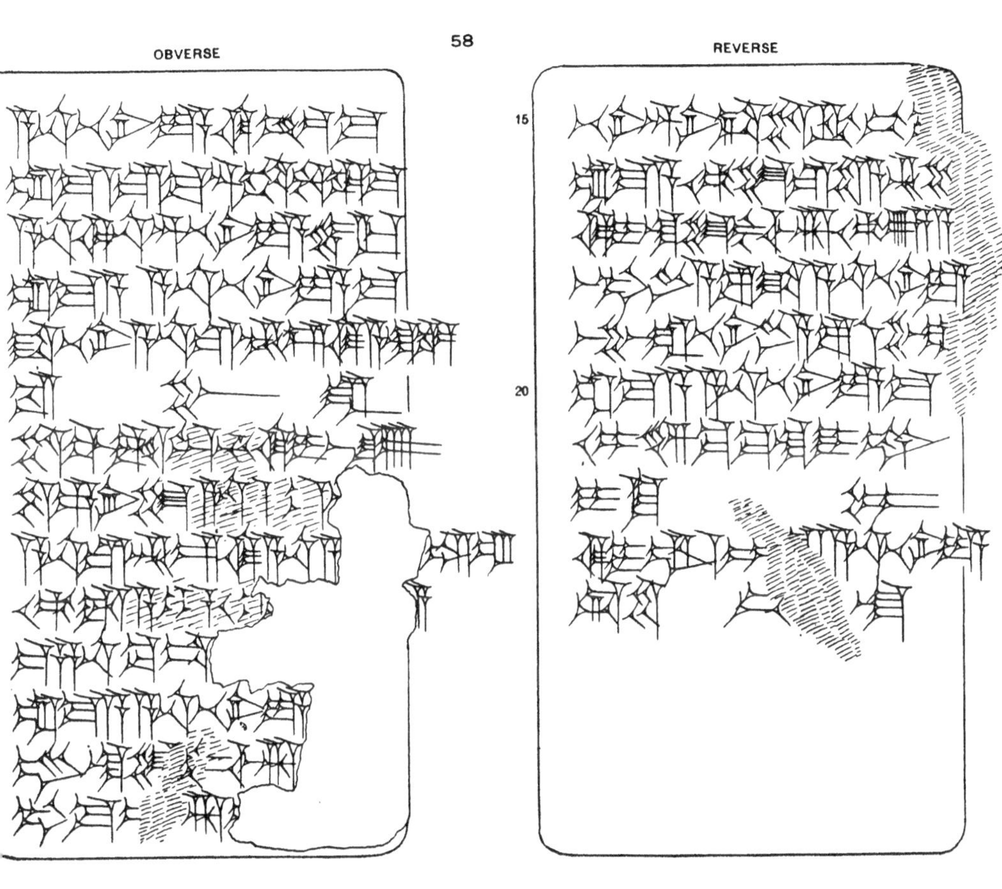

59

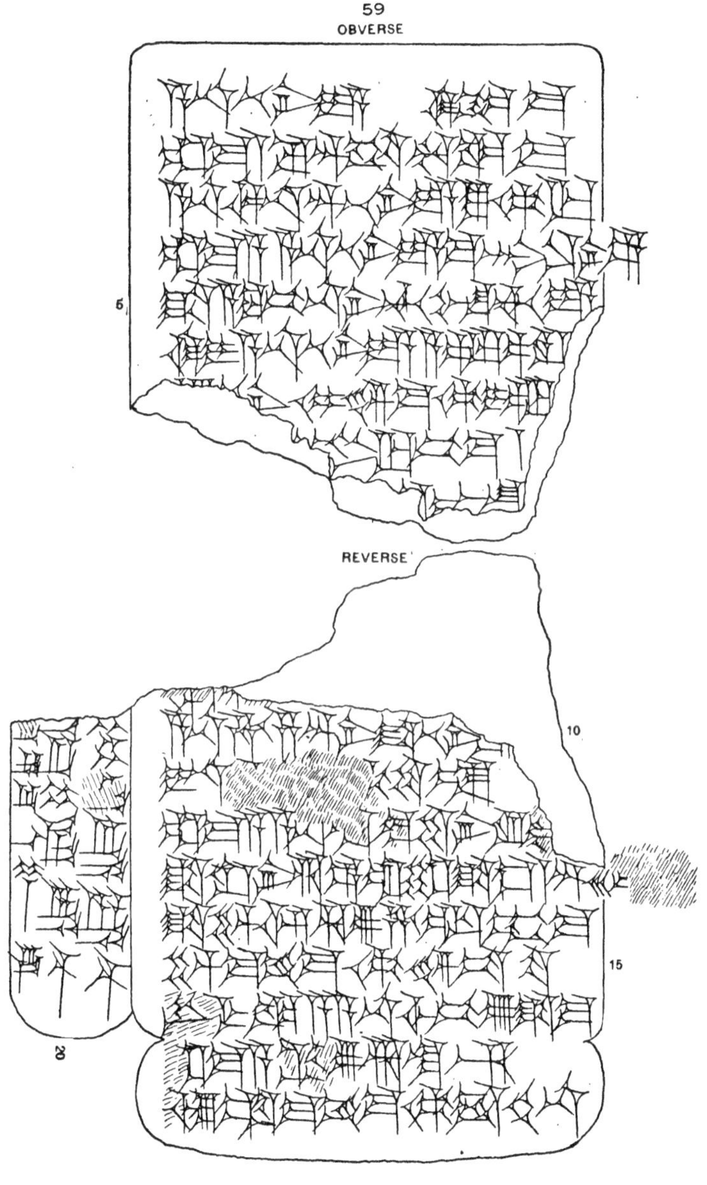

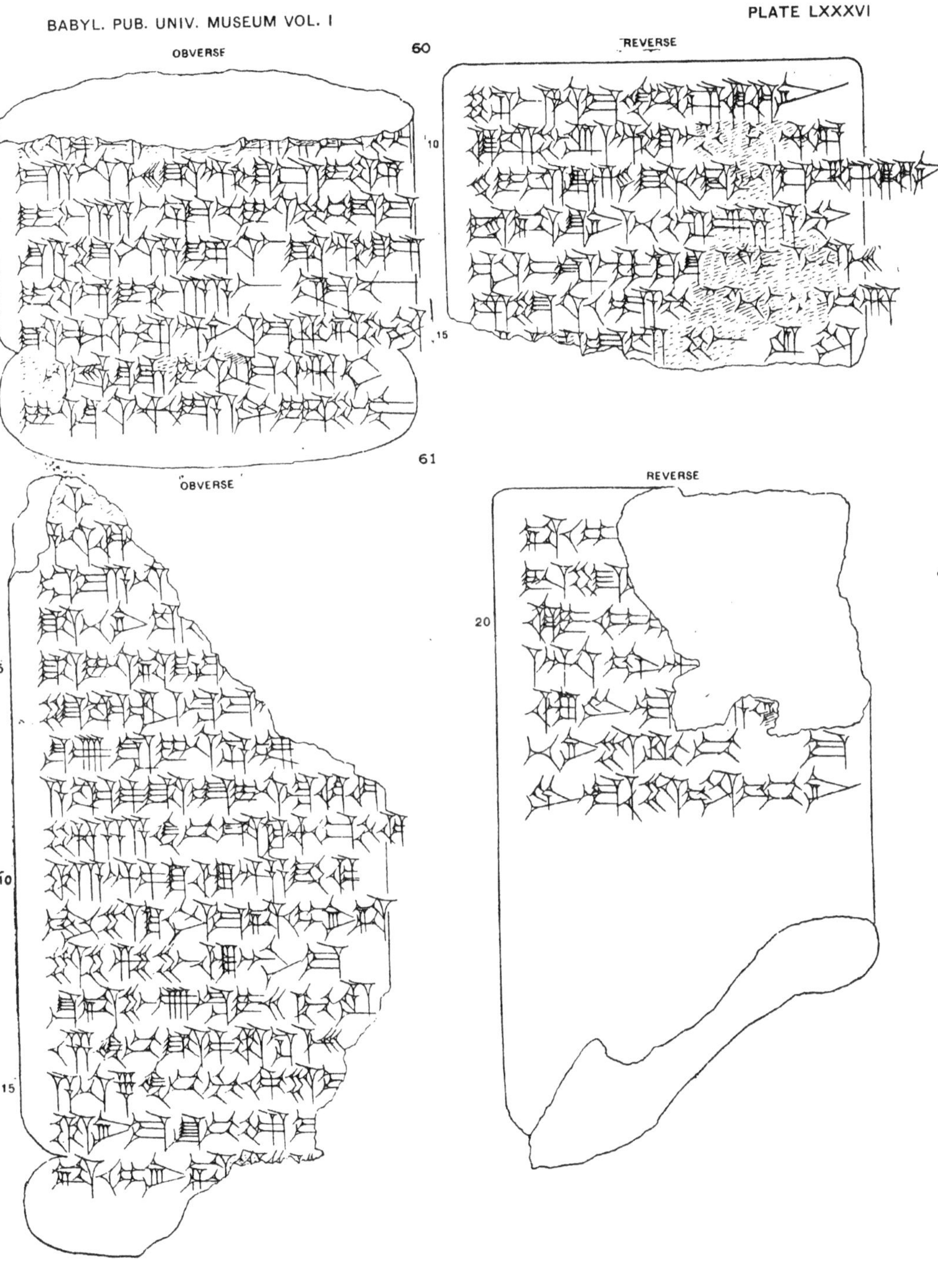
60
OBVERSE
REVERSE
61
OBVERSE
REVERSE

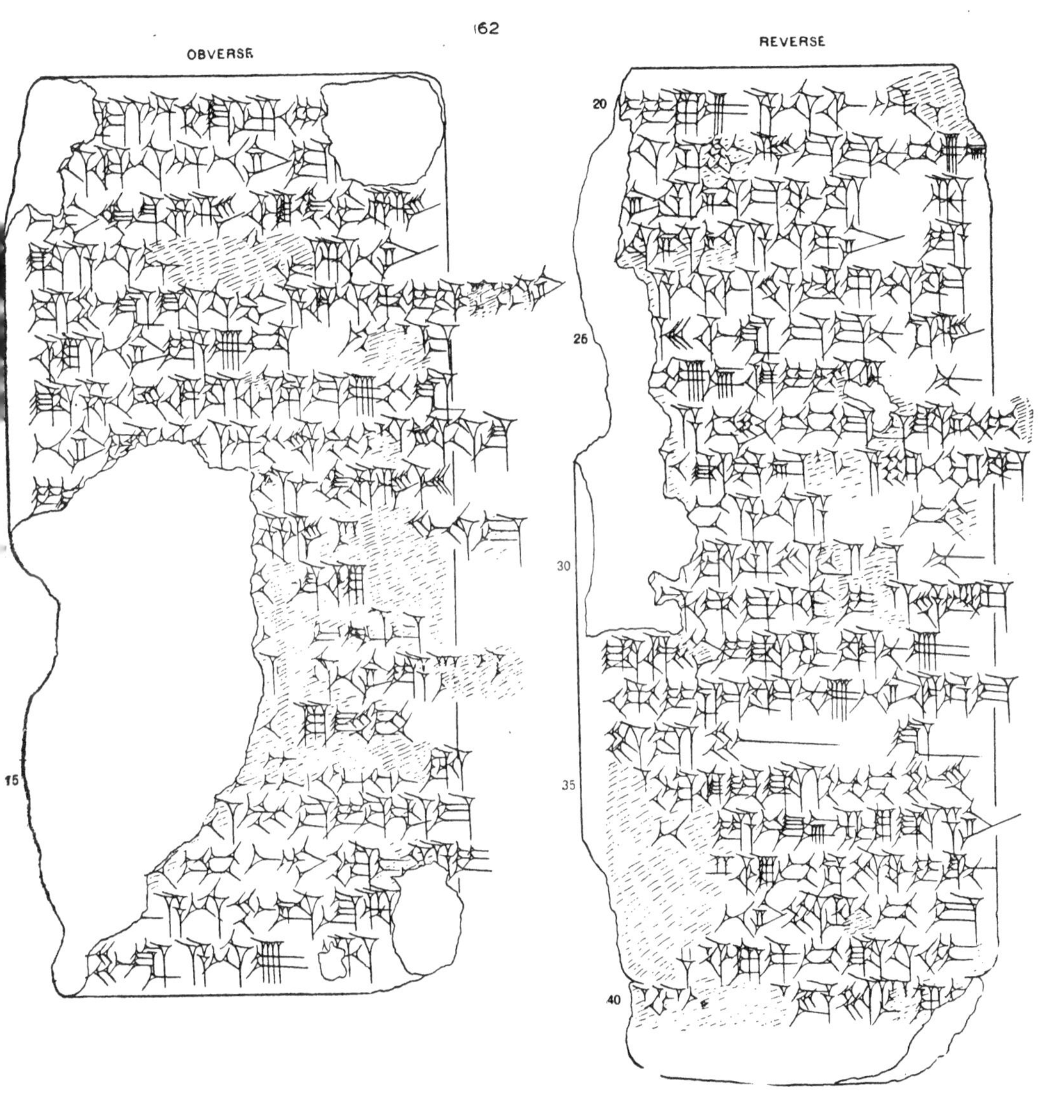
162
OBVERSE
REVERSE

63

OBVERSE

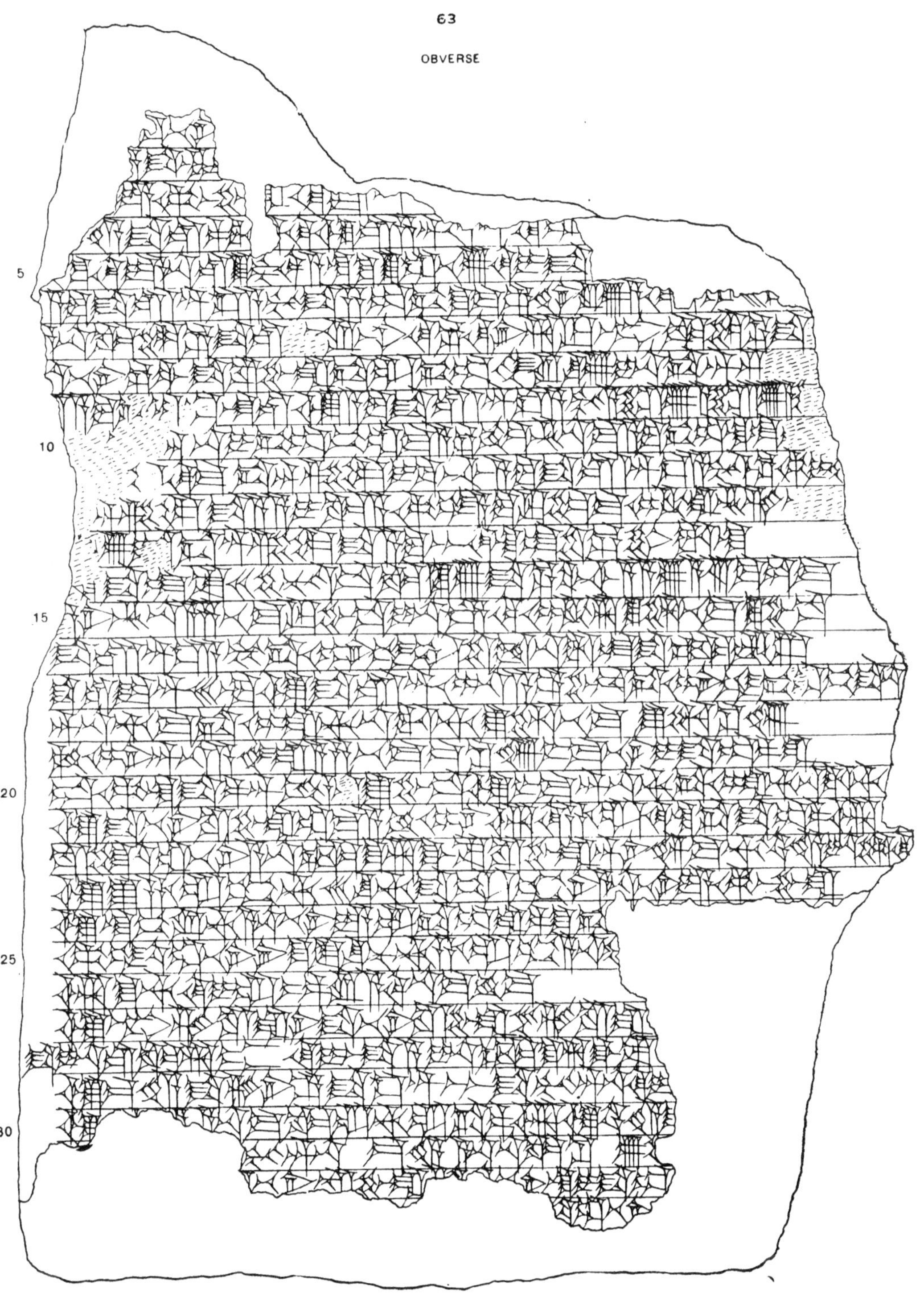

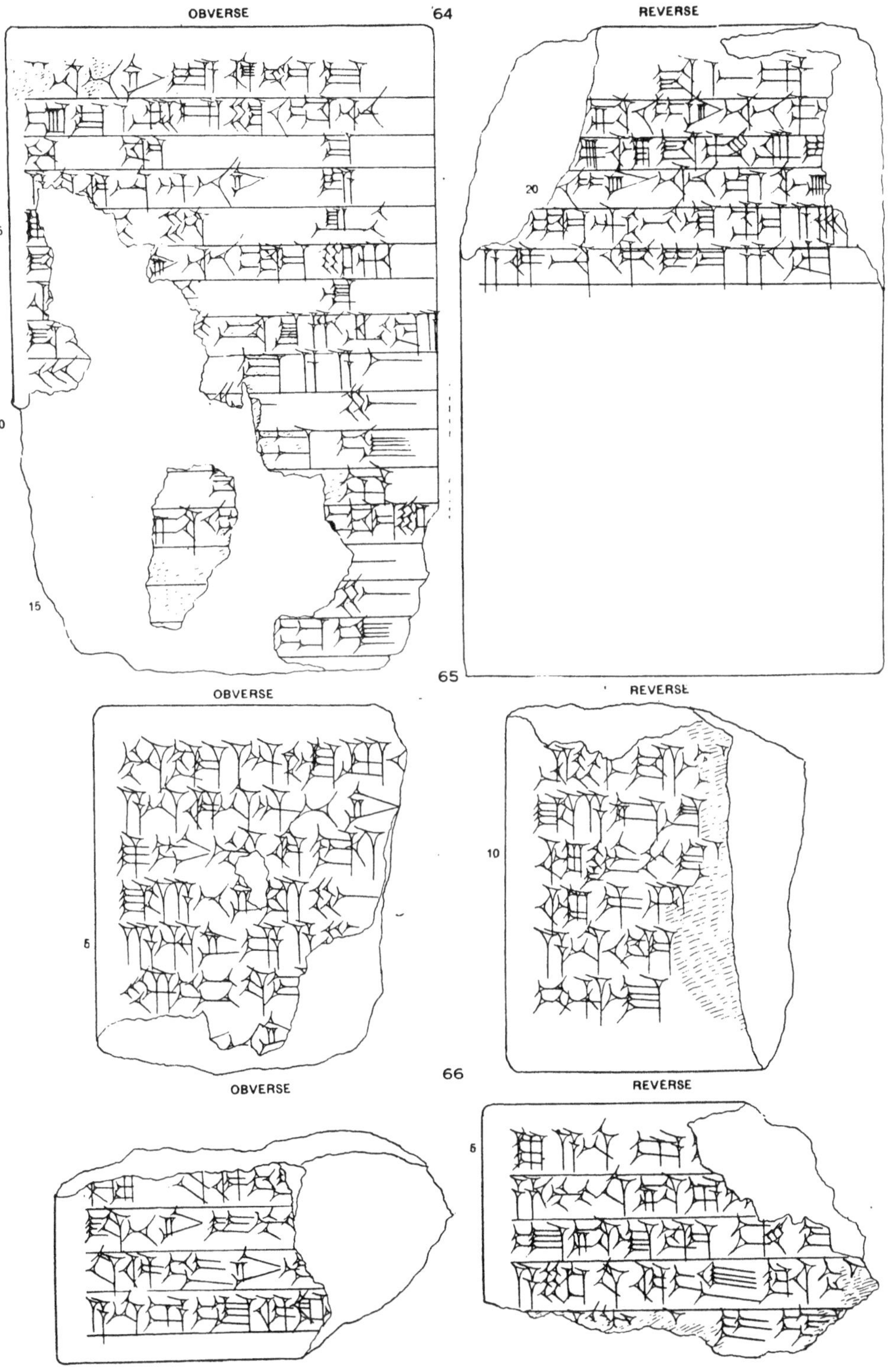
64
OBVERSE
REVERSE
65
OBVERSE
REVERSE
66
OBVERSE
REVERSE

67

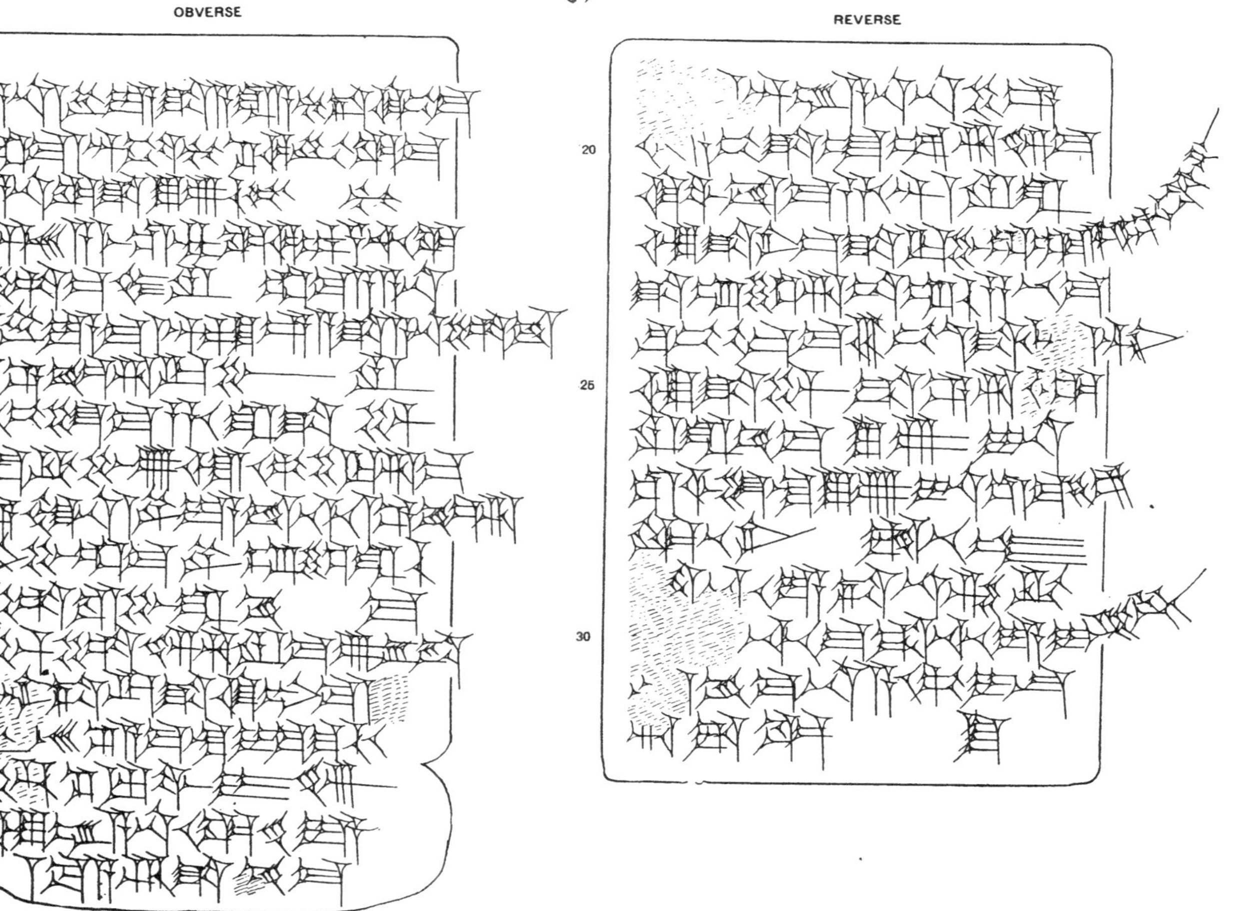

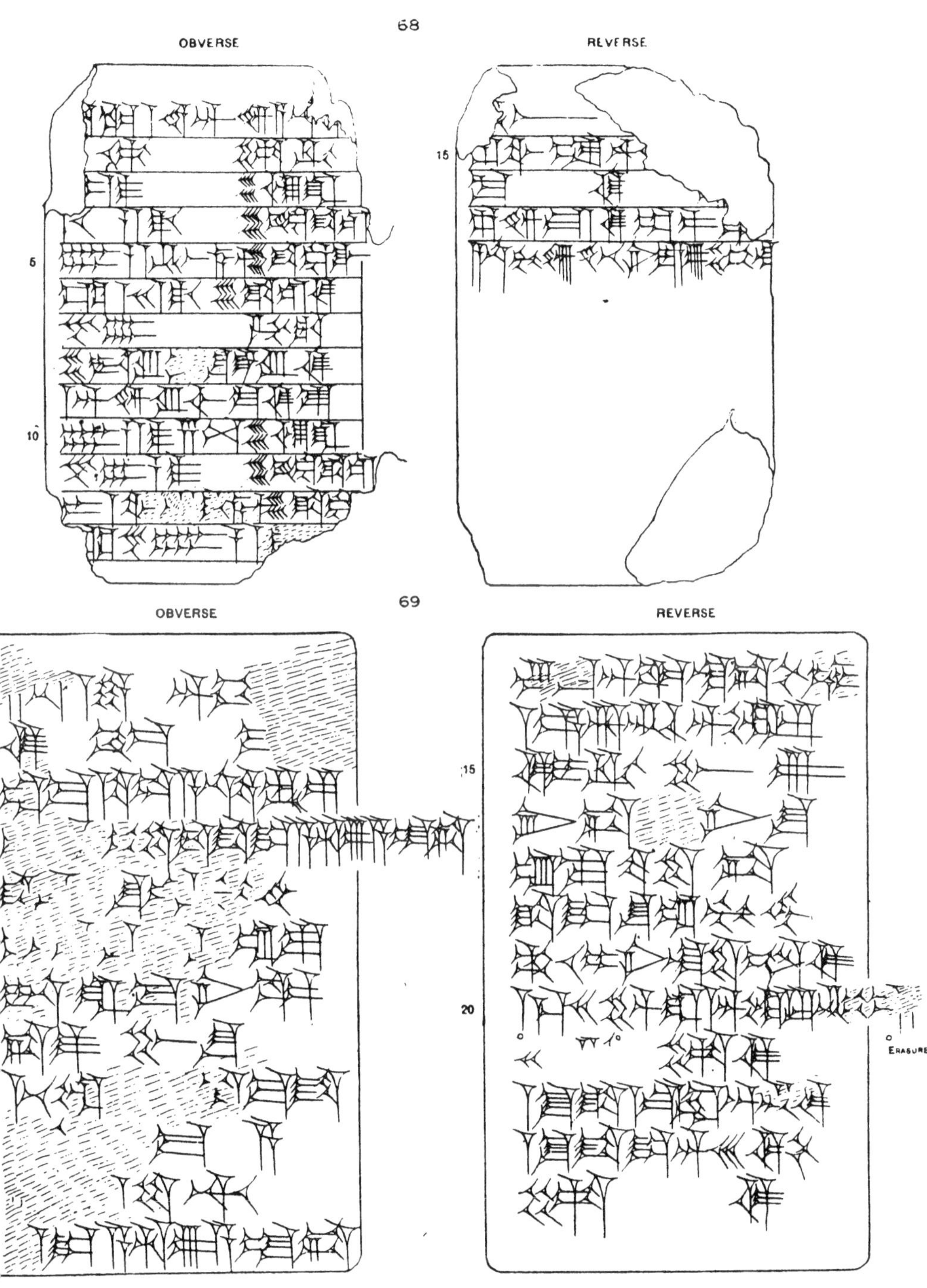
68
OBVERSE
REVERSE
69
OBVERSE
REVERSE
ERASURE

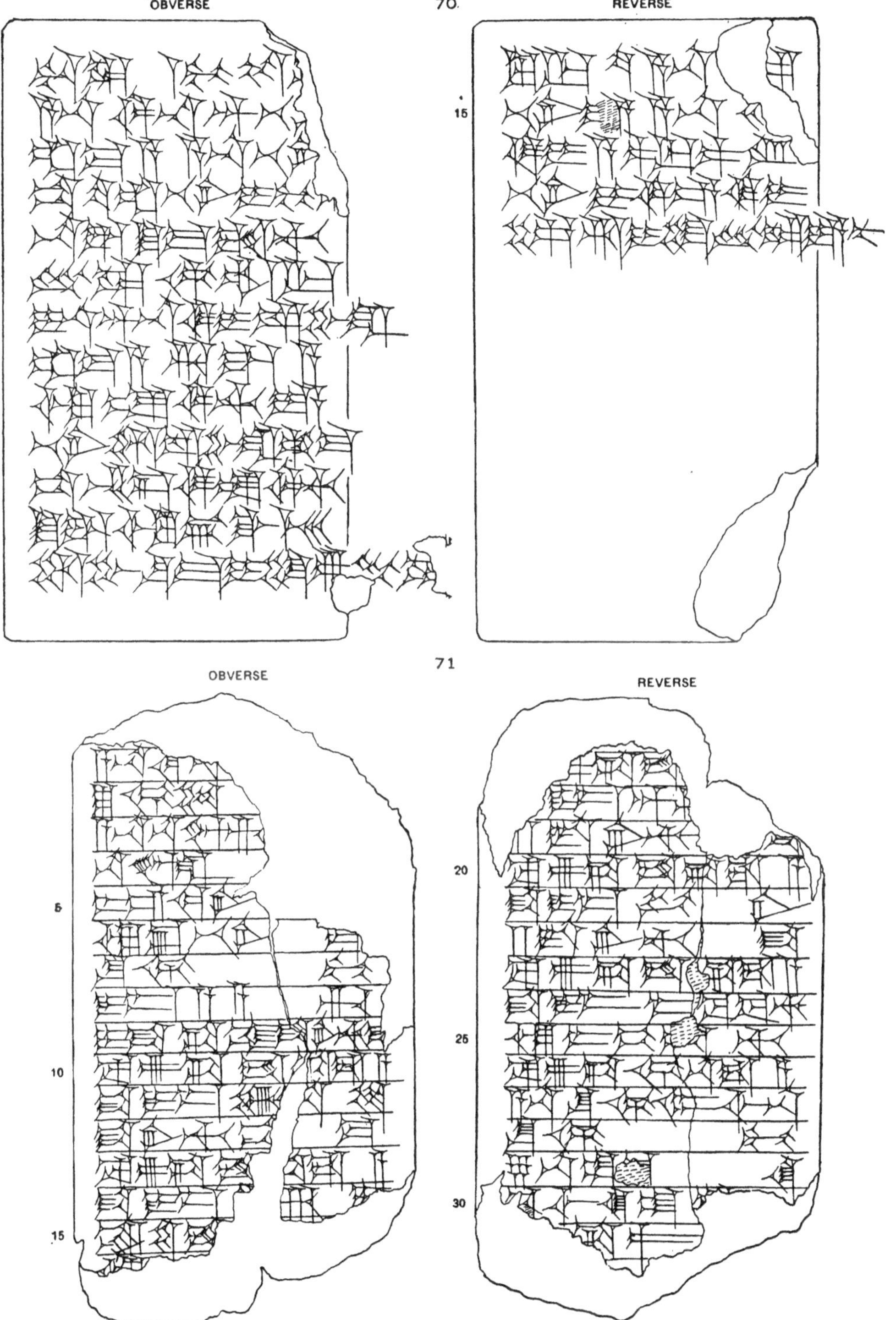
70.
OBVERSE
REVERSE
71
OBVERSE
REVERSE

72

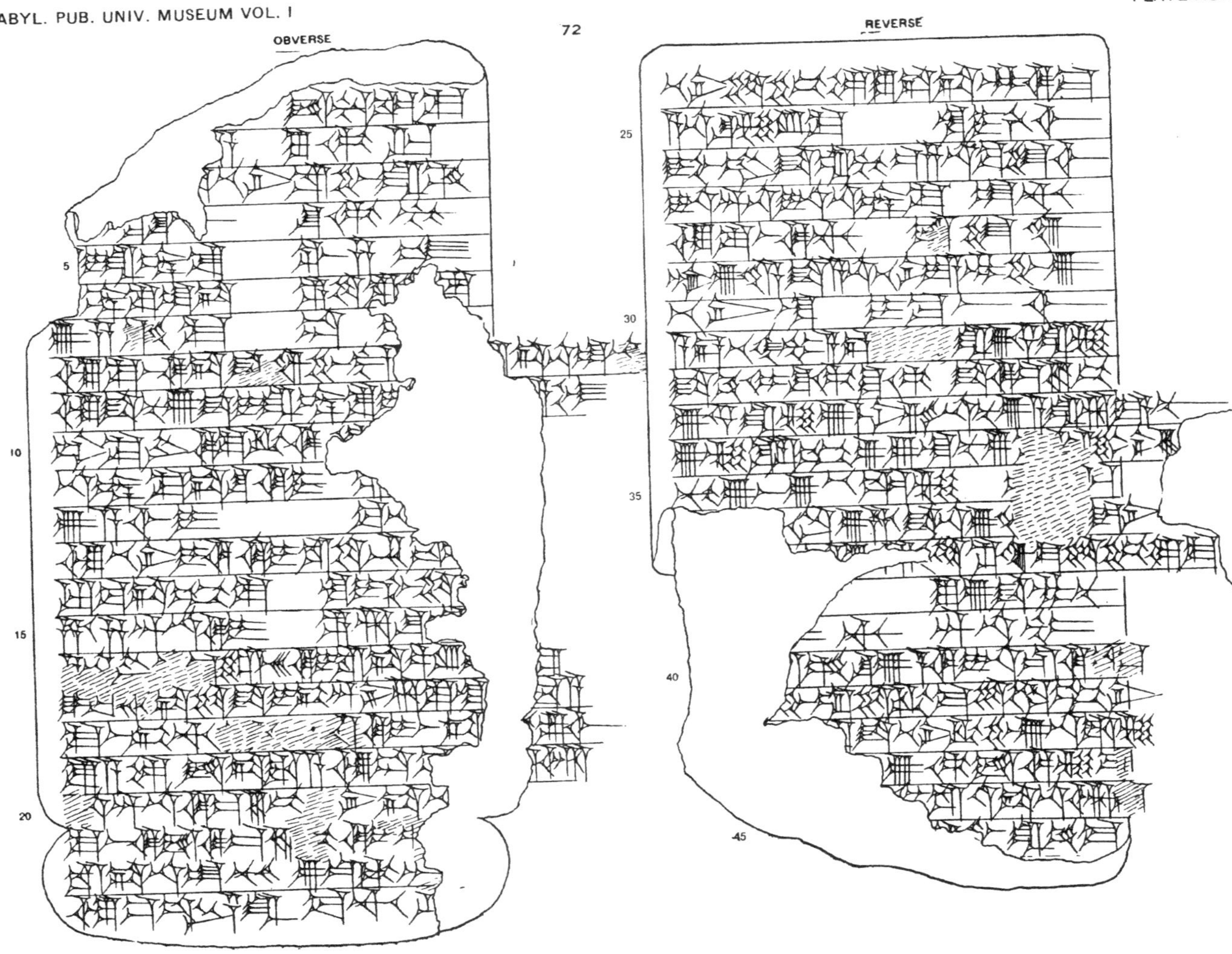

73

OBVERSE

REVERSE

74

OBVERSE

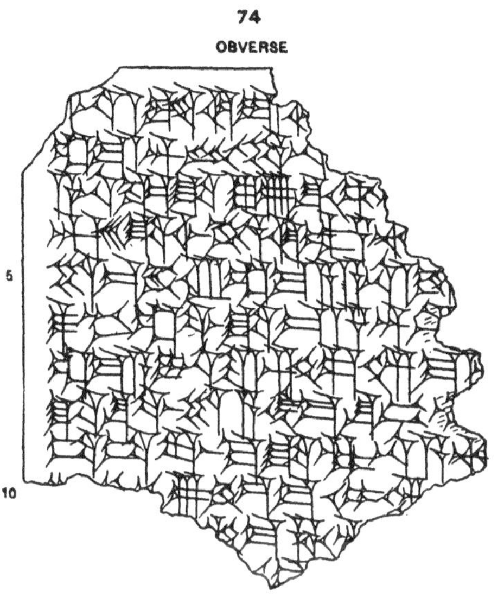

75

OBVERSE

REVERSE

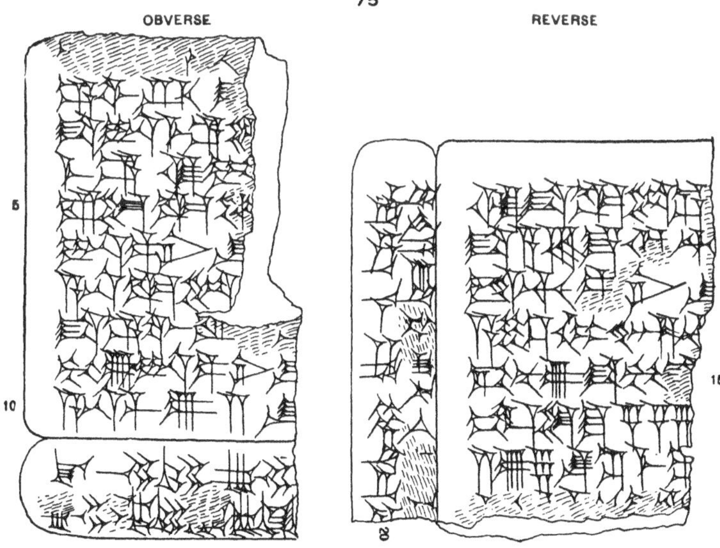

76

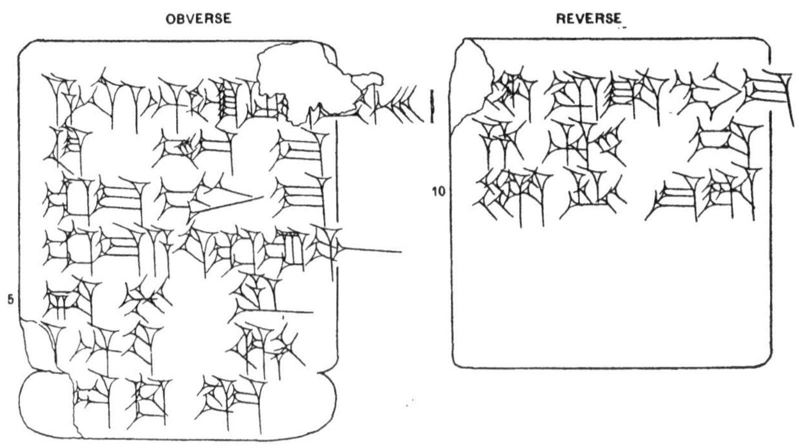

77

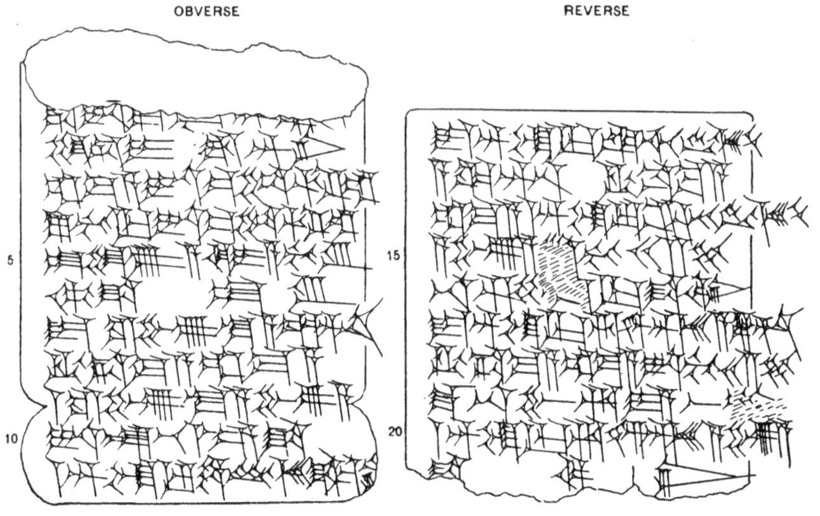

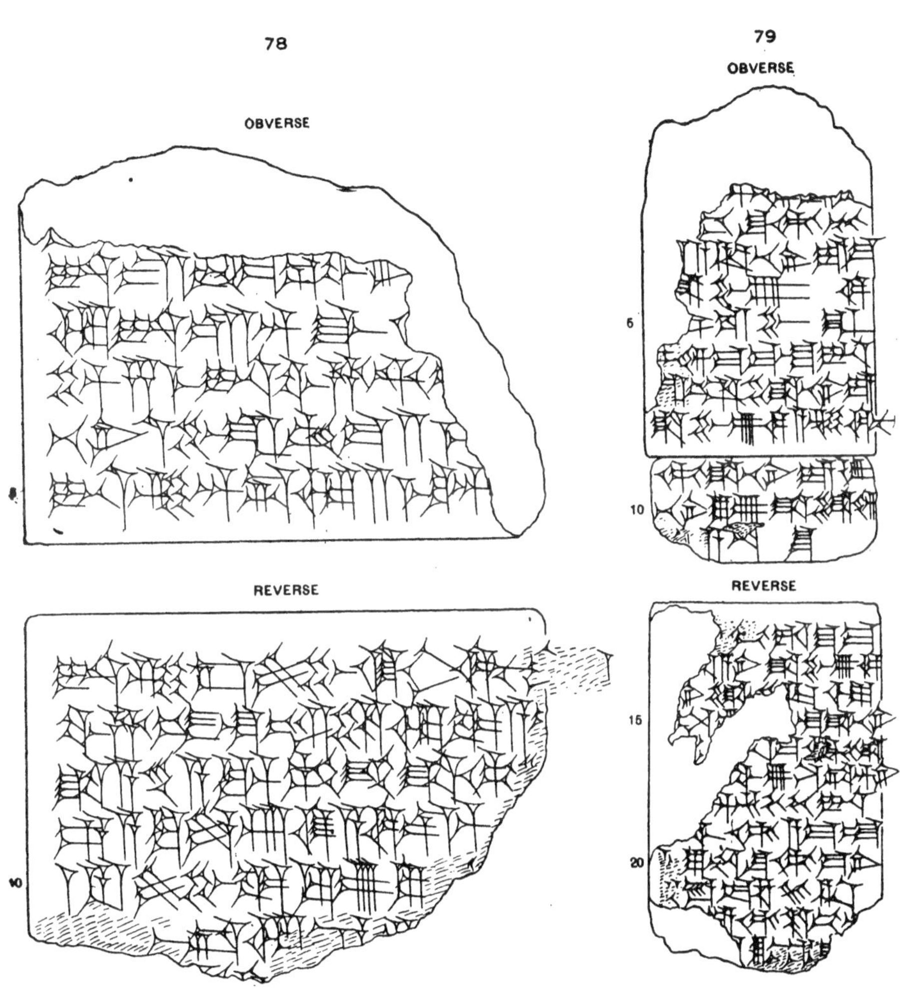
78
OBVERSE
REVERSE
79
OBVERSE
REVERSE

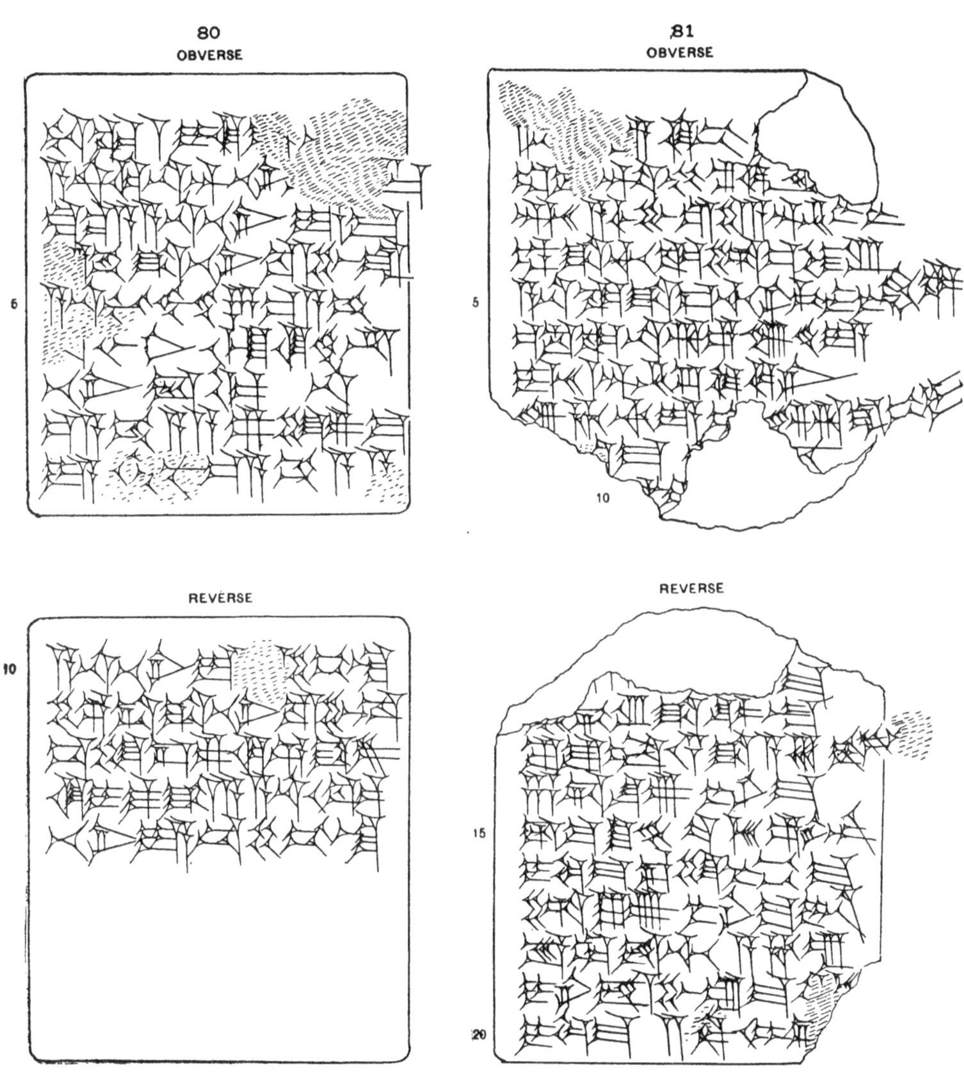
80
OBVERSE
81
OBVERSE
REVERSE
REVERSE

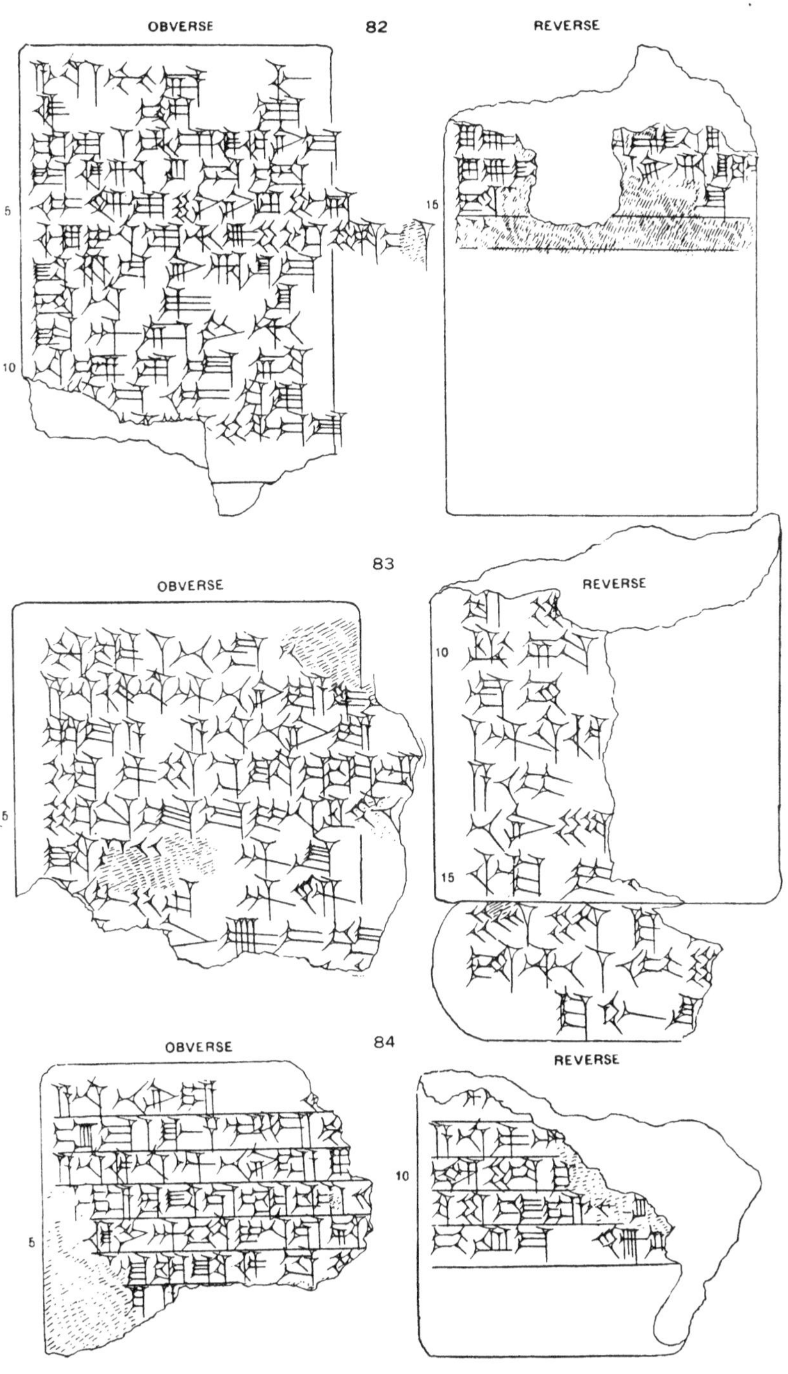
OBVERSE
82
REVERSE
83
OBVERSE
REVERSE
OBVERSE
84
REVERSE

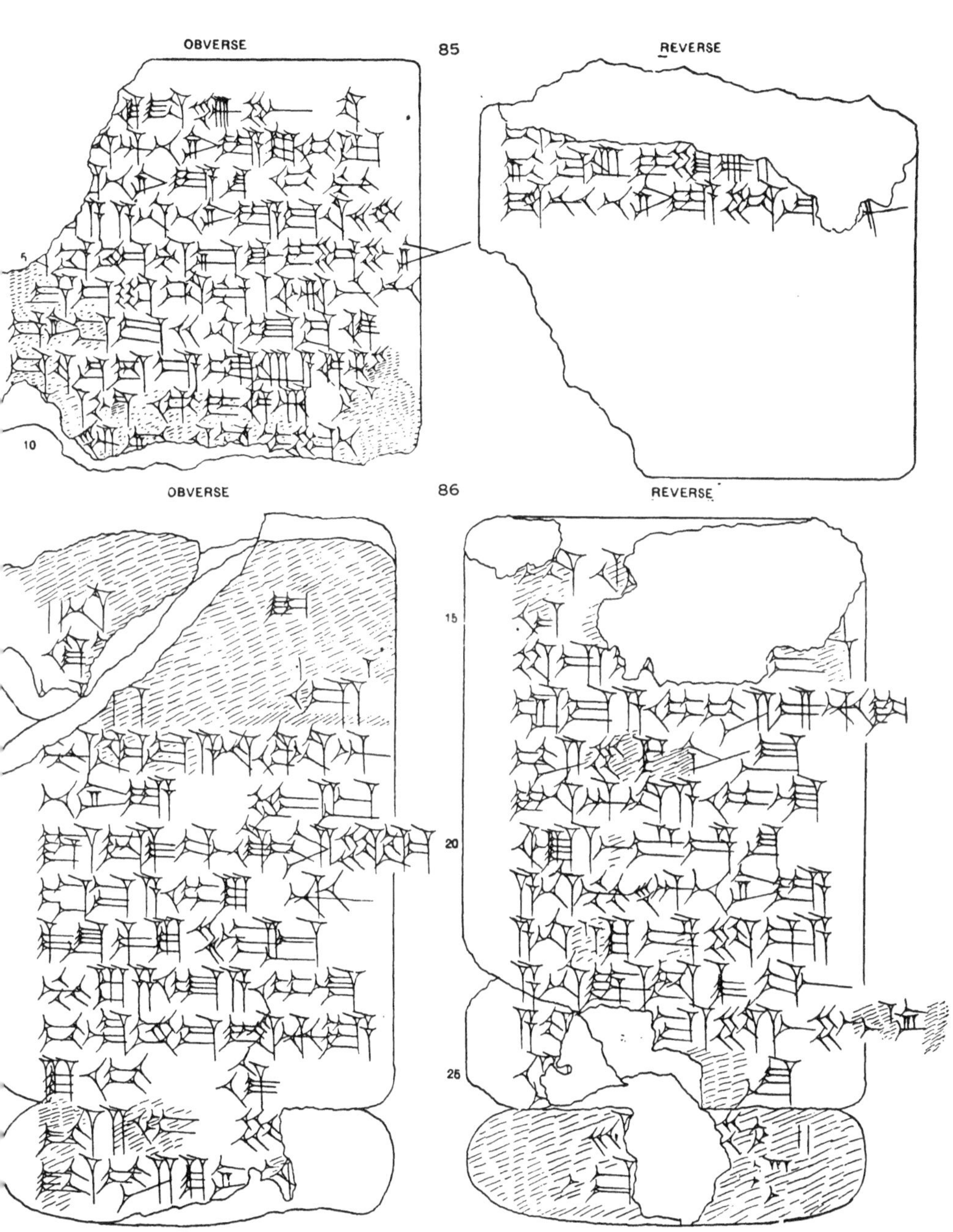
OBVERSE
85
REVERSE
OBVERSE
86
REVERSE

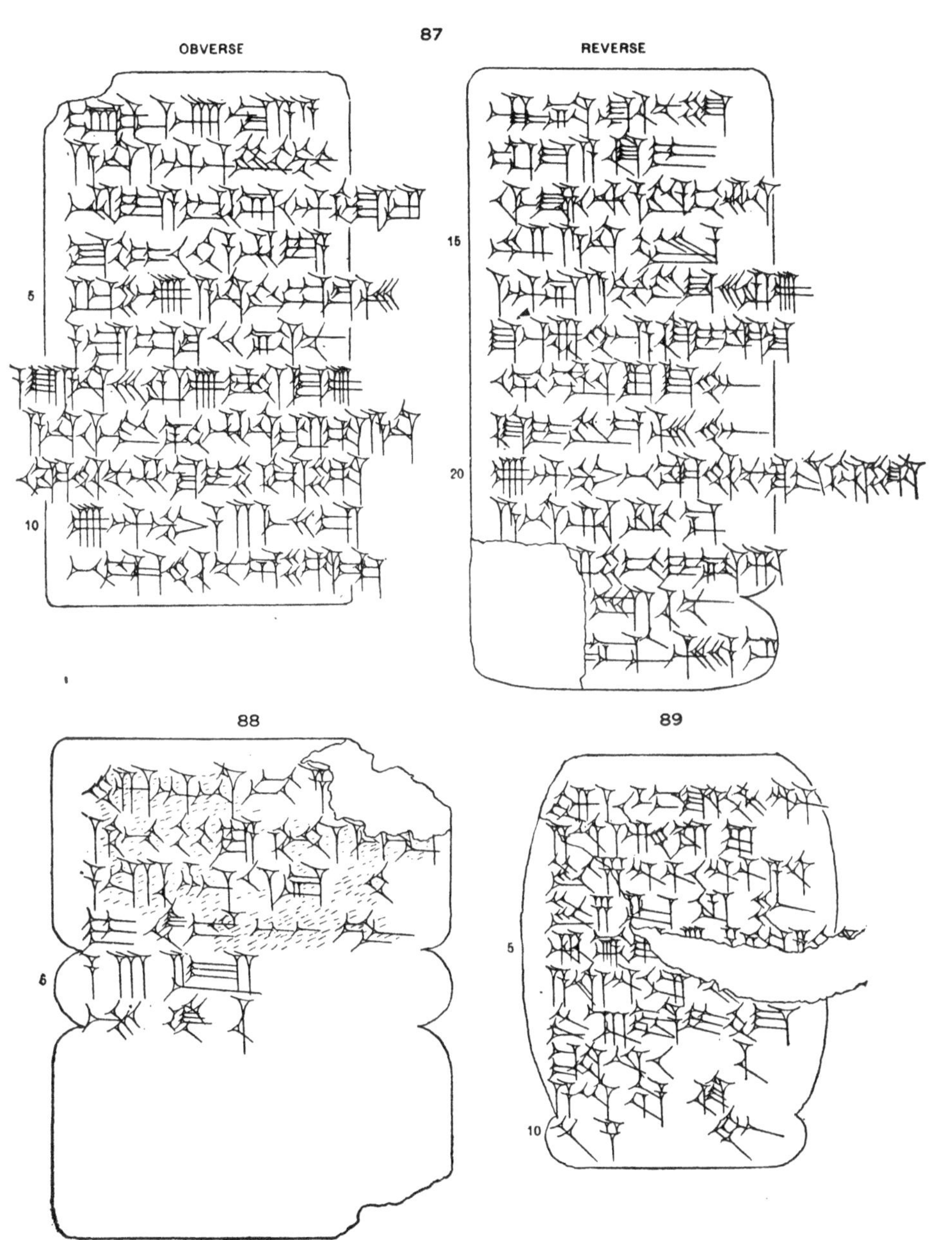
87
OBVERSE
REVERSE
88
89

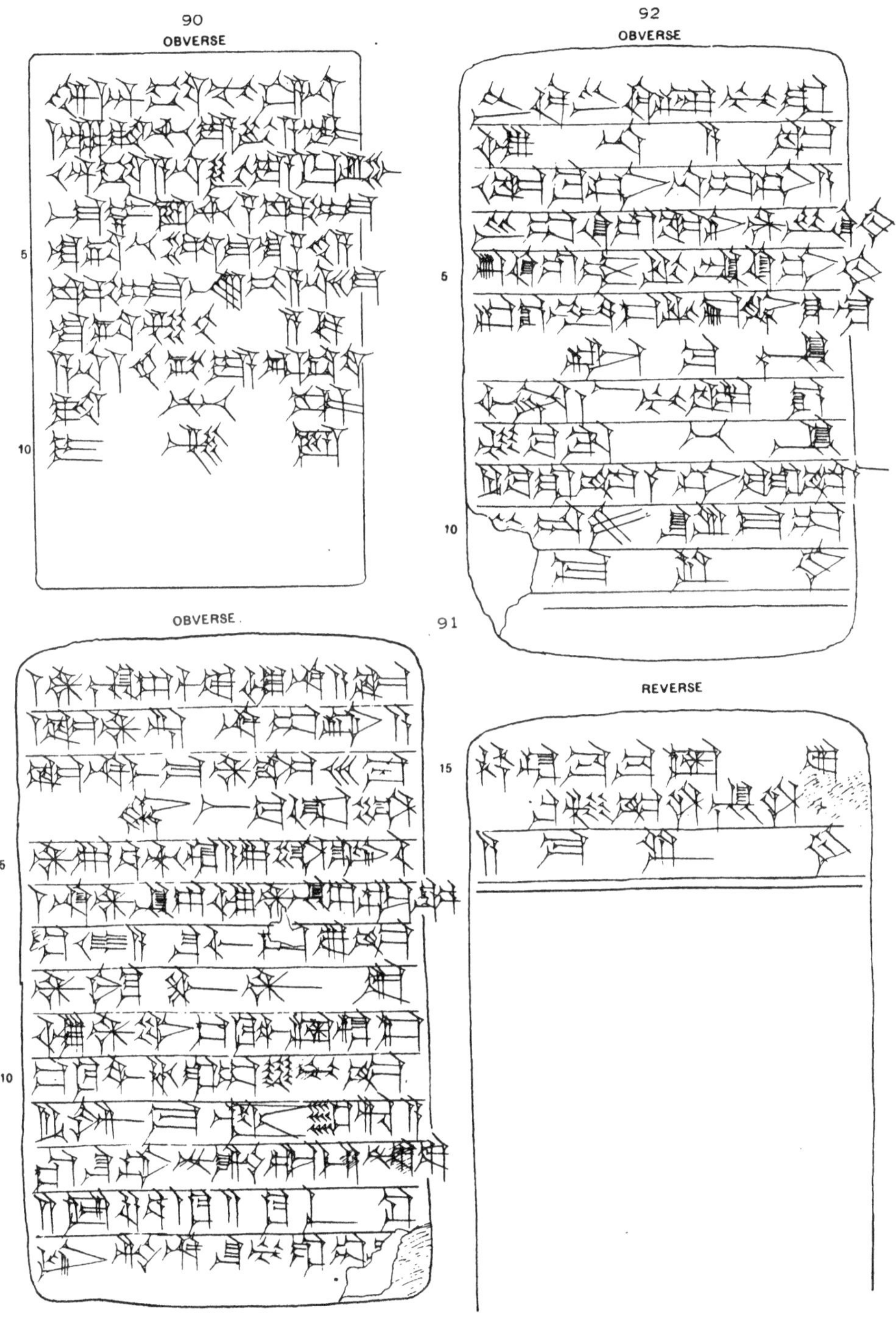
90
OBVERSE
92
OBVERSE
OBVERSE
91
REVERSE

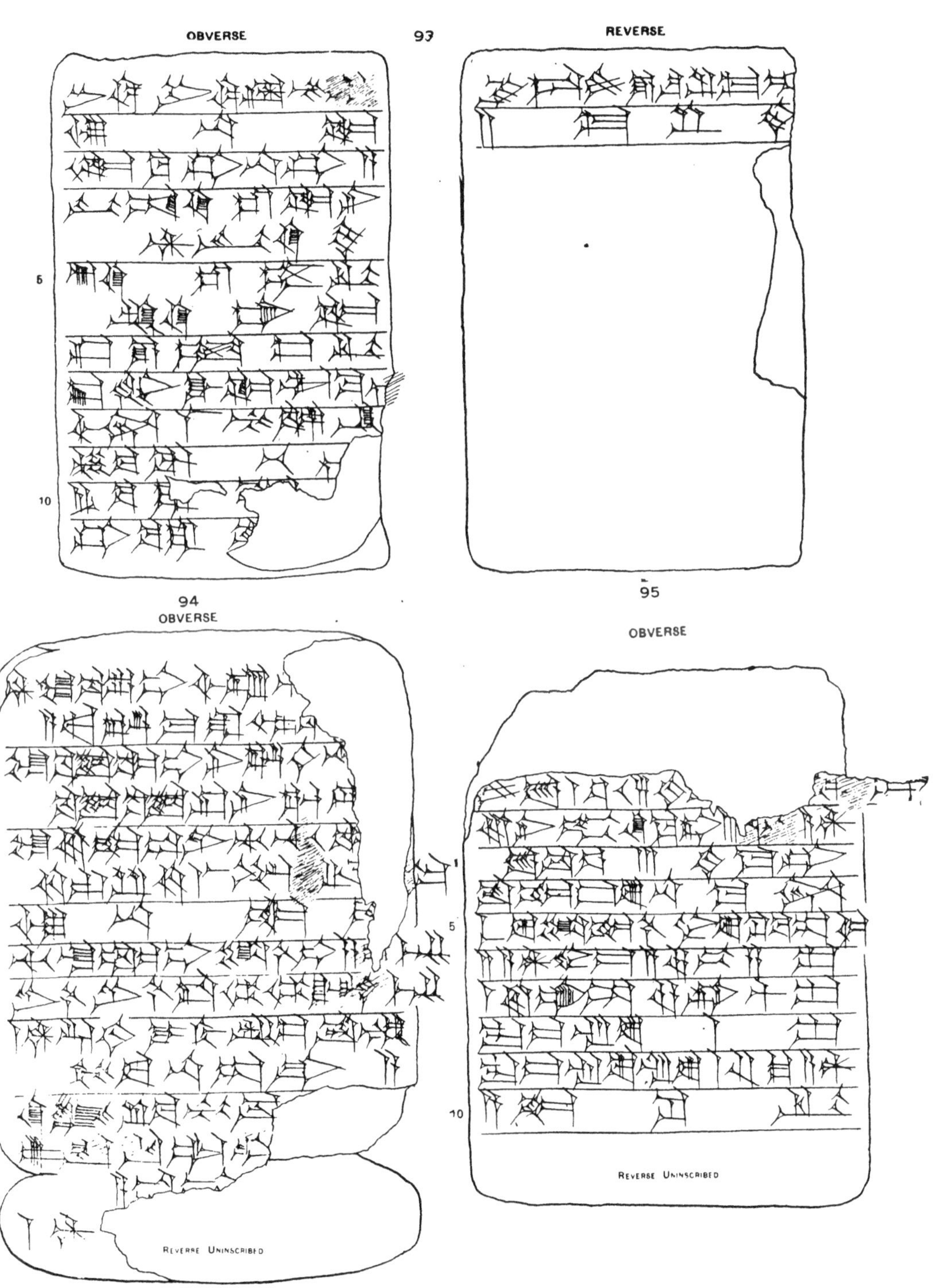
93
OBVERSE
REVERSE
94
OBVERSE
REVERSE UNINSCRIBED
95
OBVERSE
REVERSE UNINSCRIBED

96

OBVERSE

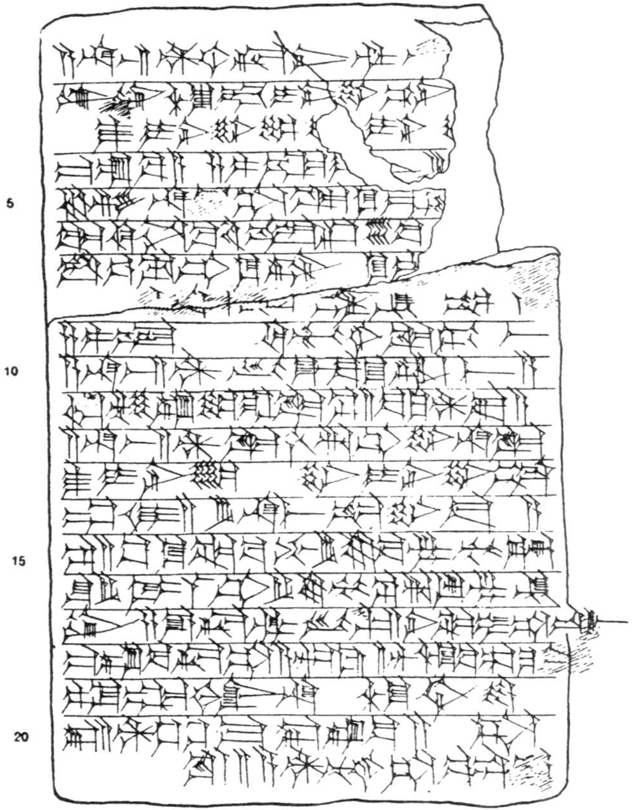

Rest Nearly Destroyed

97

OBVERSE

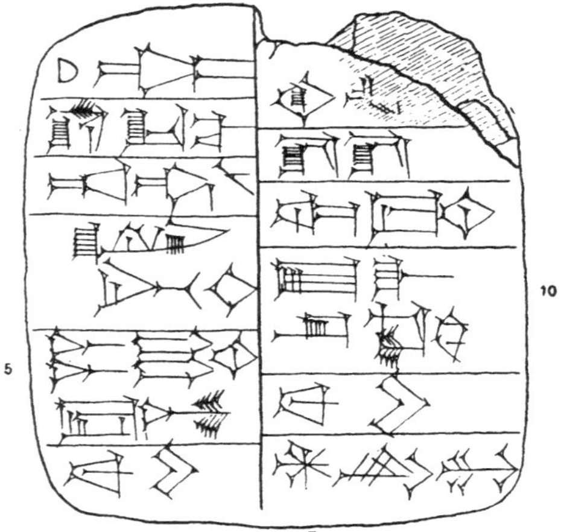

REVERSE

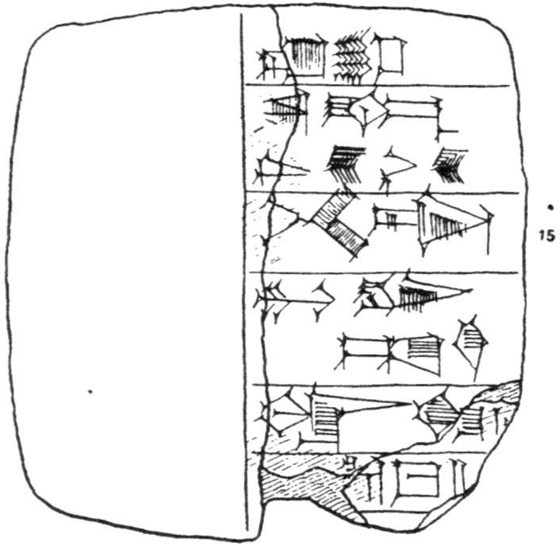

98

OBVERSE

REVERSE

99

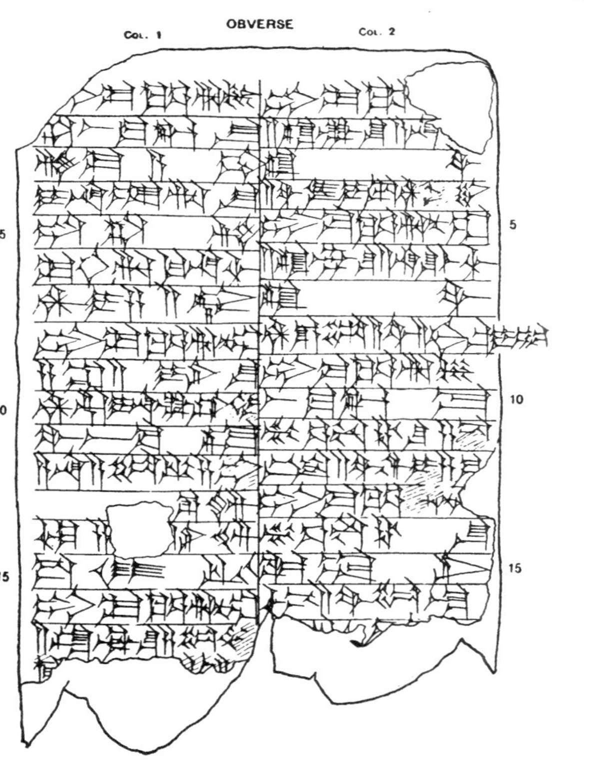

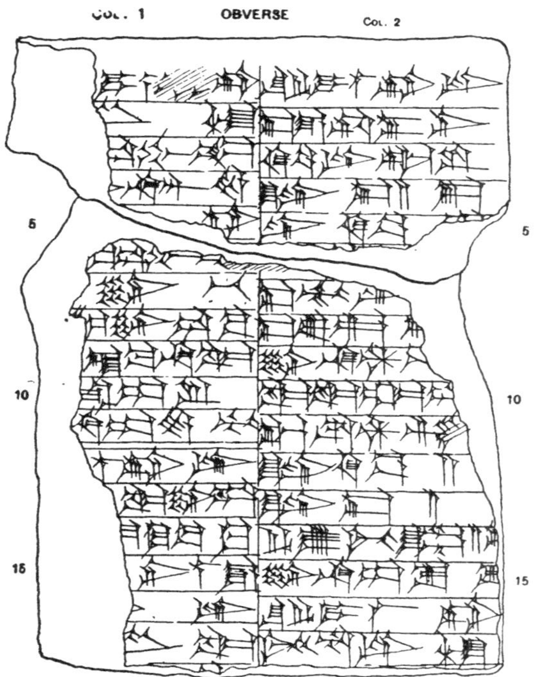
Col. 1
OBVERSE
Col. 2

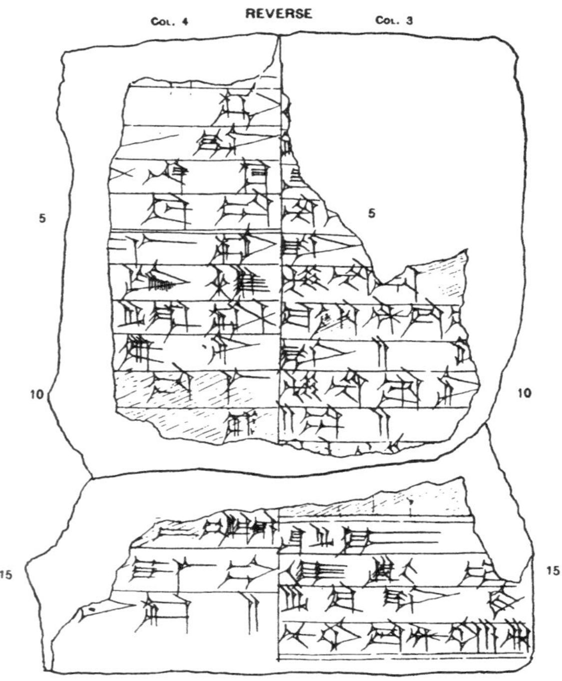
Col. 4
REVERSE
Col. 3

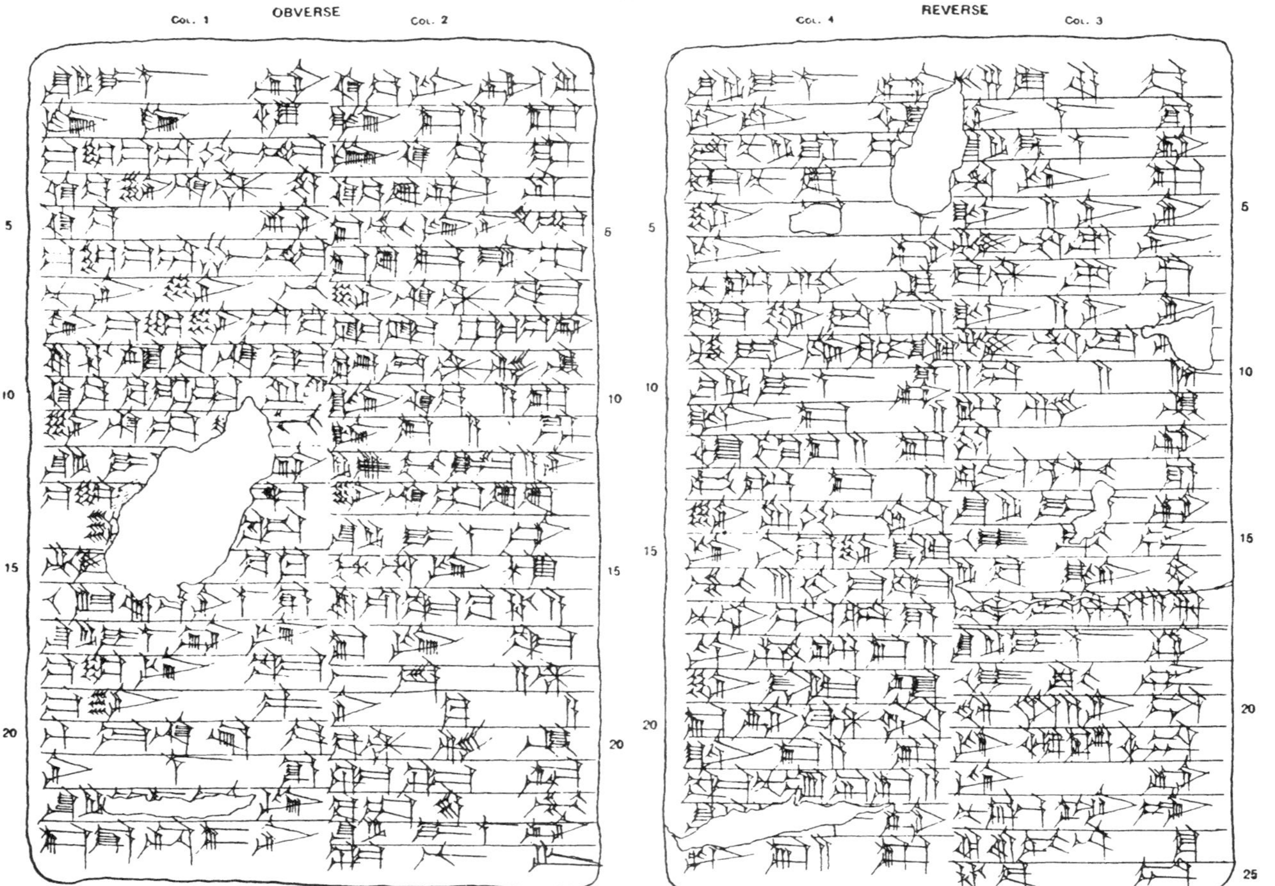
OBVERSE
Col. 1
Col. 2
REVERSE
Col. 4
Col. 3

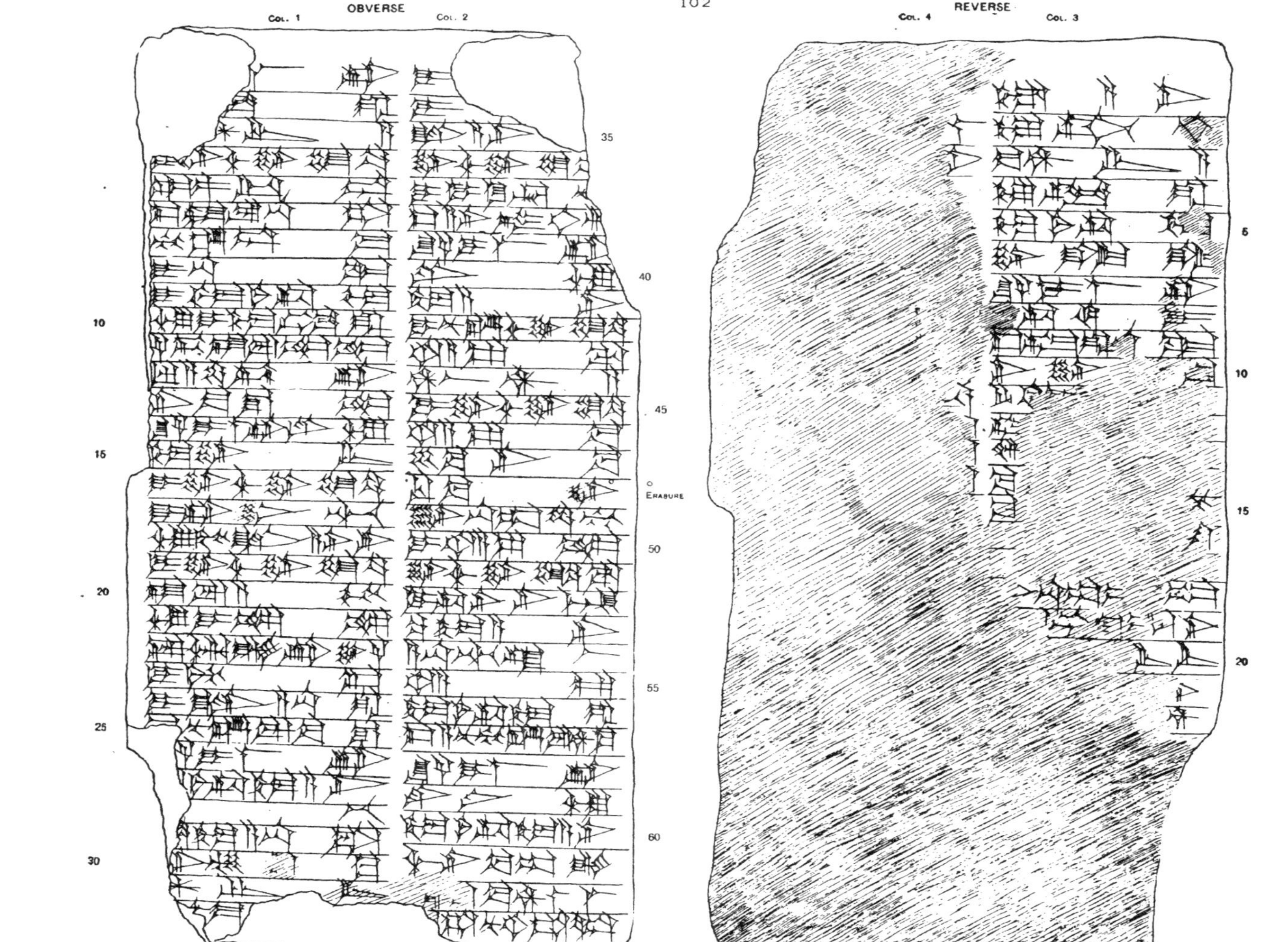
OBVERSE
Col. 1
Col. 2
Erasure
REVERSE
Col. 4
Col. 3

103

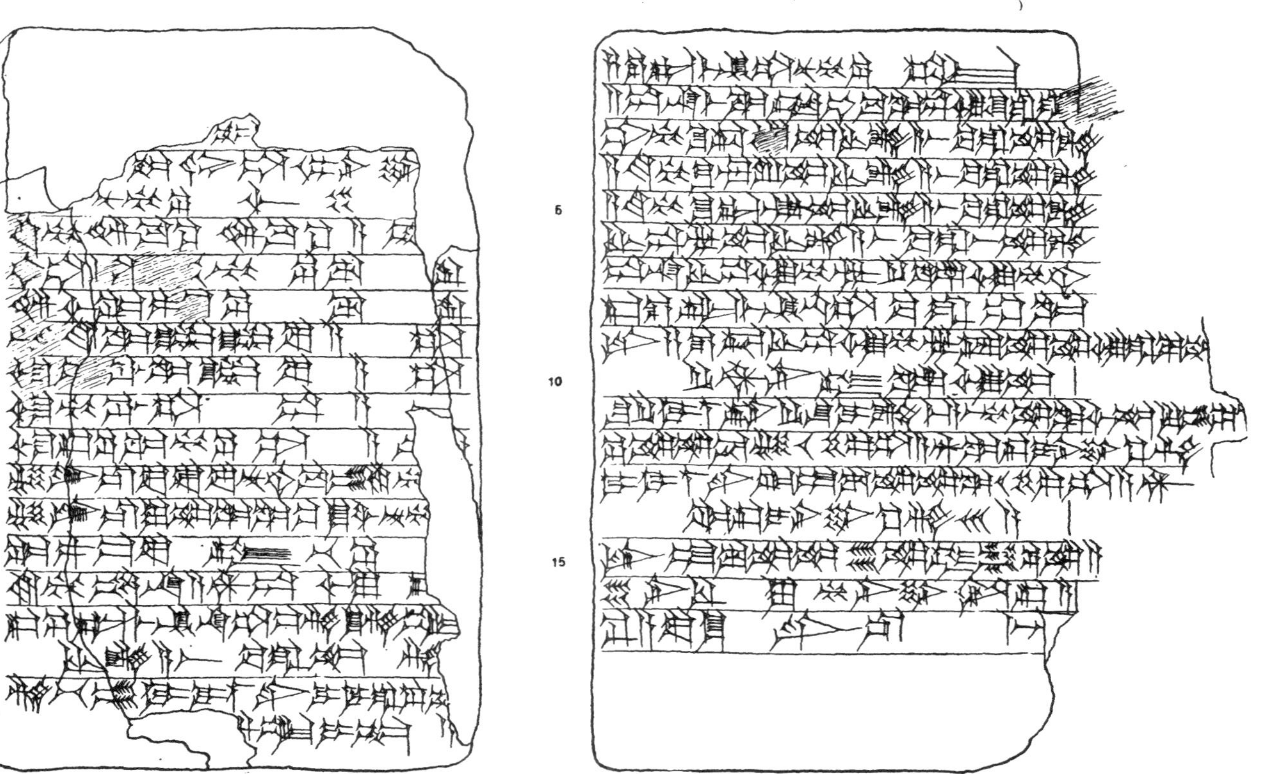

104

OBVERSE

REVERSE

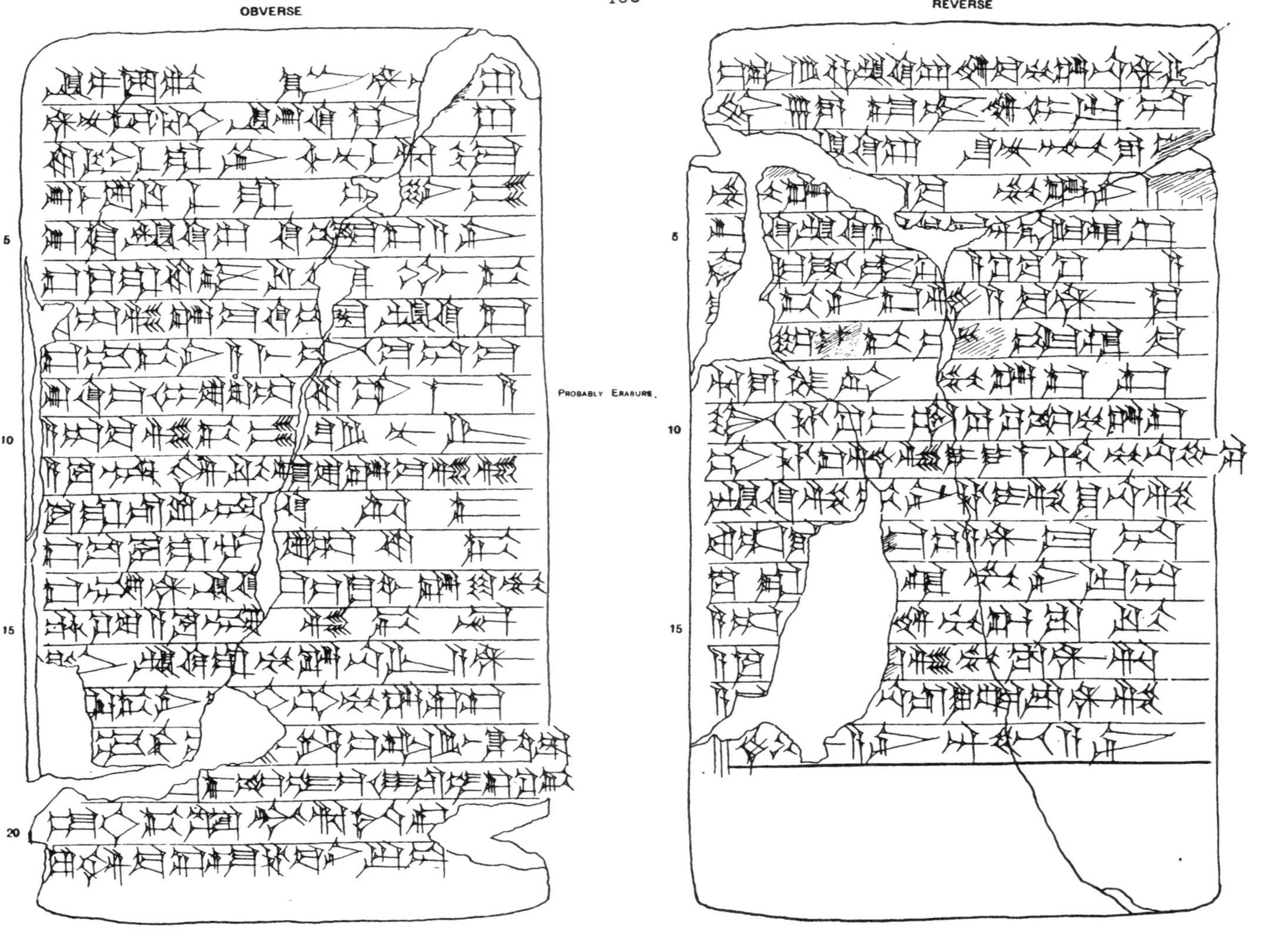
OBVERSE
REVERSE
Probably Erasure.

106

OBVERSE

REVERSE

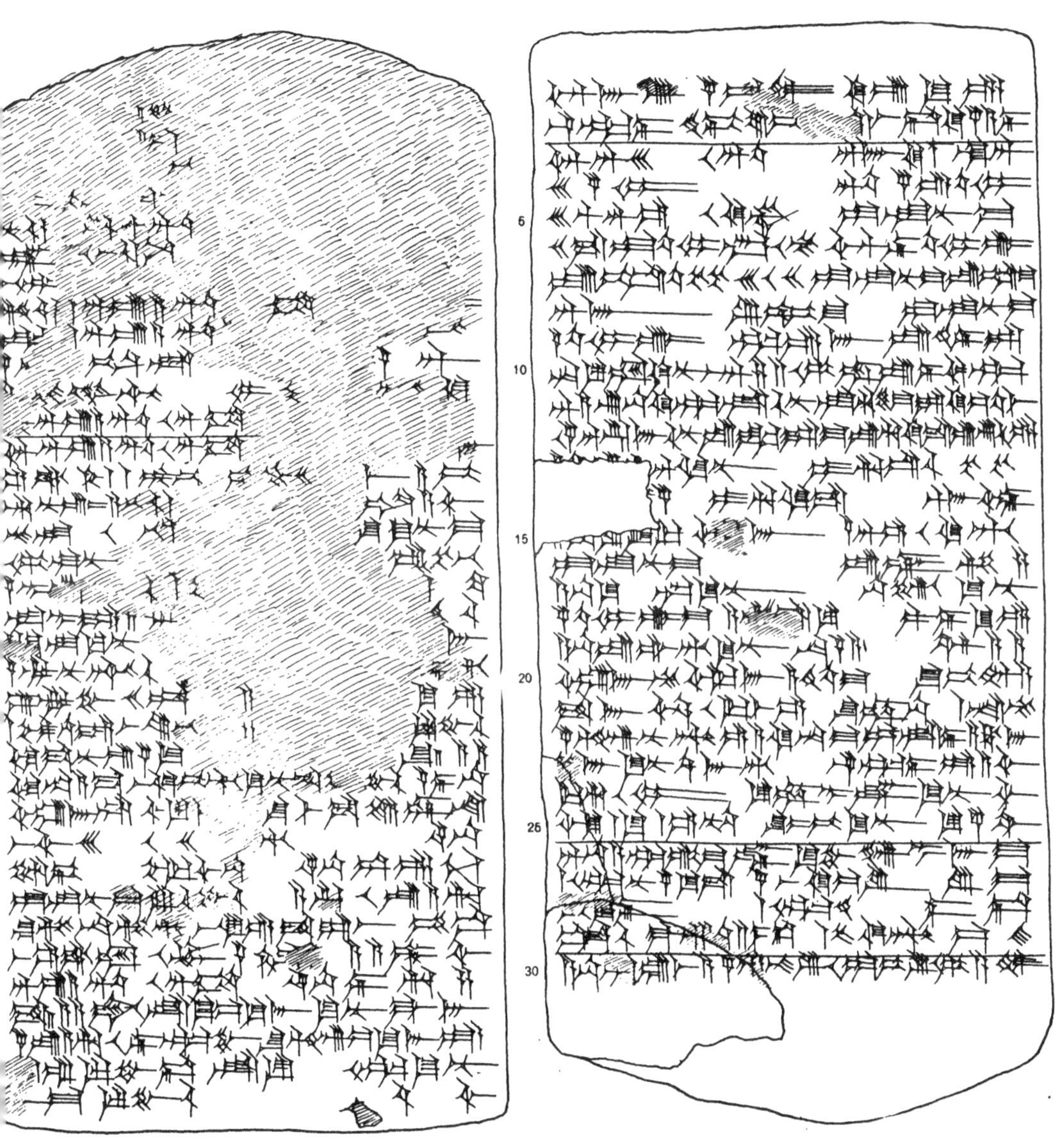

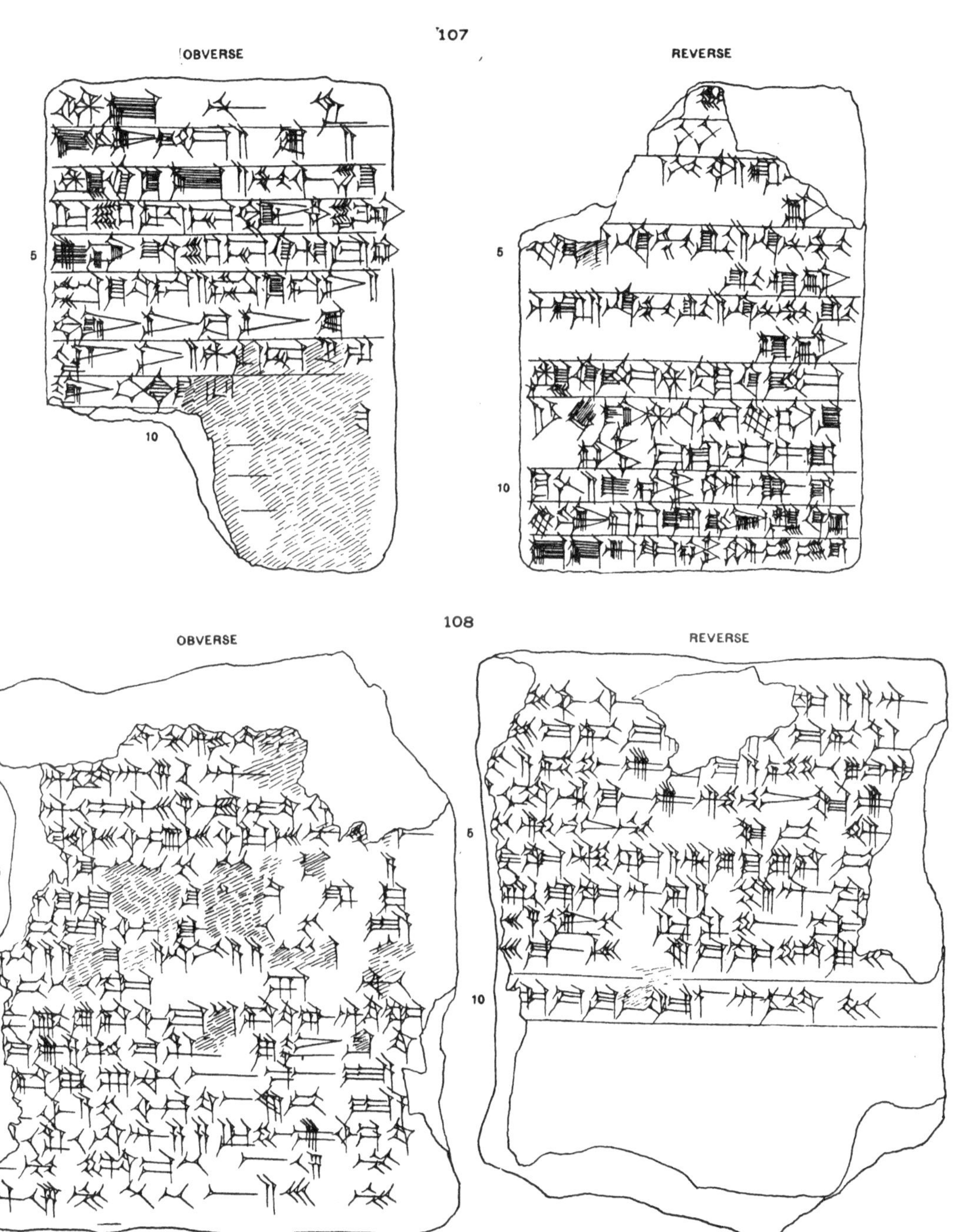
107
OBVERSE
REVERSE
108
OBVERSE
REVERSE

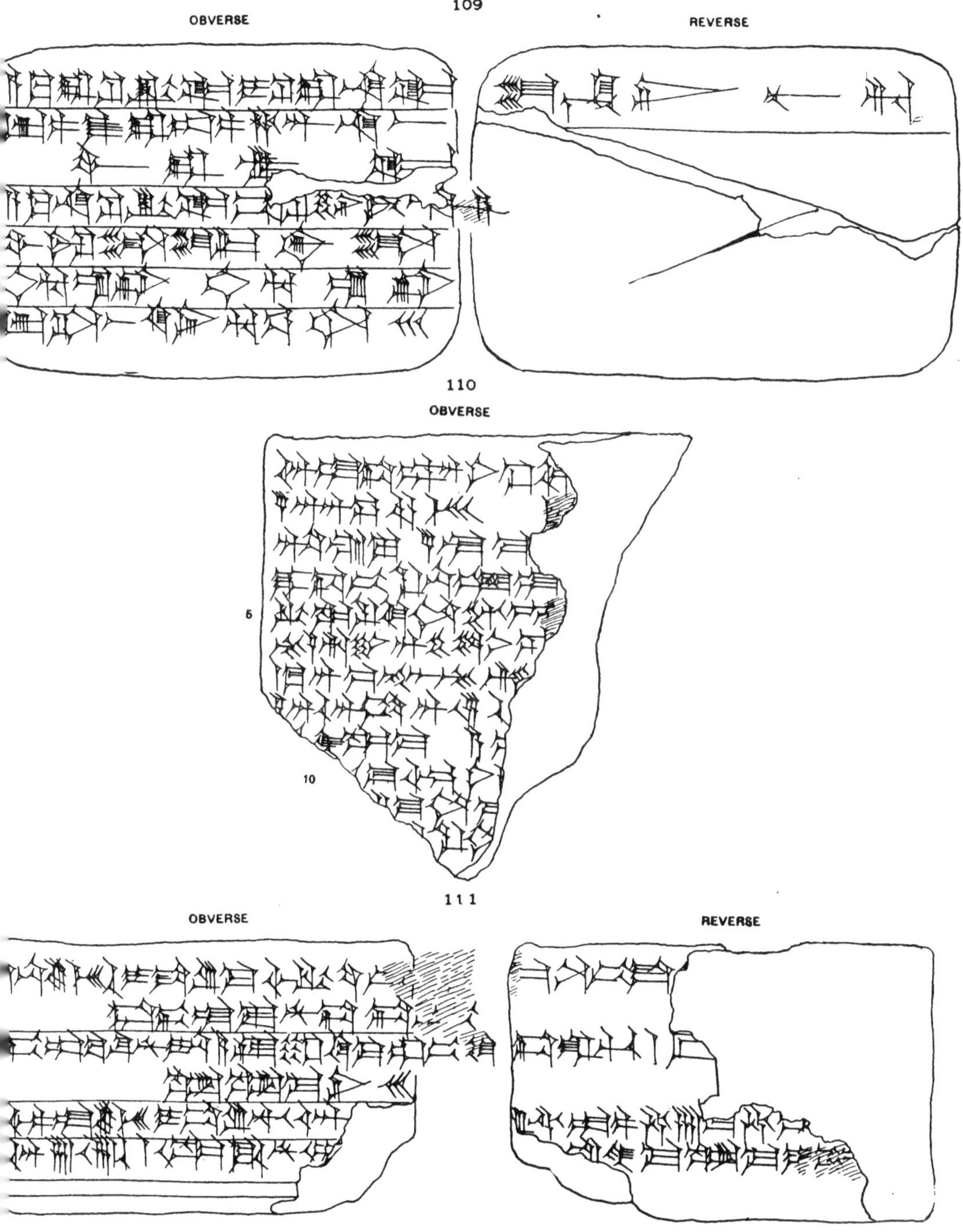
109
OBVERSE
REVERSE
110
OBVERSE
5
10
111
OBVERSE
REVERSE

112

OBVERSE

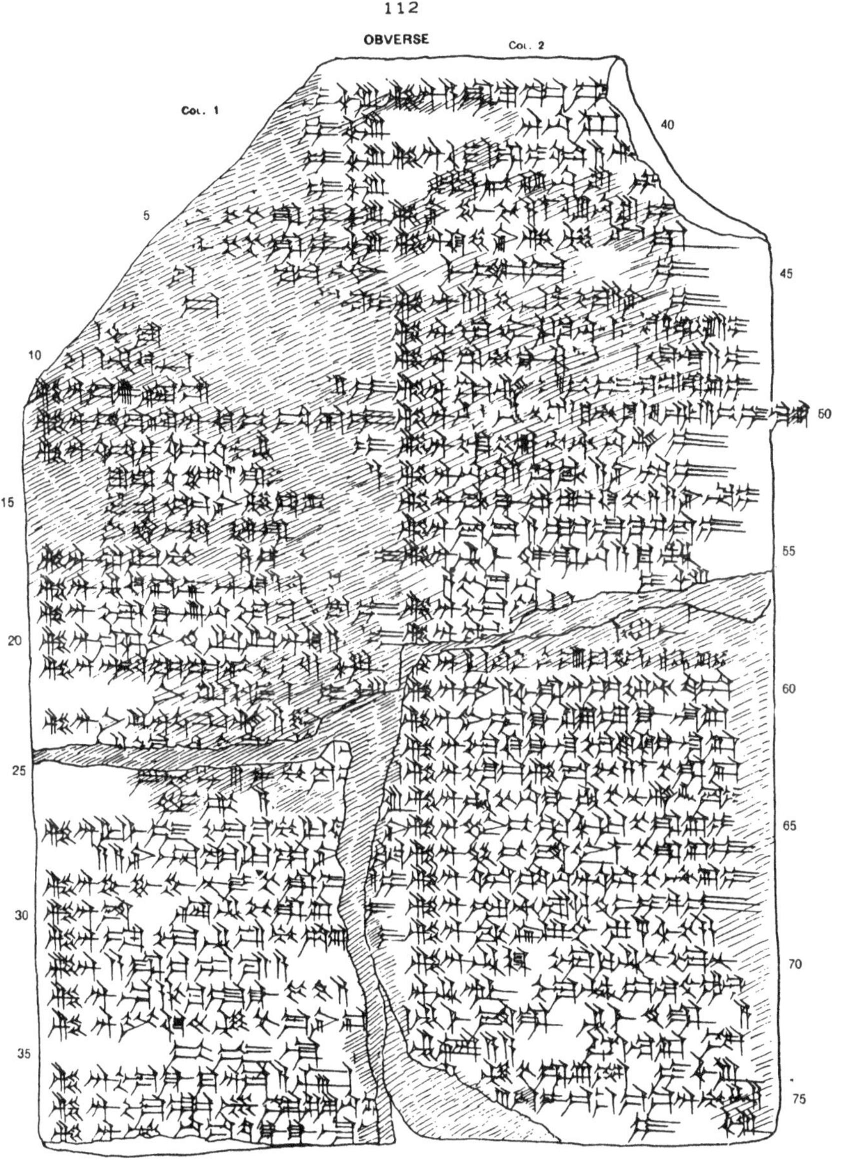

112

REVERSE

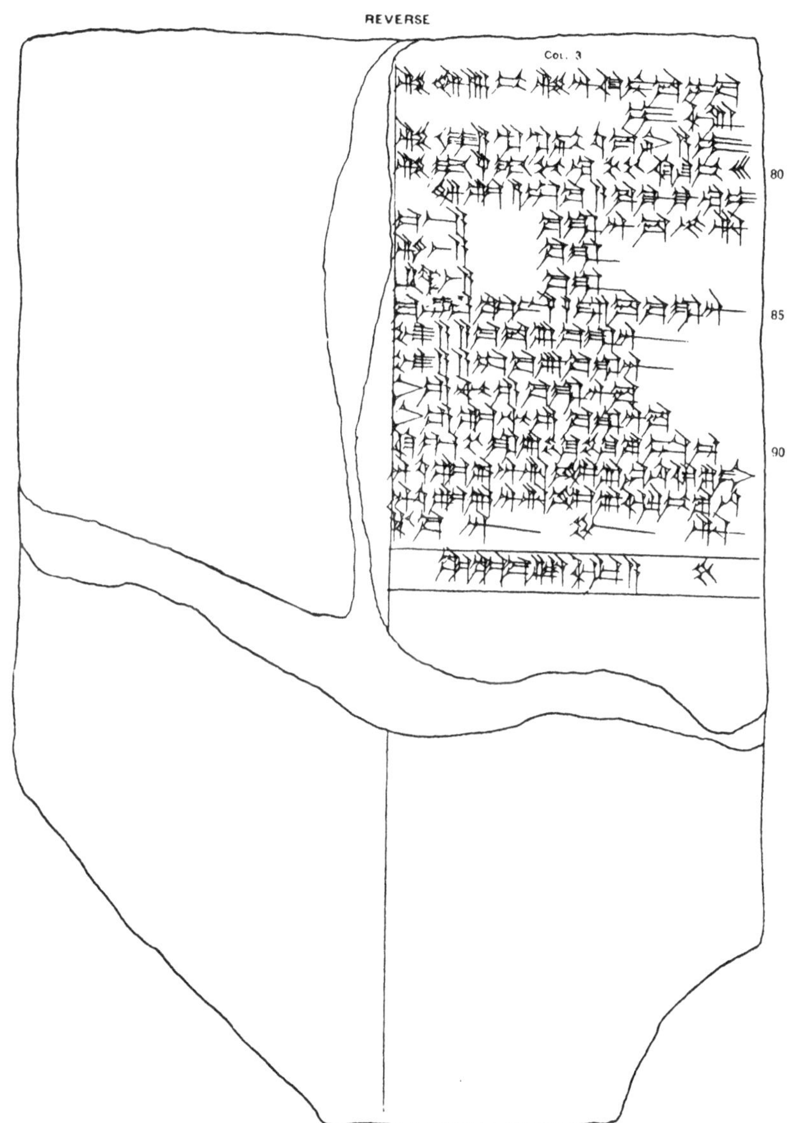

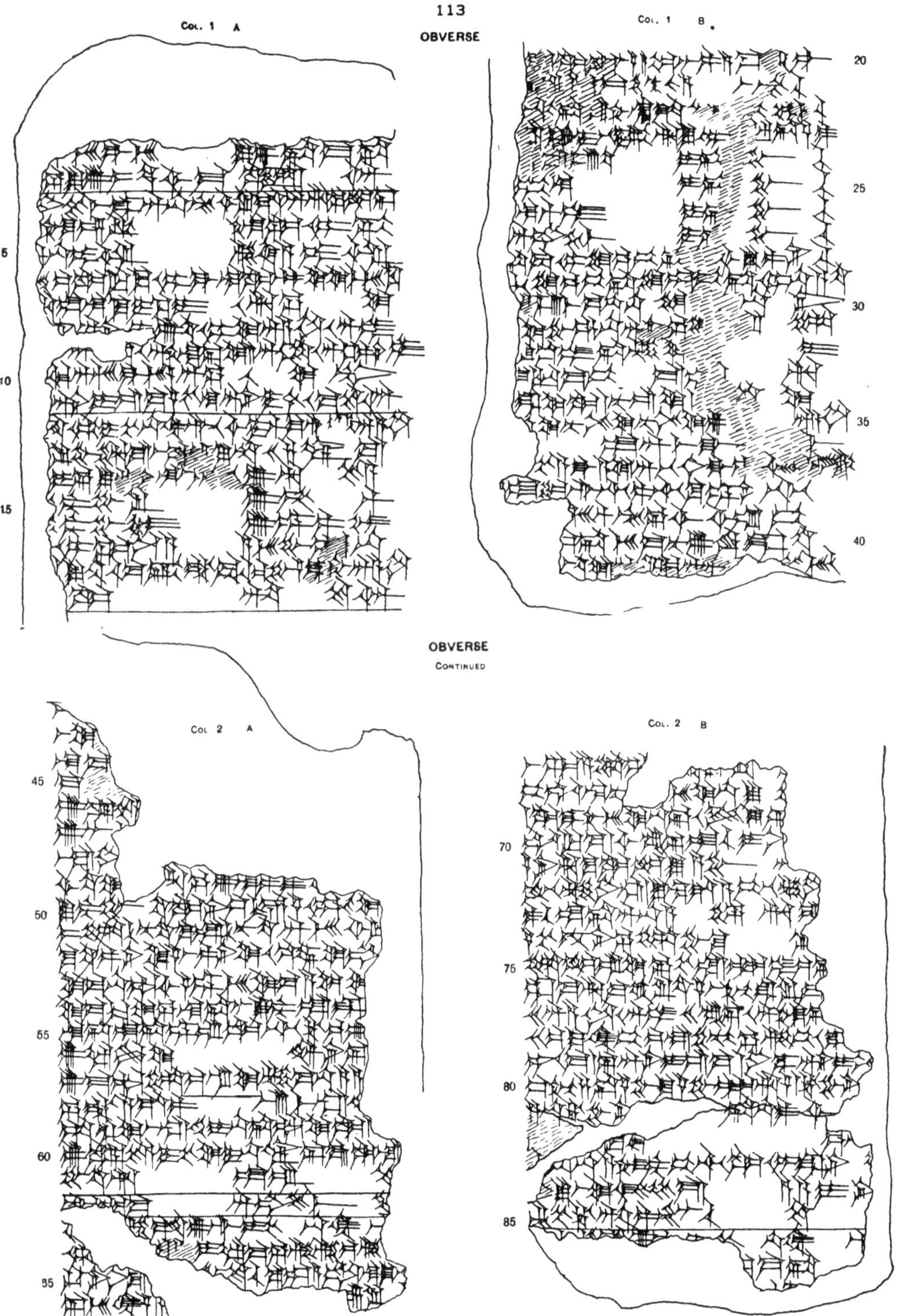
113
OBVERSE
Col. 1 A
Col. 1 B
OBVERSE
Continued
Col 2 A
Col. 2 B

113

REVERSE

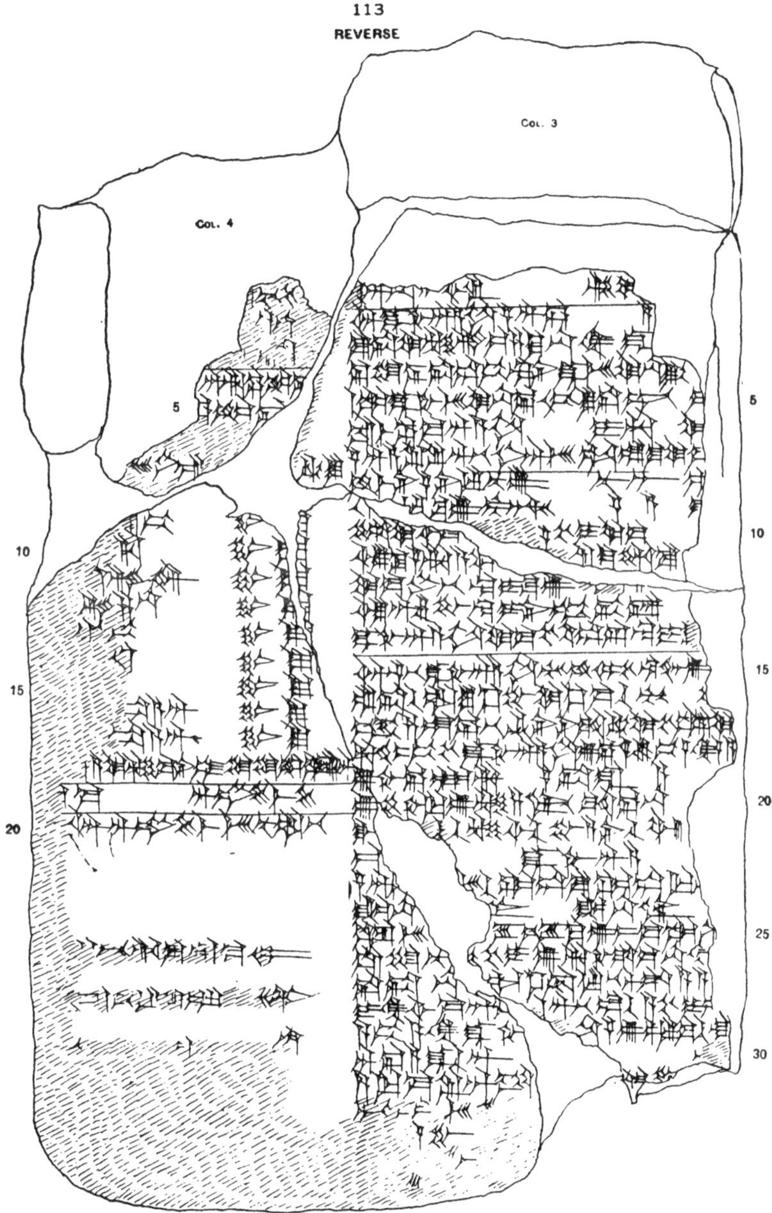

114

OBVERSE

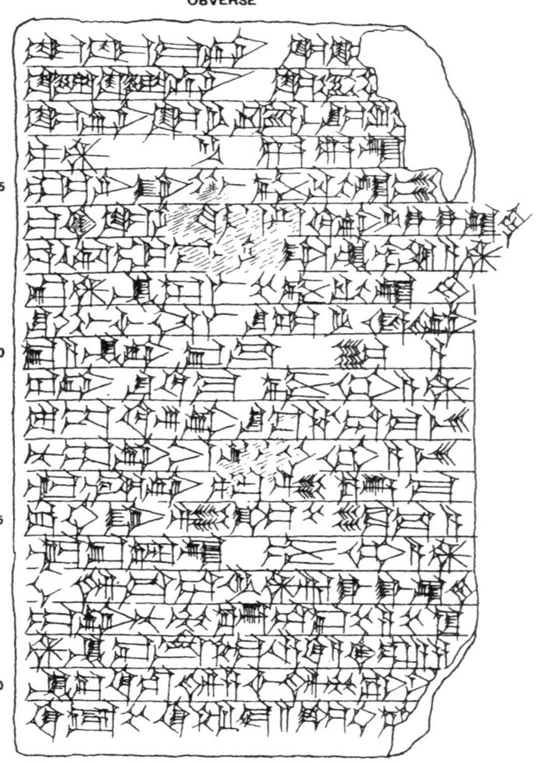

REVERSE

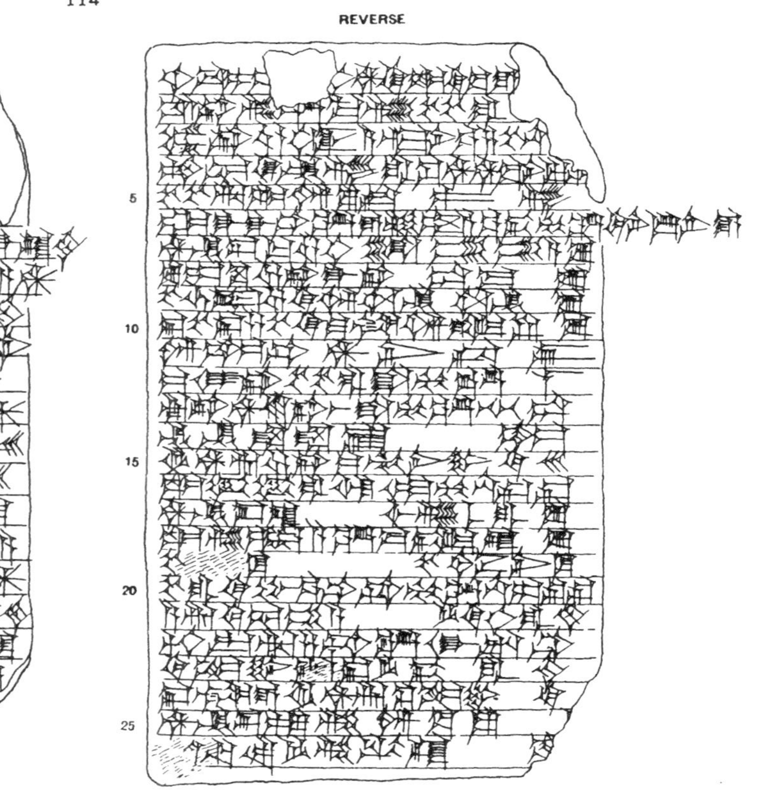

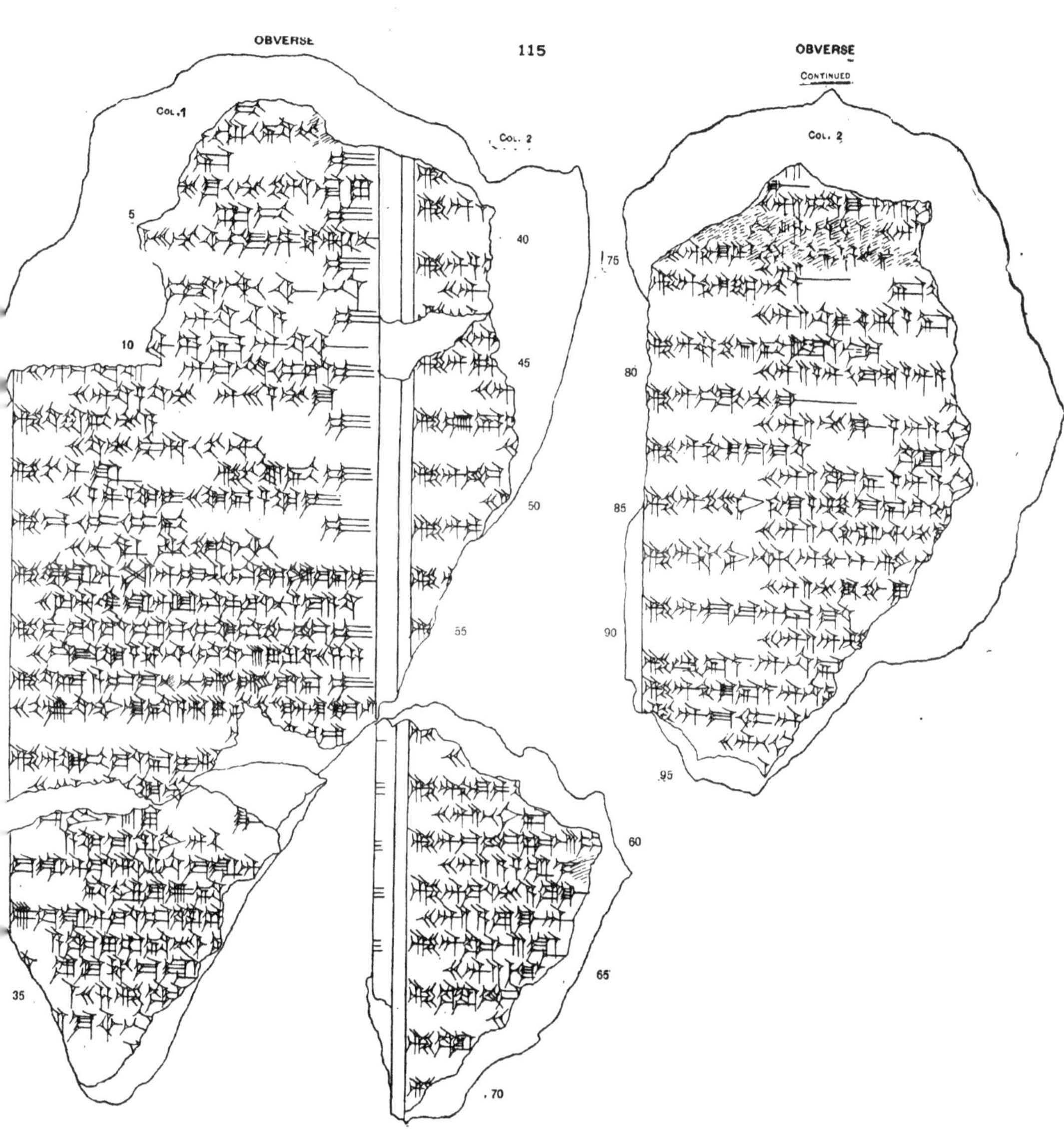
OBVERSE
115
Col. 1
Col. 2
OBVERSE
CONTINUED
Col. 2

116

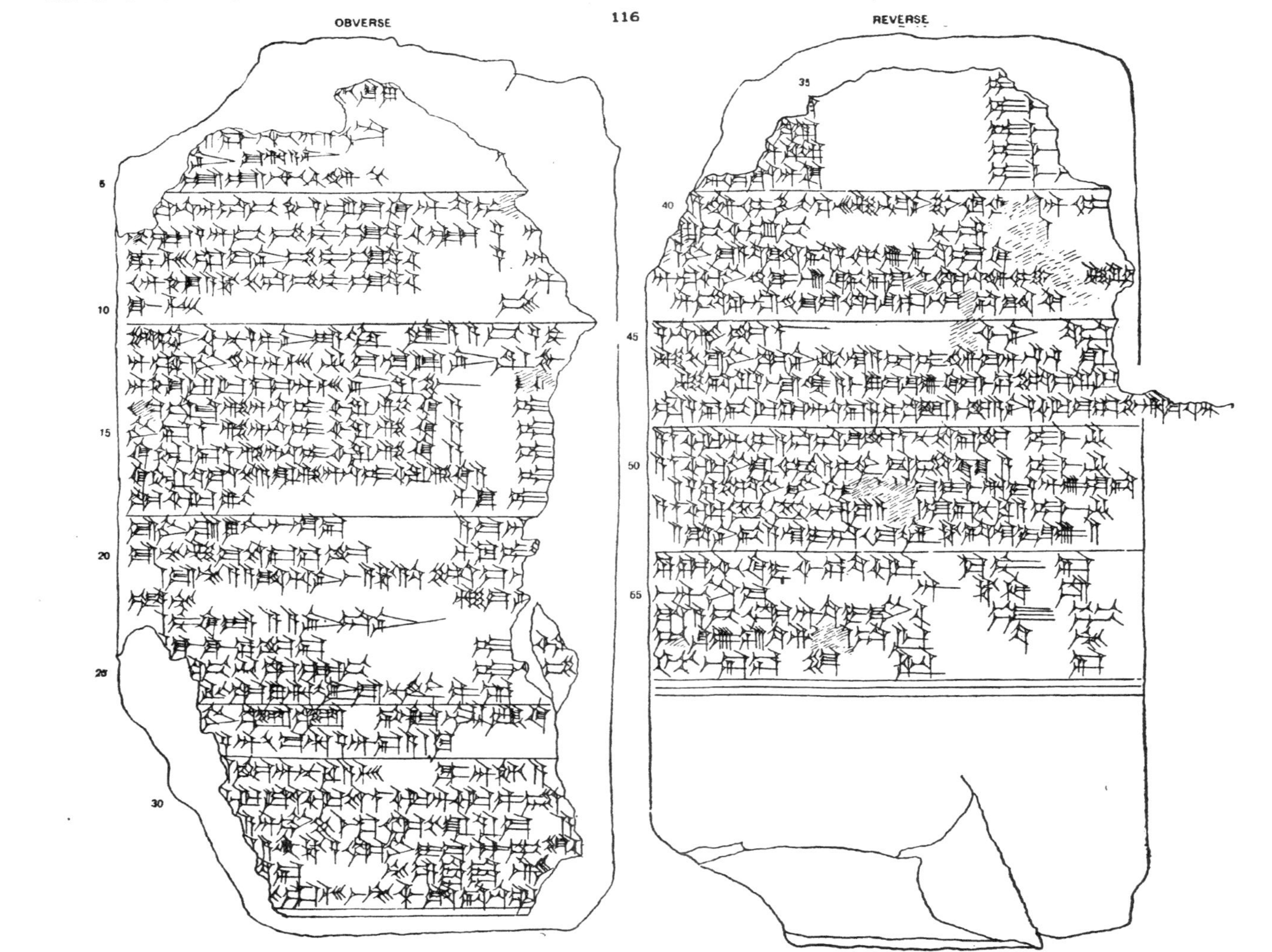

117

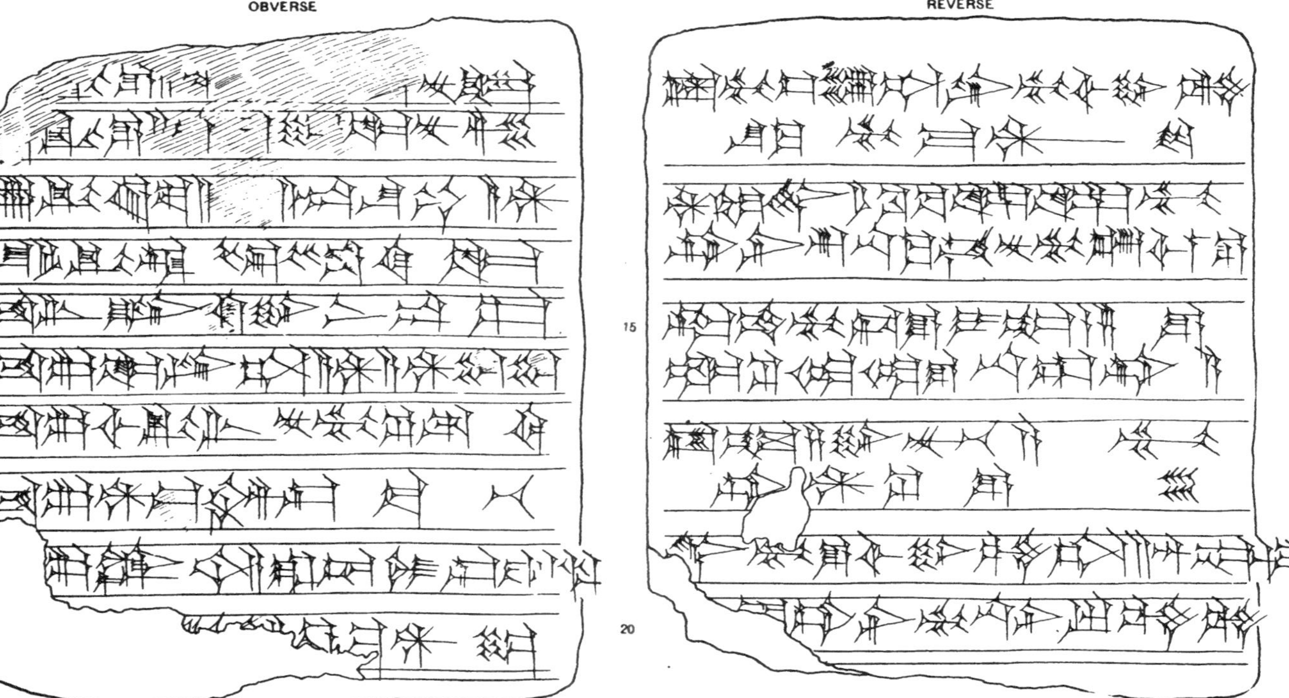

118

REVERSE

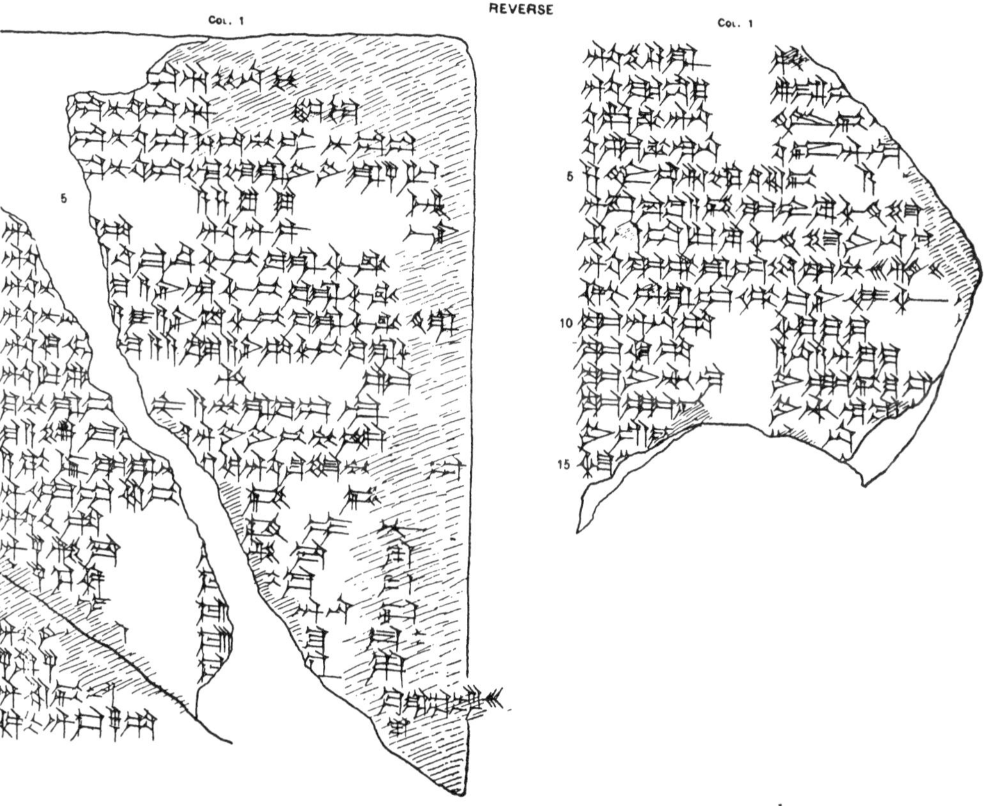

118

REVERSE

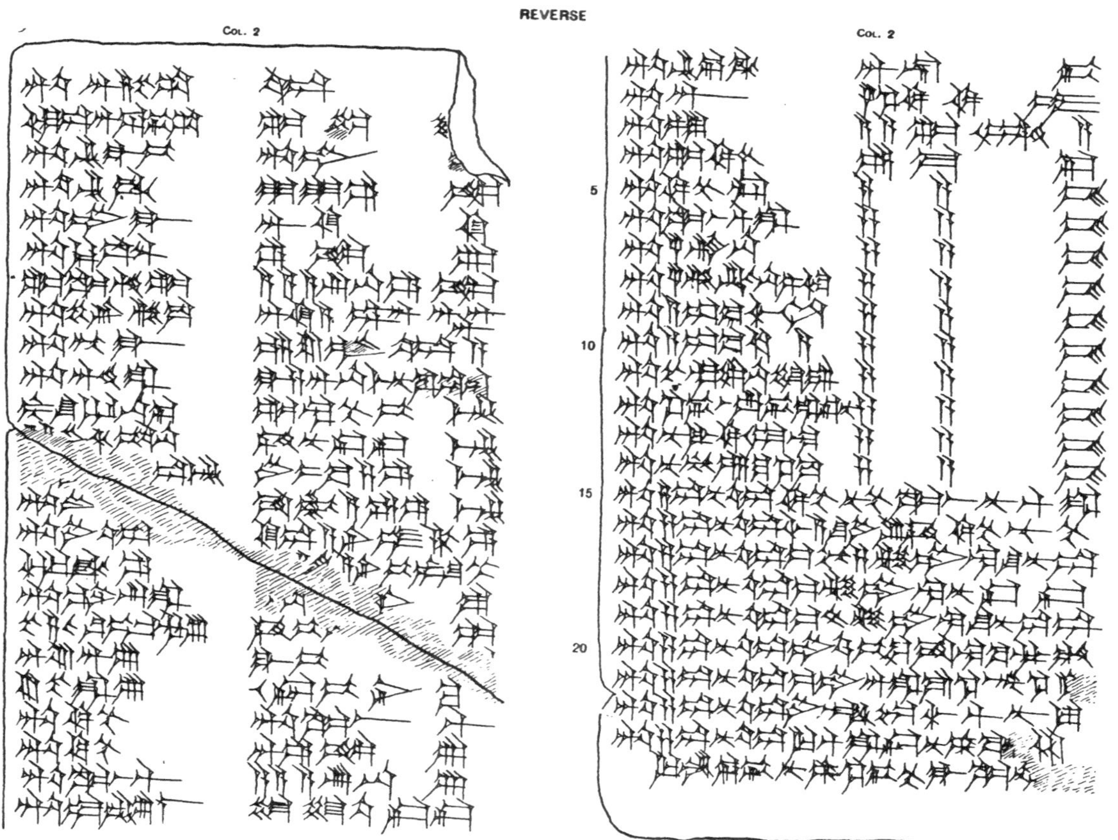

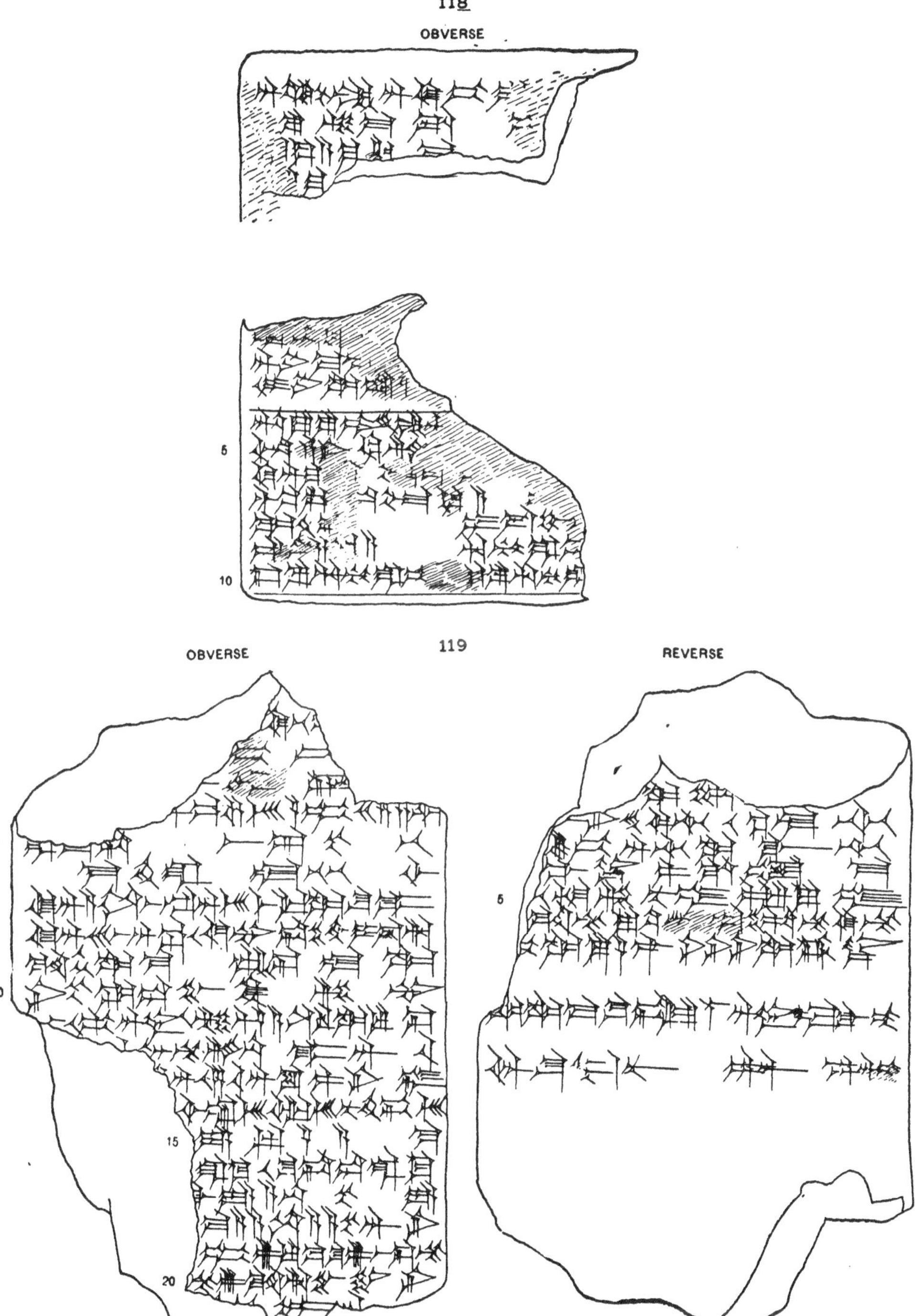
118
OBVERSE
119
OBVERSE
REVERSE

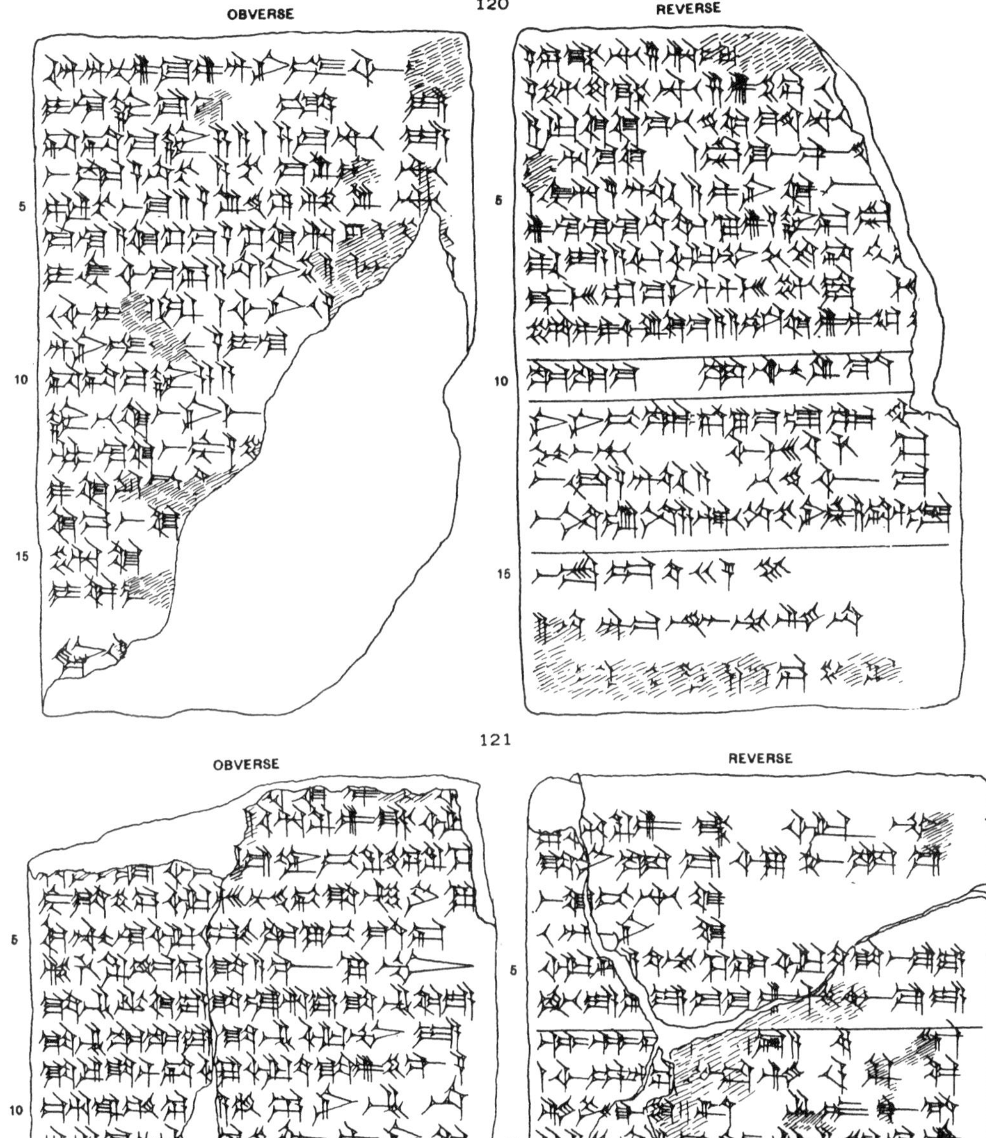
120
OBVERSE
REVERSE
121
OBVERSE
REVERSE

1122

OBVERSE

OBVERSE

CONTINUED

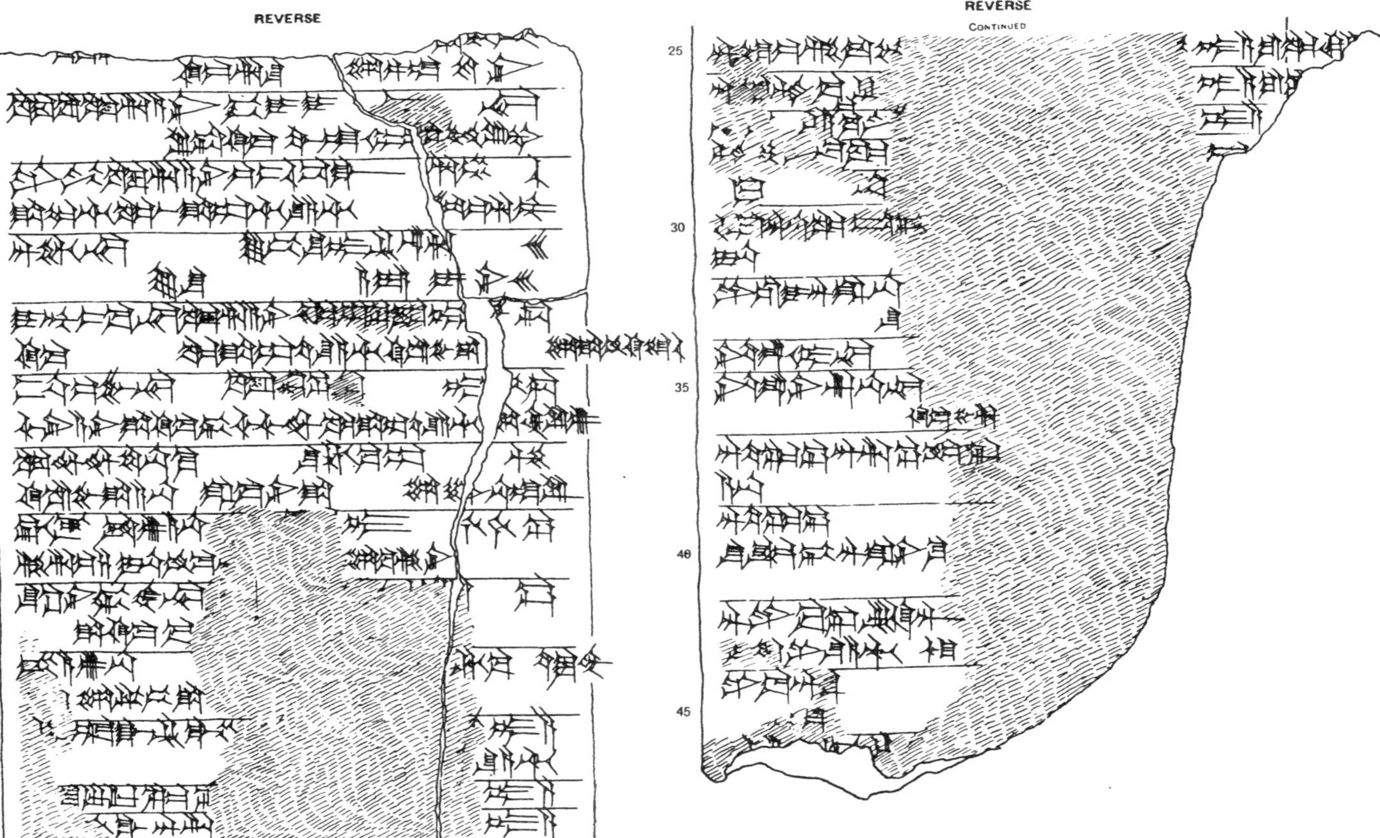
REVERSE
REVERSE
CONTINUED

123

OBVERSE

REVERSE

124

OBVERSE

REVERSE

125

OBVERSE

REST DESTROYED

126

OBVERSE

REVERSE

127

OBVERSE

Col. 1 Col. 2 Col. 3

REVERSE

Col. 6 Col. 5 Col. 4

128

OBVERSE

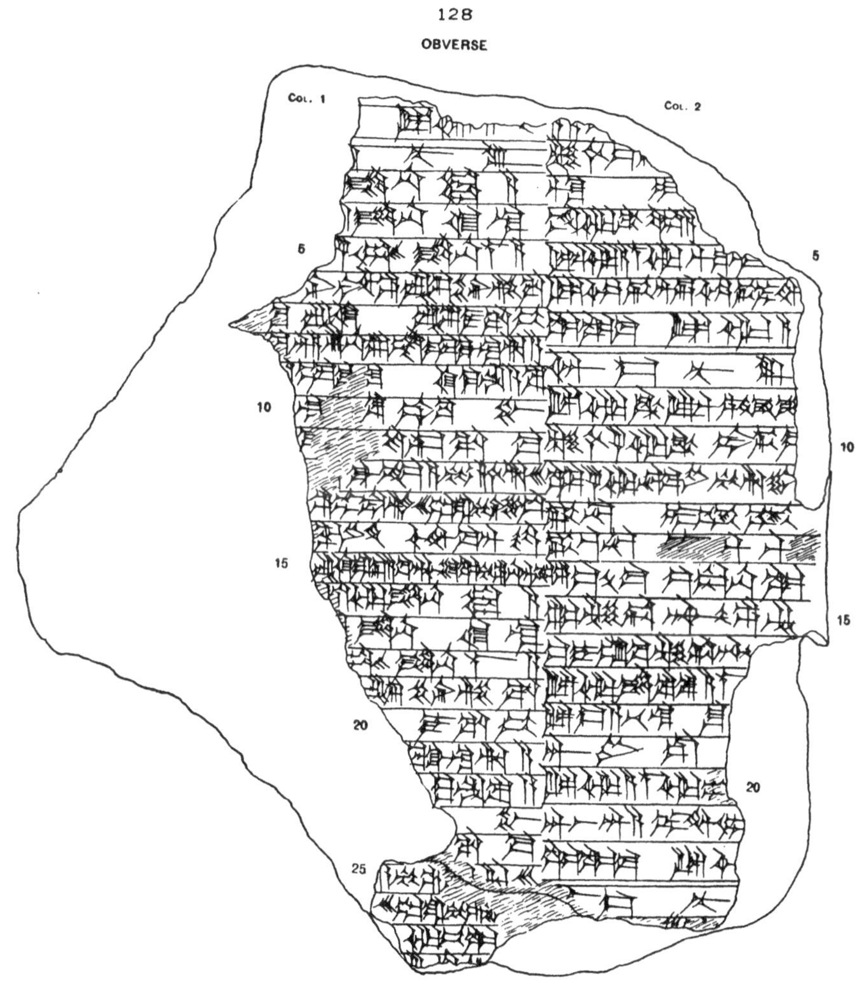

128

REVERSE

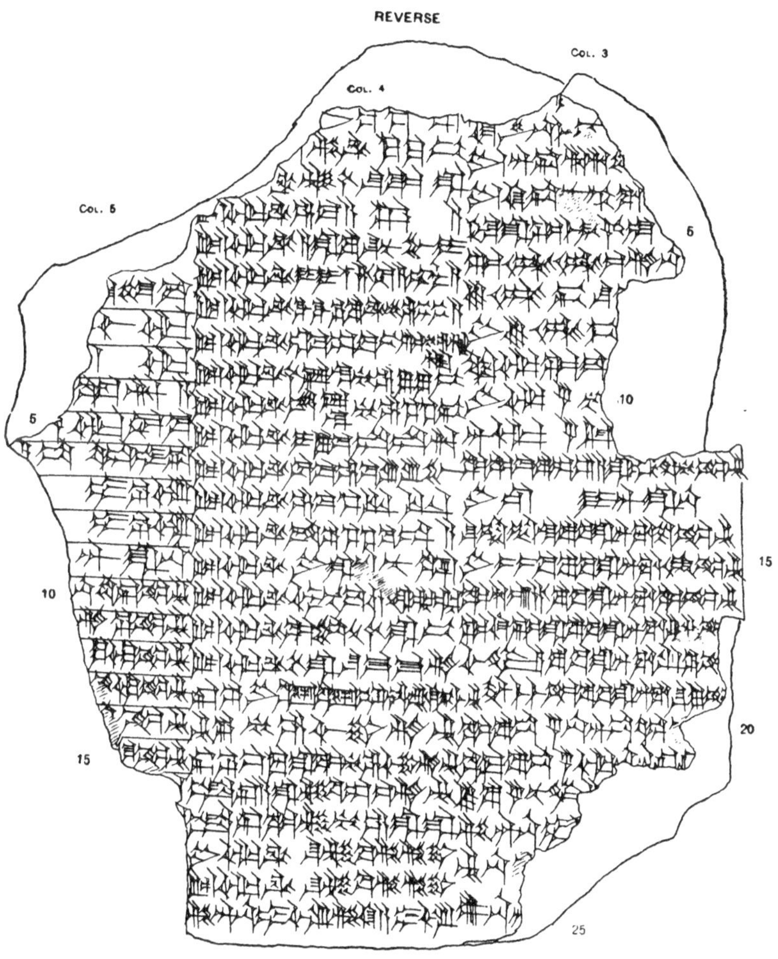

129

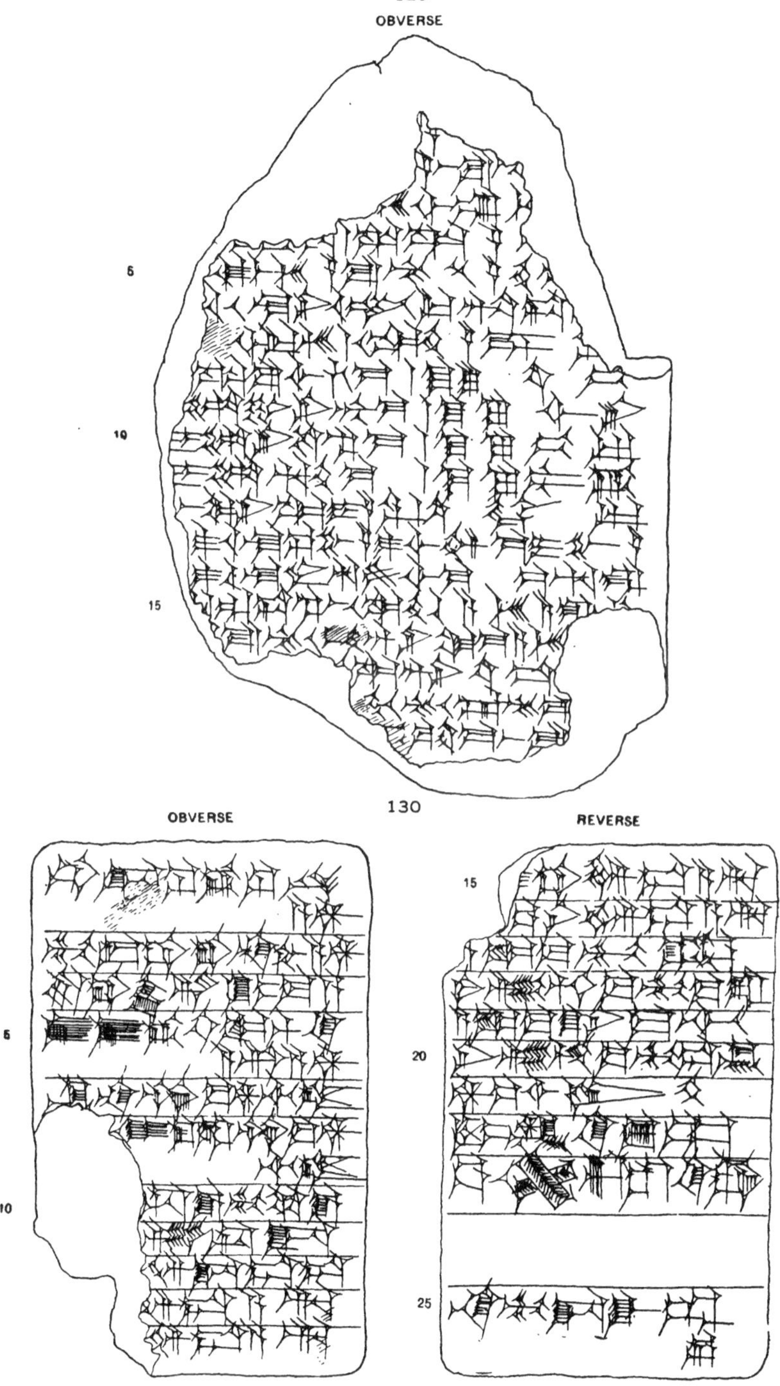

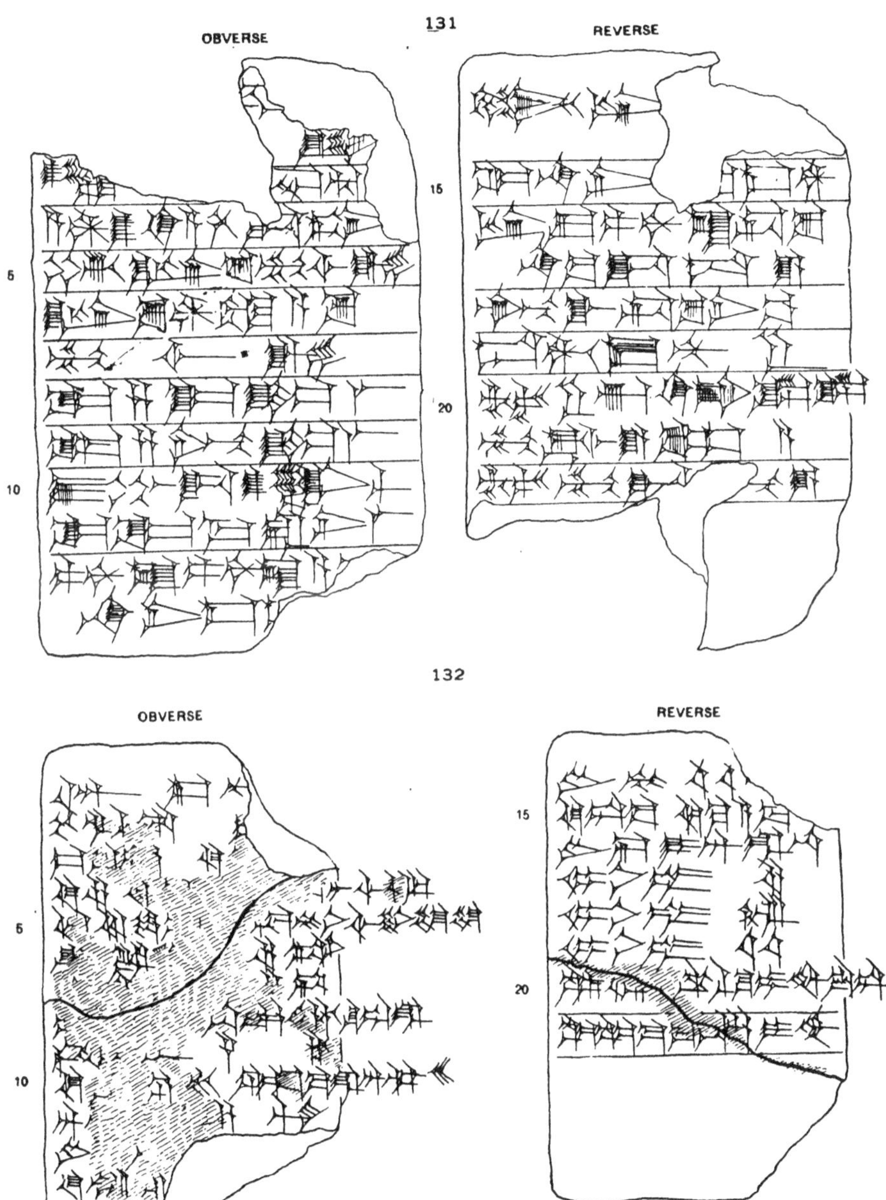
131
OBVERSE
REVERSE
132
OBVERSE
REVERSE

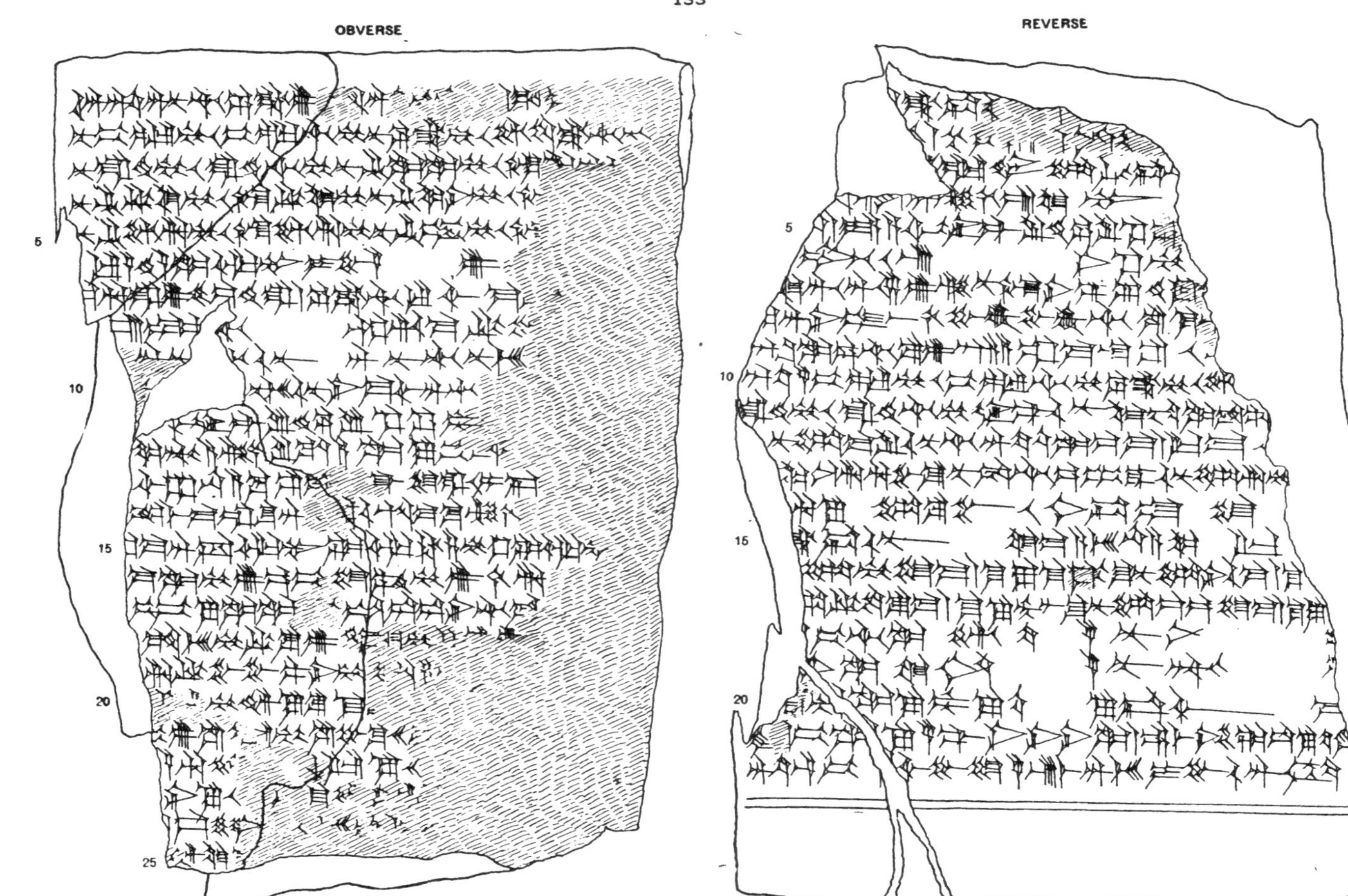
OBVERSE
REVERSE

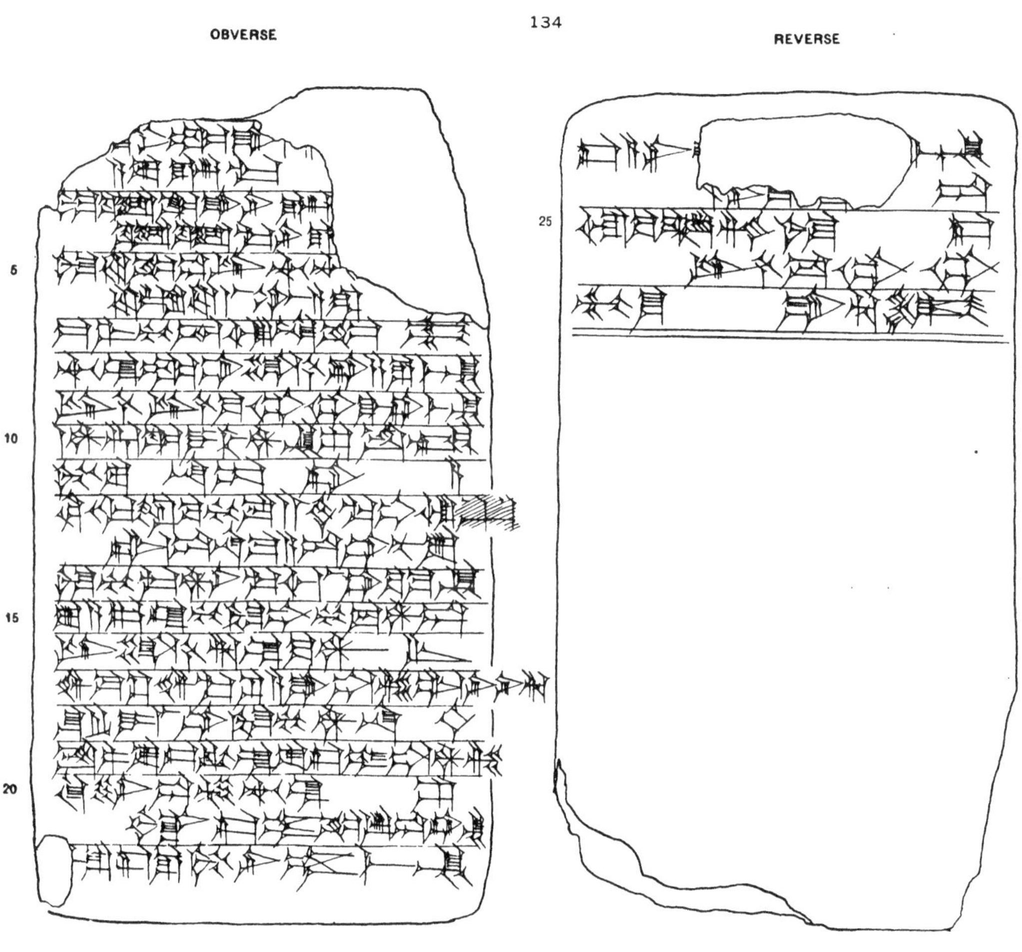
134
OBVERSE
REVERSE

135

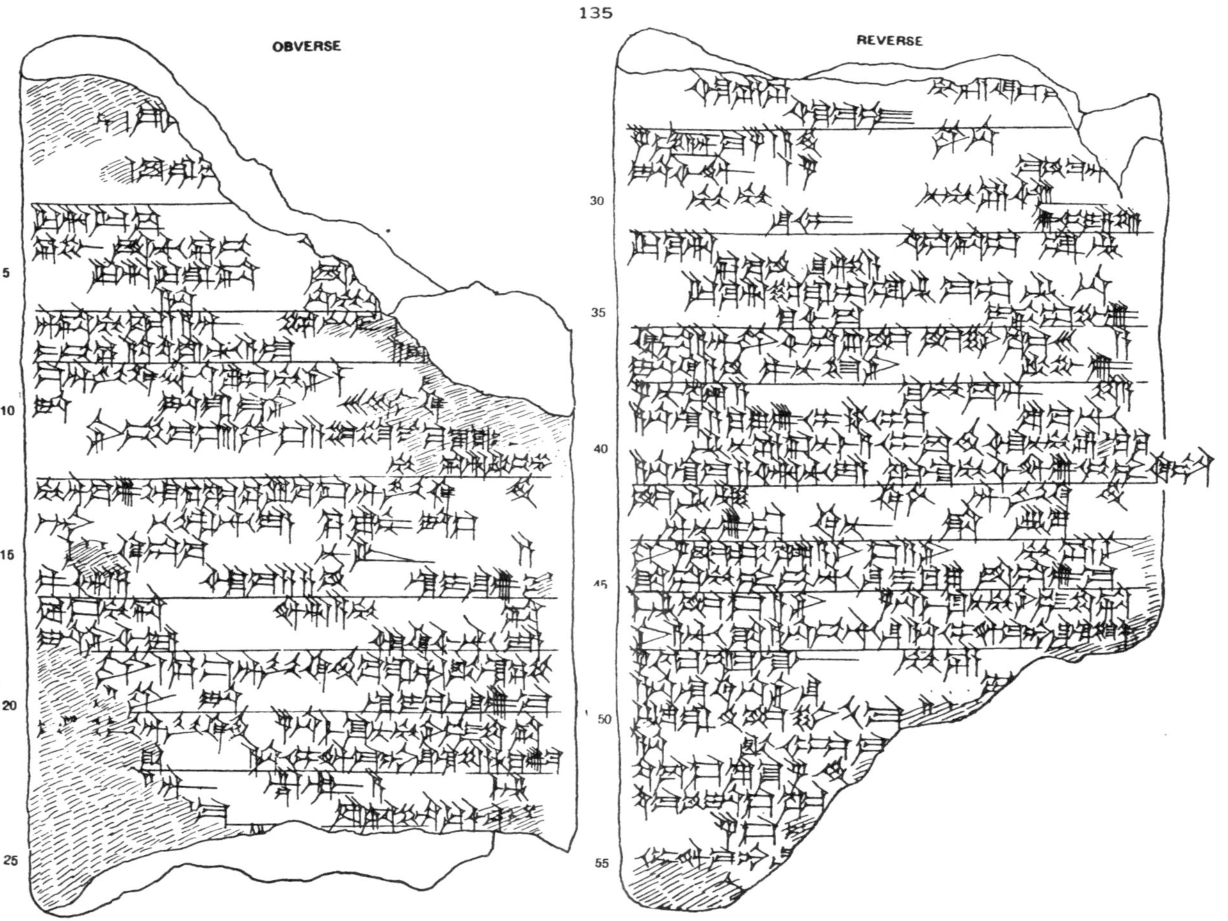

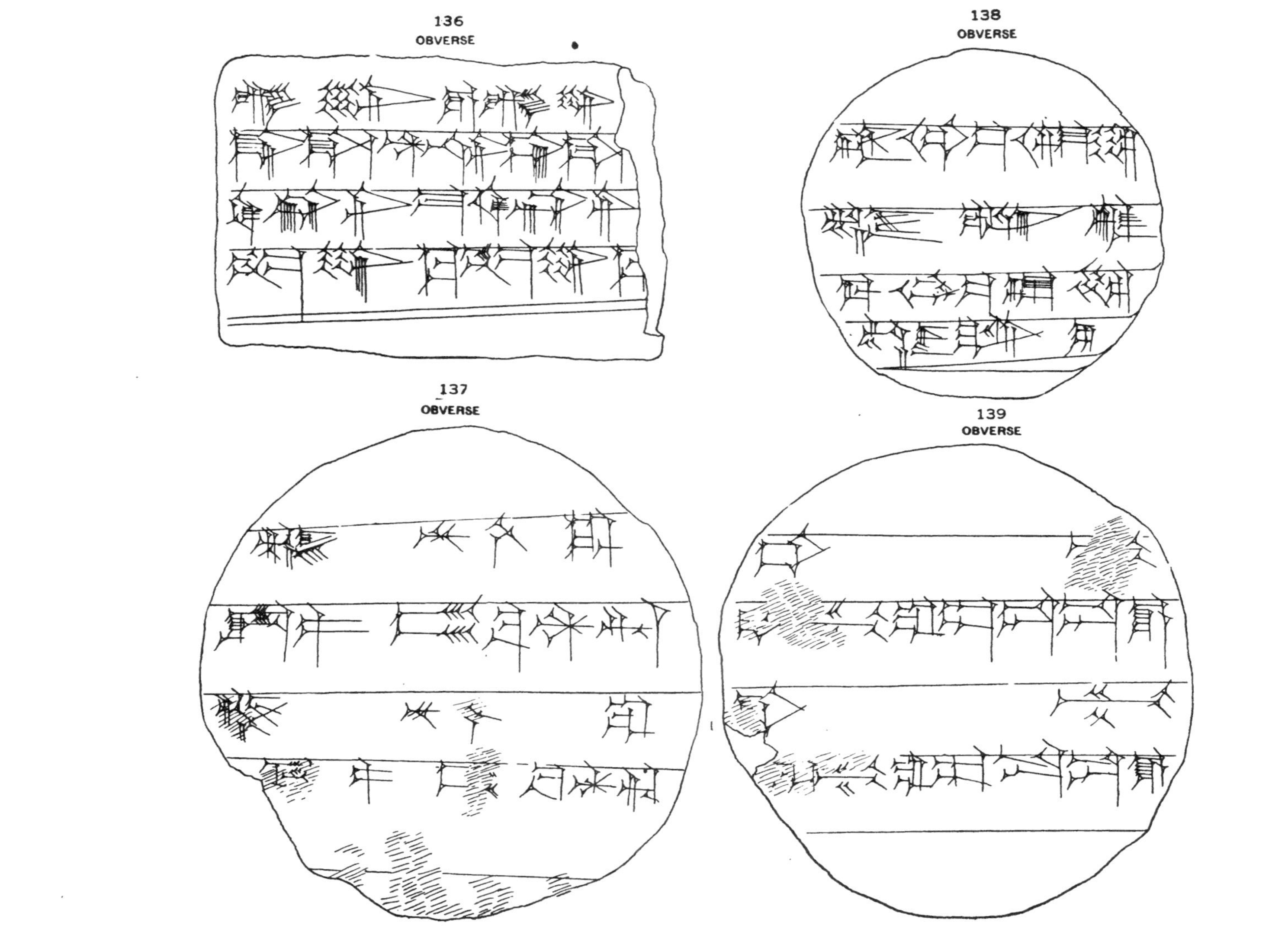
136
OBVERSE
138
OBVERSE
137
OBVERSE
139
OBVERSE

www.ingramcontent.com/pod-product-compliance
Lightning Source LLC
LaVergne TN
LVHW011201110826
845150LV00006B/1281

* 9 7 8 1 4 2 5 5 7 2 8 5 3 *